CORE TEACHINGS OF
THE DALAI LAMA

Our Human Potential

*The Unassailable Path of Love,
Compassion, and Meditation*

The Dalai Lama

TRANSLATED AND EDITED BY
Jeffrey Hopkins

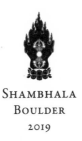

SHAMBHALA
BOULDER
2019

Shambhala Publications, Inc.
4720 Walnut Street
Boulder, Colorado 80301
www.shambhala.com

This book was previously published under the title *The Dalai Lama at Harvard*.

9 8 7 6 5 4 3 2 1

Printed in the United States of America

∞ This edition is printed on acid-free paper that meets the American National Standards Institute Z39.48 Standard.
♲ This book is printed on 30% postconsumer recycled paper. For more information please visit www.shambhala.com.

Shambhala Publications is distributed worldwide by Penguin Random House, Inc., and its subsidiaries.

Library of Congress Cataloging-in-Publication Data
Names: Bstan-'dzin-rgya-mtsho, Dalai Lama XIV, 1935– author. | Hopkins, Jeffrey, translator, editor.
Title: Our human potential: the unassailable path of love, compassion, and meditation/The Dalai Lama; translated and edited by Jeffrey Hopkins. Other titles: Dalai Lama at Harvard.
Description: Boulder: Shambhala, 2019. | Series: Core teachings of the Dalai Lama | "This book was previously published under the title The Dalai Lama at Harvard"—Title verso. | Includes bibliographical references and index.
Identifiers: LCCN 2018041969 | ISBN 9781611806786 (pbk.: alk. paper)
Subjects: LCSH: Buddhism—Doctrines.
Classification: LCC BQ7935.B774 D34 2019 | DDC 294.3/4—dc23
LC record available at https://lccn.loc.gov/2018041969

CONTENTS

Translator's Preface

In August of 1981, His Holiness the Dalai Lama of Tibet gave a series of lectures at Harvard University under the auspices of the American Institute for Buddhist Studies and the Center for the Study of World Religions. Organized principally by Professor Robert Thurman, president of AIBS, the Dalai Lama's lectures, which were given in Emerson Hall in Harvard Yard, fulfilled superbly the intention of providing an in-depth introduction to Buddhist theory and practice.

The lectures occurred over five days with sessions of approximately two hours each in the mornings and afternoons. Using the format of the four noble truths, the Dalai Lama depicted the situation of beings trapped in a round of suffering that is impelled by counterproductive actions that are themselves founded on a basic misunderstanding of the nature of persons and other phenomena. Ignorance being the root cause of suffering, he described, in considerable detail, the path out of this situation—the motivation to extricate oneself from uncontrolled repetition of unhealthy attitudes, the extension of this realization of one's own plight to that of others, and the consequent generation of universal compassion. He particularly emphasized the development of wisdom penetrating the veil of false appearance of phenomena, arriving at their true nature, unadulterated with false superimpositions.

After the first lecture on Monday morning, the Dalai Lama answered questions at the beginning of each session. Since the topics were concerned with the relationship between science and religion, the nature and levels of consciousness, the meaning of being a person in a system of selflessness, dualism, and non-dualism, the difference between low self-worth and selflessness, techniques for curing depression, the types of rainbow bodies, the difference between afflictive and non-afflictive attachment, the position of women in Buddhism, the conflict between evolution and the Buddhist theory of devolution, the usage of sex in the tantric path, how to conduct daily practice without becoming attached to it, and balancing altruistic activity and internal development, the answers covered the spectrum of issues that everyone with even a passing interest in Buddhism has wanted to probe for the last several decades. The Dalai Lama's answers revealed his deeply thoughtful and yet practical orientation to these crucial issues, balanced with self-effacing humor.

The lectures, translated and edited here in book form, provide technical information on a Buddhist perspective on the human situation as well as inspirational advice on love and compassion. The combination of intellect and impressive expository ability, coupled with practical, compassionate implementation that characterizes the Dalai Lama's personality, resounds throughout the talks. He speaks from the heart with insight drawn from a Buddhist tradition that reached high levels of development in the Tibetan cultural region, which stretches from Kalmuck Mongolian areas near the Volga River (in Europe), where it empties into the Caspian Sea, Outer and Inner Mongolia, the Buriat Republic of Siberia, Ladakh, Bhutan, Sikkim, much of Nepal, and all of present-day Ch'ing-hai Province as well as parts of Gansu, Yunnan, and Sichuan Provinces (which were part of Tibet before the Chinese conquest in the 1950s). In this vast region of Inner Asia, the language of prayer and philosophical discourse was Tibetan, and the large monastic universities of Tibet, until the Communist takeovers, drew students from all of these areas. The Dalai Lama speaks out of this centuries-old tradition of Buddhist studies with a voice of experience—of the implementation of Buddhist principles and techniques in a very difficult period of loss of homeland. With particular poignancy, he speaks of the value of enemies and the pressing need for compassion, patience, and tolerance. As the lectures unfold, a picture of the Dalai Lama as striving to bring peace on the individual, family, local, national, and international levels emerges—a leader of humankind suggesting techniques and advising on attitudes for actively converting conflict to peace.

I served as the interpreter for these lectures and have retranslated them for this book in order to attempt to capture the detail and nuance often missed in the pressure of immediate translation. I wish to thank Kensur Yeshi Thupten, former abbot of a Tibetan monastic college now re-established in south India, for identifying numerous quotations and Dr. Elizabeth S. Napper, Executive Director of the Tibetan Studies Institute, for making copious editorial suggestions. Thanks also to Gareth Sparham for reading the entire manuscript and making many helpful suggestions.

Occasional footnotes have been provided in order to explain translation choices and to give references to supplementary material as well as references for quotations. The names of Tibetan authors and orders are given in "essay phonetics" for the sake of easy pronunciation; for a discussion of the system used, see the technical note at the beginning of *Meditation on Emptiness*. Transliteration of Tibetan in parentheses and in the glossary is done accordance with a system devised by Turrell Wylie; see "A Standard System of Tibetan Transcription," *Harvard Journal of Asiatic Studies* 22 (1959): 261–67. For the names of Indian scholars and systems used in the body of the text, *ch*, *sh*, and *ṣh* are used instead of the more usual *c*, *ś*, and *ṣ* for the sake of easy pronunciation by non-specialists.

Jeffrey Hopkins
University of Virginia

Our Human
Potential

1. THE BUDDHIST ANALYTICAL ATTITUDE

Monday Morning

I AM VERY GLAD and deeply honored to speak here in this renowned university about Buddhism and particularly about its philosophy. I will speak about Buddhism from the broad perspective of the four noble truths, expressing points through my own broken English when I feel I can. Otherwise, I will speak through my interpreter.

My topics are the Buddhist schools of tenets and the views expressed in them. From among them, I will mainly speak about the systems of the Middle Way School[1] and the Mind Only School.[2] If I explained all of the schools, not only would you get confused but also I probably would too!

The teacher of the Buddhist doctrine in terms of this era was Gautama Buddha, who was born in the Shākya clan in India. The story of Buddha's life is told in three parts: an initial generation of an altruistic intention to become enlightened, in the middle his accumulation of the collections of merit and wisdom, and in the end his attaining enlightenment and turning the wheel of doctrine. The reason why his story is presented this way is that in Buddhism there is no teacher who was already enlightened from beginningless time; instead, a person must become newly enlightened.

Because there are four schools of tenets within Buddhism, there are many different explanations of how to generate an altruistic intention to become enlightened, how the collections of merit and wisdom are accumulated, and how to become enlightened. From a general point of view, however, Shākyamuni first developed an aspiration to attain Buddhahood in order to bring about the welfare of sentient beings—their welfare being his primary intent, and his enlightenment being the means to bring it about. Then, in the middle, he accumulated the collections of merit and wisdom for three periods of countless eons, at the end of which he became fully and thoroughly enlightened. Since Shākyamuni's life story is widely available in Buddhist literature, it is not necessary to repeat it here.

For me, it has great significance that the way of life of Buddha, Jesus Christ, and other past teachers is marked by simplicity and devotion to the practical benefit of others. All of these leaders supremely exemplify in their behavior voluntary assumption of suffering—without consideration of hardship—in order to bring about the welfare of other persons. Although Buddha, for instance, was born in a wealthy family, he sacrificed all these worldly facilities, remaining in a remote area to practice under great hardship. Only after that did he become fully enlightened. As followers of these faiths, we must make sure to consider this essential similarity.

After Shākyamuni became a Buddha at Bodhgayā, he stayed for several weeks without teaching, without turning the wheel of doctrine. He had attained enlightenment on the fifteenth day of the fourth month [of the Indo-Tibetan calendar] and began to speak about his doctrine on the fourth day of the sixth month. That is tomorrow; so, we are one day too early! He began turning the wheel of doctrine with a discourse in Varaṇāsi on the four noble truths mainly for five ascetics. Before considering his teaching of the four truths, let us become oriented by discussing the basic topic of the three refuges.

REFUGE

What kind of refuge does Buddhism offer? How are Buddhists and non-Buddhists differentiated? From the viewpoint of refuge, a Buddhist is someone who accepts Buddha, his doctrine, and the spiritual community as the final refuge. From the viewpoint of philosophy, a Buddhist is someone who asserts the four views [to be explained later] that guarantee a doctrine as being Buddhist. With respect to the three refuges, called the Three Jewels,[3] it is said that the Buddha is the teacher of refuge but that the *actual* refuge is the dharma, the doctrine. Buddha himself said, "I teach the path of liberation. Liberation itself depends upon you."[4] From the same perspective, Buddha said, "You are your own master." The spiritual community are those who assist one in achieving refuge.

Buddha

What, according to the higher systems of tenets, is a Buddha? Primordially, all of us have the substances for becoming a Buddha—essential factors of body, speech, and mind—and, due to these, it is possible to develop the exalted body, speech, and mind of Buddhahood, the culmination of the path. In terms of the exalted mind of a Buddha, two factors are differentiated—one being the knowing factor of the mind and the other being the suchness or final mode of being of that mind. These two are the called the Wisdom Truth Body[5] and the Nature Body[6] of a Buddha, and together they are referred to as the Truth Body.[7]

Within the one entity of the Nature Body itself, two types are differentiated—the final reality or sphere of reality[8] into which defilements are extinguished and the factor of having separated from those defilements through the power of their antidote. These are factors of natural purity and purity from adventitious defilements—the two aspects of the Nature Body.

Doctrine

From among the Three Jewels that constitute a Buddhist's refuge—Buddha, doctrine, and spiritual community—the Doctrine Jewel is twofold: true cessations and true paths. True cessations are the actual refuge in that they afford protection from the unwanted since they are states of separation from suffering and its causes.

True paths are the means of directly attaining these. This is why true cessations and true paths are the actual refuge. The ensuing series of lectures will be concerned to a large extent with the sphere of reality into which defilements are extinguished.

The doctrine is divided into verbal and realizational forms, the latter being comprised by true cessations and true paths. These are the doctrine that is realized. True paths are mainly those that actually overcome defilements—the training in wisdom—but also include the basis that makes wisdom possible, the training in meditative stabilization, as well as the basis that makes meditative stabilization possible, the training in ethics. These three trainings in ethics, meditative stabilization, and wisdom are realizational doctrine, and texts that take these three trainings as their topics are the verbal doctrine, the means of expressing those topics, the three scriptural collections—manifest knowledge,[9] sets of discourses,[10] and discipline.[11]

As Maitreya's *Ornament for the Great Vehicle Sūtras* says,[12] "The scriptural collections are either three or two." Thus, the scriptural collections are either the three just mentioned or two, those of the Hearer and Solitary Realizer Vehicles and those of the Bodhisattva Vehicle.

Spiritual Community

The spiritual community is comprised by Bodhisattvas, Hearers, and Solitary Realizers who have reached at least the level of the path of seeing, at which point emptiness is realized directly. Due to this realization, they are called Superiors.[13] Bodhisattva Superiors are those who have gained realization of any of the ten grounds.[14] There are many ways of dividing the levels or grounds of practice into different numbers—one in which the levels of the path of accumulation and the path of preparation, called the grounds of practice through belief,[15] are included as an additional single category and another in which, even within just considering the levels of Superiors, further distinctions are made in the tenth ground, etc. Thus, there come to be explanations of eleven, thirteen, or fifteen grounds. Also, especially in connection with tantra, there are many ways of enumerating the grounds. On the other hand, from the viewpoint of a highly developed practitioner whose mode of procedure is very swift due to making use of the uncommon mantric [or tantric] path of the mind of clear light, some scholars maintain that it is mistaken to enumerate paths and grounds, this being especially so with respect to those having realization of the final great seal.[16] The reason cited is that it is mistaken to utilize explanations of a very slow mode of procedure for this very swift mode of procedure in Mantra.

In terms of Hearers and Solitary Realizers, eight grounds or levels are described.[17] These are more conveniently explained in terms of four fruits of practice:

1. Stream Enterer:[18] one who has perceived the truth directly.
2. Once Returner:[19] one who has abandoned the first six gradations of afflictive emotions pertaining to the Desire Realm.
3. Never Returner:[20] one who has abandoned all nine gradations of afflictive emotions pertaining to the Desire Realm.
4. Foe Destroyer:[21] one who has abandoned all eighty-one gradations of afflictive emotions pertaining to all three realms—Desire Realm, Form Real, and Formless Realm.

Thus many divisions are explained with respect to the spiritual community that assist one in accomplishing refuge.

Those are the three refuges—Buddha, his doctrine, and the spiritual community. However, in Tibet it is said that there are four refuges—Lama, Buddha, doctrine, and spiritual community. A woman from Germany who was interested in Buddhism asked me with considerable amazement, "How is it that the lama is considered to be even greater than Buddha? I cannot accept this. What does it mean?" I told her that she was right. For, actually the refuges of Buddhists are only three—Buddha, doctrine, and the spiritual community. The reason for separate consideration of the lama or guru, however, is that the lama is like a messenger from Buddha, the one who at this point introduces us to the path. Furthermore, a fully qualified lama is the equivalent of a Buddha. Thus, even though there is a purpose for treating the lama separately, in fact there is no lama or guru not included among Buddhas or the spiritual community; there are only three refuges, not four. Lamas who are not properly qualified are again a different matter.

FOUR DISTINCTIVE VIEWS

As mentioned above, in terms of view or philosophy, whether someone is a Buddhist or non-Buddhist is posited by way of whether that person asserts the four views that guarantee a doctrinal system's being Buddhist. These four are:

1. All products are impermanent.
2. All contaminated things are miserable.
3. All phenomena are empty and selfless.
4. Nirvana is peace.

There is a complication, however, because a subschool of the Great Exposition School—the Vatsīputrīya[22]—asserts an inexpressible self, and thus there is debate as to whether or not adherents to this school are Buddhist in terms of view.

TWO LEVELS OF THE HISTORY OF BUDDHISM

The *Sūtra Unravelling the Thought*,[23] a Great Vehicle sūtra, explains that Buddha set forth three turnings of the wheel of doctrine—the first being the turning of the wheel of the four noble truths, the middle one being the turning of the wheel of no character, and the final one being the turning of the wheel of good differentiation. In the first turning of the wheel of doctrine, Buddha said that almost all phenomena exist by way of their own character. Then, in the middle wheel of doctrine Buddha said that all phenomena are without their own entityness. Then, in the final wheel of doctrine he differentiated phenomena, teaching that imputational natures[24] are not established by way of their own character[25] but thoroughly established natures[26]—emptiness—and other-powered natures[27] are established by way of their own character.[28]

Many historians have debated about whether the Great Vehicle in general is the Buddha's word and, within that, whether the Secret Mantra Vehicle is Buddha's word. Let us speak about this from a Buddhist point of view. Buddha expounded doctrines for Hearers in a popular way; among the fruits of the path mentioned in the Hearer scriptures, there are three levels of enlightenment— those of Hearers, of Solitary Realizers, and of Buddhas, and thus even the Hearer scriptures teach a path of Bodhisattvas for achieving the enlightenment of a Buddha. The Hearer scriptures do not just teach the paths of Hearers and Solitary Realizers. I do not use the terminology of "Low Vehicle" and "Great Vehicle" because there are complications that come from using such terminology; it seems better to use "Hearer Vehicle" and "Bodhisattva Vehicle." Still, when the term "Low Vehicle" is used, it is not a case of considering something to be inferior and thus to be despised. In this vein, in Mantra it is a root infraction of the tantric vows if one considers that through the Hearer Vehicle one cannot overcome the obstructions to liberation from cyclic existence. Therefore, it is clearly explained that one must greatly respect the Hearer Vehicle; it is not described as inferior. Also, in terms of practice, a single person should implement all of the practices of all of the vehicles, with very few exceptions. Hence, an explanation of greater and lesser vehicles is made in terms of greater and lesser motivation, in dependence upon which there come to be greater and lesser trainings, in dependence upon which there are greater and lesser fruits of the path. Even though this is the case, because of misunderstandings when the terms "Lesser Vehicle" and "Great Vehicle" are used, I prefer the terms "Hearer Vehicle" and "Bodhisattva Vehicle." In some Buddhist conferences, it has been advocated that the former terms no longer be used.

In the scriptures of the Hearer Vehicle itself, three types of fruits of the path are described: the enlightenment of a Hearer, the enlightenment of a Solitary Realizer, and the enlightenment of a Bodhisattva as a Buddha. Thus, even the scriptures of the Hearers speak of Bodhisattvas who work at achieving Buddhahood by accumulating the collections of merit and wisdom over three periods of countless eons. Still, the Hearer scriptures do not clearly set forth the mode of achieving the path of a Bodhisattva; they speak only of the path of the thirty-seven harmonies with enlightenment.

Therefore, Nāgārjuna says in his *Precious Garland*[29] that if, through merely cultivating in meditation the paths of the thirty-seven harmonies with enlightenment as causes of achievement, one nevertheless achieved an unsurpassed enlightenment that exceeded the enlightenment of a Hearer or Solitary Realizer, then this would be a case of the causeless production of an effect. Hence, the Hearer scriptures, since they also speak of Buddhahood, implicitly indicate that there is a separate mode of achieving the Bodhisattva path. Thus, even according to the Hearer scriptures, it appears that for select trainees of pure karma, among whom there were both humans and gods, Buddha set forth the Bodhisattva vehicle.

Still, not all of Buddha's teachings and activities are available in popular accounts. For example, Buddha set forth the middle turning of the wheel of doctrine at Vulture Peak, during which time he spoke the Perfection of Wisdom Sūtras, and in those sūtras it is indicated that a great many trainees—humans, gods, demigods, and so forth—were present. However, when you go to Vulture Peak itself, it is a fact that only about ten, or a maximum of fifteen, people could fit on the tiny hill that is the actual Vulture Peak perceptible with the eye. Hence, this is a case of an appearance [of a much larger place of teaching] to trainees of pure karma; such appears to their more pure perspective.

Since there was much controversy on whether or not the Great Vehicle is the word of Buddha, Maitreya establishes in his *Ornament for the Great Vehicle Sūtras*[30] that it was actually spoken by Buddha, as does Nāgārjuna in his *Precious Garland*,[31] Bhāvaviveka in his *Blaze of Reasoning*,[32] and Shāntideva in his *Engaging in the Bodhisattva Deeds*.[33] However, that the Great Vehicle scriptures were actually spoken by Buddha is something that is not clear in the commonly renowned historical records. This is my estimation of the situation.

Even more, Secret Mantra was not generally set forth in public; rather, it was disclosed individually for uncommon persons whose mental continuums had been ripened to that level. There are also cases in which tantric teaching has occurred by way of the appearance of the principal figure of a mandala [a sacred residence]—the Buddha—in visions to uncommonly qualified trainees due to their special karma and merit. Thus, these teachings could occur while Shākyamuni Buddha was still alive or even after his passing away. In this way, these are events that are not within the province of the records of ordinary history.

THE NEED FOR ANALYSIS

About the doctrine, the higher schools of tenets—the Mind Only School and the Middle Way School—set forth systems for distinguishing between what is definitive[34] and what requires interpretation.[35] This means that even if a particular doctrine is set forth in Buddha's scriptures, one must examine to determine whether or not it is damaged by reasoning. If there is damage by way of reasoning, it is not suitable to assert the literal reading of the passage just as it is; rather, it must be interpreted otherwise.

All four schools of tenets—the Great Exposition School,[36] the Sūtra School,[37] the Mind Only School,[38] and the Middle Way School[39]—cite Buddha's word as sources for their tenets, and there are similarly many different ways of positing what is definitive and what requires interpretation. Hence, since all of the schools have quotations that can serve as sources for the particular tenets of their schools, it is impossible merely through reliance on scripture to understand which teachings represent Buddha's final thought and which were spoken only due to a certain purpose. Therefore, Buddha himself said:[40]

> Like [analyzing] gold through scorching,
> Cutting, and rubbing it,
> Monks and scholars are to adopt my word
> Not for the sake of respecting [me],
> But upon analyzing it well.

Hence, it is said that if someone asserts a tenet contradicting reason, that person is suitable to be a valid, or authoritative, being with respect to this topic.[41] Therefore, *reasoning* is taken as the prime means of differentiating what is definitive and what requires interpretation.

Then, how is analysis to be done? About this, Buddha set forth the principle of four reliances:

1. Do not rely on the person, rely on the doctrine.
2. About the doctrine, do not rely on the words, rely on the meaning.
3. About the meaning, do not rely on interpretable meaning, rely on definitive meaning.
4. About the definitive meaning, do not rely on [ordinary] consciousness, rely on exalted wisdom.

One is to analyze doctrines by way of the four reliances in order to determine whether a particular doctrine is incontrovertible with respect to its meaning.

It is important to know how to differentiate between the thought of the speaker and the thought of the scripture. In this sense, the Consequence School represents Buddha's thought as the speaker of the scriptures, and the uncommon tenets of the other, lower schools represent the thought of scriptures spoken at particular times for particular purposes. When Buddhist studies are done, the perspective of multiple systems should be kept in mind; otherwise, if you take just one page, memorize it, and remain repeating just its meaning, you will become very confused when you see another page!

The Six Ornaments of the World and the Two Supreme Persons, depicted in the paintings displayed behind me, are persons who provided means of analyzing scripture such that their texts are real eye-openers. To say a little about them, the first two saint-scholars, Nāgārjuna and Āryadeva, mainly wrote on the philosophy of emptiness according to the Middle Way School, the highest interpretation. The next two are Asaṅga and Vasubandhu; their work is mainly on the moral, ethical side and the class of method rather than theory; in terms of theory, they mostly follow Mind Only. Since we Tibetans mostly follow the philosophy of the Middle Way School, we side with Nāgārjuna and Āryadeva and make critical objections to Asaṅga and Vasubandhu!

The next two are the great Buddhist logicians, Dignāga and Dharmakīrti. All of Buddhist logic is based on Dignāga's works, especially as they are expanded upon by Dharmakīrti. Without the works of these two great persons, Buddhist logic might not have had any sharpness. The Two Supreme Persons are Guṇaprabha and Shākyaprabha, who mainly wrote about the discipline—conduct, how to behave, how to become a monk or nun, the lifestyle of ordained persons. The Six Ornaments of the World and the Two Supreme Persons are true, ancient scholars.

THE FOUR NOBLE TRUTHS

Now, the actual topic—the four noble truths. The four truths involve two explanations of cause and effect, one being within the afflicted class of phenomena and the other being within the purified class of phenomena.

What is the relevance of these two sets of cause and effect? They are described because we want happiness and do not want suffering. Since we want happiness, the cause and effect of the purified class of phenomena is explained, and since we do not want suffering, the cause and effect of the afflicted class of phenomena is explained.

These two groups of cause and effect can be set forth either in terms of their actual temporal sequence or in terms of the process of their realization, the emphasis being respectively on objective and subjective factors. For example, Maitreya in the fourth chapter of his *Ornament for Clear Realization*[42] presents the four noble truths in terms of temporal sequence:

> In accordance with the order of cause and path
> And suffering and cessation . . .

"Cause" and "path" are the two causes—true origins and true paths—and "suffering" and "cessation" are the two effects—true sufferings and true cessations. This is a description from the objective point of view of actual temporal sequence, the second and fourth truths being presented before the first and third, respectively—causes before effects. Then, Maitreya in his *Great Vehicle Treatise on the Sublime Continuum*[43] presents the four in the subjectively oriented order of their realization:

> The illness is to be recognized; the causes of the illness are
>   to be abandoned.
> The state of bliss is to be attained, and the medicine is to be
>   taken.
> Likewise, suffering, cause, cessation of those, and path
> Are to be recognized, abandoned, known, and undertaken.

Here, suffering is first; then causes of suffering, then its cessation, and then the path for achieving cessation. This is in terms of the procedure of the *realization* of the four truths.

This latter order is clear when put together with an example. Suffering is like a sickness. Sicknesses are unwanted, but in order to make effort at a cure it is necessary first to recognize that you are sick. If you think that the sickness is a state of happiness, you will not have any wish to become free from it. Thus, first you should recognize the illness.

Once you identify it, since you do not want that suffering, you will investigate to determine what the real cause of the illness is. This is why the true sources of suffering are the second of the four truths. Even though when you identify suffering, you have an attitude of wanting to be rid of it, at that time you still have not determined its root, its causes; thus, you cannot have confidence that you can be cured of this illness. However, once you find the real cause of the sickness, you have the confidence, "Now I can get rid of this illness." This brings us to true cessations, the third noble truth. For, after identifying the cause of suffering, you can confidently think, "Now I can achieve cessation, a curing of the illness."

Once you know that life in cyclic existence has a nature of suffering and know its causes and that there is a cessation of suffering, you develop a wish to investigate the path out of suffering as well as a wish to enter onto such a path. When you see that an illness can be cured, you seek the medicine for curing it, and even if you have to have an operation, you are willing to undergo temporary hardship in order to bring about the happiness that is its result. To gain a better or bigger benefit, you sacrifice a smaller one. This is our nature, a natural law.

The Need for Detailed Examination

Sixteen attributes are explained, four for each of the four truths. What is the reason for presenting these topics in such great detail? In the Buddhist explanation, the root of suffering comes through the force of ignorance, and the destruction of ignorance is to be brought about by analytical wisdom. In terms of the way in which analytical wisdom researches or investigates its objects, there are six modes of research or investigation, done with the purpose of eventually eradicating suffering. The first is to research the meaning of words, that is, to investigate word by word their meaning. The second is to research the actualities of things in terms of whether they are internal or external. The third is to research the character of phenomena—their individual, particular character and their general character. The fourth is to research the classes of phenomena in terms of where favorable and unfavorable qualities lie. The fifth is to research time, because the transformation of phenomena depends upon time. The sixth is to research reasoning, within which there are four types:

1. The reasoning of dependence: that effects depend upon causes.
2. The reasoning of the performance of function: for example, that fire performs the function of burning or that water performs the function of moistening.
3. The reasoning of nature: that each phenomenon has its own nature; for example, that fire has a nature of heat and water has a nature of wetness.
4. The reasoning of valid establishment: non-contradiction with direct perception and inference.

Valid cognition is of two types, direct and inferential valid cognition, the latter having three forms—inference by the power of the fact, inference through renown, and scriptural inference by way of believability.

The basis for generating an inferential consciousness is a logical sign. The importance of logical signs or reasons is due to the fact that an inferential consciousness is a figuring out of an object—usually hidden to direct perception—in dependence on a correct, unmistaken sign. The teachers of logic—Dignāga, Dharmakīrti, and so forth—made presentations of the types of reasons in very detailed ways.

A correct sign, or reason, is tri-modal. In brief, this means that (1) the sign is established as being a property of the subject, (2) the forward pervasion is established, and (3) the counterpervasion is established.[44] Such correct signs are presented from many different viewpoints. In terms of their entity, correct signs are of three types—signs that are effects [from the presence of which the existence of their causes can be inferred], signs of the sameness of nature [as in the case of proving that something is a tree because of being an oak], and signs of non-observation [as in the case of proving the absence of something through its not being perceived despite fulfillment of the conditions for its perception if it were present].

In another way, when correct signs are divided in terms of the predicate being proven, there are two types—signs of a positive phenomenon and signs of a negative phenomenon. Then, in terms of the party to whom the proof is directed, there are correct signs on the occasion of one's own purpose—proving something to yourself through reasons—and correct signs on the occasion of another's purpose—proving something to another. Then, in terms of the mode of proof, there are five:

1. Signs proving conventions—that is to say, you already know the meaning but need to know the name.
2. Signs proving meanings.
3. Signs proving mere conventions.
4. Signs proving mere meanings.
5. Signs proving both meanings and conventions.

All of these are included in signs that are effects, signs of the sameness of nature, and signs of non-observation, the first mode of division by way of entity. Relative to the specific time, situation, and person for whom one is stating a reason, one states an effect-sign, nature-sign, or non-observation sign.

Each of these three divisions by way of entity also has many subdivisions. For instance, effect signs are of five types: those proving (1) an actual cause, (2) a preceding cause, (3) a general cause, (4) a particular cause, and (5) a correct effect sign which is a means of inferring causal attributes. Similarly, among signs of non-observation, there are correct non-observation signs of the non-appearing and correct signs which are non-observations of what is suitable to appear if it were present. These are further subdivided into eleven types, some scholars even making twenty-five, such as non-observation of a related object, non-observation of a cause, or observation of a contradictory object.

Among the six modes of investigation, the last is the research of reasoning which, as mentioned above, is divided into four types. It seems that scientific investigation is mostly by way of three of these—the reasoning of nature, in which the basic character of an object is researched; the reasoning of the performance of function, in which the functions that an object performs based on having a certain nature are researched; and the reasoning of dependence, in which that on which the object depends is researched. These seem to be the basic modes of procedure of science. Therefore, it seems that the six types of investigation cover all of both scientific and spiritual research.

I believe that scientific research and development should work together with meditative research and development since both are concerned with similar objects. The one proceeds through experiment by instruments, and the other, through inner experience and meditation. A clear distinction should be made between what is not found by science and what is found to be non-existent by science. What science finds to be non-existent, a Buddhist necessarily must accept as nonexistent, but what science merely does not find is a completely different matter. It is quite clear that there are many, many mysterious things. The human senses reach a certain level, but we cannot say that there is nothing beyond what we perceive with our five senses. Even what our own grandparents did not perceive with their five senses, we are finding nowadays with ours. Thus, even within physical phenomena with shape and color, etc., those things that we can see with our five senses, many that we do not understand now will be understood in the future.

With respect to other fields such as consciousness itself, though sentient beings, including humans, have experienced consciousness for centuries, we still do not know what consciousness actually is—its functioning, its complete nature. Such things that have no form, no shape, and no color are in a category of phenomena that cannot be understood in the way that external phenomena are investigated.

2. The Situation of Cyclic Existence

Monday Afternoon

Question and Answer Period

QUESTION: Do you think that we in the West must learn to bring the paths of spiritual and scientific investigation together in order to prevent harm to humankind?

ANSWER: If we only concentrate on scientific development, without concerning ourselves with spiritual development—if we lose a sense of human value—it will be dangerous. After all, the aim of scientific progress itself is to benefit humankind. If scientific development goes wrong and brings more suffering and more tragedy on humankind, this is unfortunate. I believe that mental development and material development must go side by side.

QUESTION: Please give examples of phenomena that science does not find.

ANSWER: Consciousness itself. As I mentioned earlier, every moment we have many different levels of consciousness—coarse and subtle. Never mind the subtler levels of consciousness, it is even difficult to identify the coarser levels.

QUESTION: If mind is more than brain or a physical phenomenon, why can thinking be altered and controlled through taking drugs or through stimulation of the brain?

ANSWER: There are many different kinds of consciousness or mind. Certain ones are very much related to the physical level. For example, our present eye consciousness is dependent upon the physical eye organ; therefore, if something has happened in the organ, the consciousness cannot function normally, and if the eye organ is removed, the consciousness cannot remain, barring an organ transplant. Even in the past there were reports in Buddhist literature of persons' giving eyes or even their own bodies in order to help others. An organ, such as a heart, formed through the karma of one person is, later in that person's life, transplanted into the body of another person and is utilized. The karma that originally fanned the heart belonged to the first person; thus it seems to me that there must be an unusual karmic connection between these two people.

In any case, certain consciousnesses are very much related with present organs and brain cells; these consciousnesses can be controlled through surgery on the brain or through electronic methods. However, the subtler levels of mind are more independent of the body; thus these consciousnesses are more difficult to affect through physical means. We will return to this topic later.

QUESTION: Can there be consciousness of consciousness?

ANSWER: Some systems of tenets assert self-knowing consciousnesses. For instance, the Mind Only School uses the existence of self-knowing consciousness as the main reason to prove that consciousness is truly established. This is a case of consciousness knowing consciousness.

However, in all Buddhist systems of tenets, whether something exists or not depends upon a validly perceiving consciousness that establishes it. With regard to establishing a consciousness as a valid one, only the Consequence School[1] explains that this is done in dependence upon the object of comprehension. In the Mind Only School, the existence of an object of comprehension is determined in dependence upon a valid consciousness, and the existence of that valid consciousness is determined in dependence upon a self-knowing consciousness. In this way, two types of consciousnesses are set forth—those that are directed outward and those that are directed inward. A consciousness that is directed inward does not take on the aspect of an apprehended object but is only directed inward, taking on the aspect only of the apprehending consciousness. Thus, this is a case of a presentation of consciousness knowing a consciousness.

The Consequentialists, however, reject this. They say that except for some schools stubbornly swearing that there is self-knowing consciousness, there are no valid proofs. They do not assert a consciousness that knows itself and do not need such in their system, but they still hold that it is possible for a particular consciousness to know another particular consciousness. For example, even though, in general, in meditative practices one meditates not on external objects but on an internal object such as a visualization of a Buddha, sometimes one concentrates on mind itself. Though, technically speaking, this is not a matter of a consciousness knowing itself, it can be said that a later instant of consciousness knows a former moment of consciousness or that a particular aspect of a consciousness knows the general consciousness. Thus, in this sense also, consciousness can know consciousness.

QUESTION: Please repeat the four reliances.

ANSWER: The first is to rely not on the person but on the doctrine. Even though someone is famous, one is not to accept whatever that person says just because he or she said it. Therefore, the first reliance means that one should *examine* what the person says.

The second is to rely not on the words but on the meaning; this means that one should not look to the beauty and euphony of the words. For, even if the words are beautiful, if they do not have good content, they should not be accepted. Also, if something is set forth without beautiful words and so forth but has proper content, it should be accepted.

The third is, with respect to the meaning, to rely not on what requires interpretation but on what is definitive. As mentioned earlier, there are different interpretations, in the various schools of tenets, of what requires interpretation and what is definitive. For instance, in the Mind Only School, it is said that what is literally acceptable is definitive and what is not literally acceptable must be interpreted. That which is nonliteral is to be interpreted by way of showing the basis in Buddha's thought, the damage to the literal reading, and the purpose of such a teaching. In the Middle Way School and particularly in the Consequence School, there is a twofold identification of what is definitive and what requires interpretation, one from the point of view of the objects of expression and one from the point of view of the means of expression. With respect to objects of expression, the final reality, emptiness, is definitive, whereas all other phenomena require interpretation in that they are not the final mode of subsistence of phenomena. With respect to the means of expression, those texts that set forth the emptiness of inherent existence are definitive since they present the final mode of subsistence of phenomena. Those texts that, even if they are literally acceptable, set forth any of the many different types of conventional phenomena need to be interpreted in order to determine the final mode of subsistence of those phenomena; these texts require interpretation because their objects of expression are included within the conventional level of phenomena and are variegated and not final. On the other hand, since the reality of the emptiness of inherent existence is the final mode of subsistence of phenomena, no matter how much one analyzes, there is no final mode of subsistence other than it, and thus it is definitive, as are texts that teach it.

Therefore, with respect to the meaning, it is said that one should rely not on that which requires interpretation but on the definitive. Then, with respect to the definitive, one should rely not on the mode of perception of consciousnesses that are affected by dualistic appearance but on a Superior's exalted wisdom consciousness in which all dualism has been utterly extinguished.

QUESTION: What is the relationship between the rational analytical and the nonverbal?

ANSWER: In the scriptures, it is stated again and again that the profound experience of the definitive reality of the emptiness of inherent existence is unthinkable and inexpressible. However, it is also said again and again that in order to understand this very mode of subsistence, it is necessary to engage in hearing the great texts and engage in analytical thinking. Therefore, when it is said that reality is unthinkable and inexpressible, the reference is to a state that has passed beyond the range of objects of conception and analysis, since reality *as it is experienced in meditative equipoise by a Superior*[2] cannot be expressed by terms and cannot serve as an object of a conceptual consciousness of a common being.

It is important to know that there are three types of wisdom—the wisdom arisen from hearing, the wisdom arisen from thinking, and the wisdom arisen from meditation. At the time of wisdom arising from hearing and that arisen from thinking, reality could not be unthinkable and inexpressible. Otherwise, these two types of wisdom would not exist! If reality were inexpressible in all respects, then Buddha should have remained entirely silent, and the Six Ornaments of the World also should have remained without saying anything. However, they lectured endlessly and composed many, many books. It is not that they were explaining all these topics because there was not anything to explain; they spoke because there was something to speak about.

Nevertheless, when you have thought again and again on the meaning of those topics about which you have heard a great deal and when your meditative contemplation has reached the level of ascertainment arisen from meditation, a special type of experience arises. This special understanding is not at all like your previous verbal understanding or what you understood on the level of analytical understanding; is inconceivable and inexpressible. For example, on television they are advertising many types of food, candies, and so forth that they claim are very delicious, but until you actually taste them with your tongue, they are quite unimaginable. Unless you actually experience their taste, you cannot say anything more than, "Oh, it's very sweet." You cannot say much about its sweetness, its type, degree, and so forth. Similarly, with these inner meditative experiences, their actuality is known only by an experienced person; others cannot understand.

QUESTION: What is the investigation of time?

ANSWER: In the Buddhist schools of tenets, there are many different explanations of what time is—interpretations shared by the Great Exposition School, the Sūtra School, the Mind Only School, and the Middle Way School and assertions unique to the Consequence School. However, in my reference earlier to the investigation of time, I was not speaking about that sort of time. Rather, the investigation of time in this context is a case of looking into what has occurred in the past, what is happening in the present, and what will occur in the future. This is the type of analysis that is done by historians, many of whom often say that history repeats itself, this then being an analysis of the future by investigating the past.

QUESTION: Your Holiness spoke at length about signs of non-observation, but how could one understand or know something without observing anything?

ANSWER: Non-observation here is the non-perception of something that, if it were present, would be perceptible. Therefore, its non-perception, or non-observation, under conditions suitable for its perception if it were present, can serve as a sign of its non-existence. As an example of its many subdivisions, consider a person who has doubts about the presence or absence of smoke on a lake at night. One could not say that there is not any smoke there just because one does not see any smoke, since the basic doubt comes because it is difficult to see smoke at night. Nevertheless, despite its being night, it can be proved that there is no smoke on the lake because of the non-observation of fire, since fire must necessarily precede smoke and since even a small amount of fire would be clear on a lakefront at night. This is a case of the non-observation or non-perception of a direct cause, from which one can conclude that its effect is non-existent at that place.

On the other hand, during the daytime, one could not prove the absence of smoke through the sign of not observing any fire simply because, during the daytime, it is not easy to see fire at a distance. Rather, in this instance, one could prove the non-existence of fire due to not observing any smoke. This is a non-observation of an effect, from which one can conclude that its cause is absent.

Thus, what one can prove depends on the circumstances. For instance, one could use the observation of something contradictory with a particular object to prove the absence of that object. If you had doubt about whether cold existed or not in a place in the distance, you could understand that cold is absent there due to perceiving a blazing fire at that location. Fire being contradictory to cold, observation of fire can prove the absence of cold. In this case, the observation of something contradictory serves as a sign of non-observation.

QUESTION: Could you say some more about the substances that have always been present in us and allow us to achieve Buddhahood?

ANSWER: This involves the topic of the Buddha nature, called the Buddha lineage.[3] The nature of the innermost subtle consciousness is pure; anger, attachment, and so forth are peripheral and do not subsist in the basic mind. In the system of Highest Yoga Tantra, all conceptual consciousnesses are coarser levels of mind that operate only until manifestation of the deeper minds of vivid white appearance, vivid red or orange increase, vivid black near-attainment, and the mind of clear light. The basic Buddha nature is the fundamental innate mind of clear light that is the subtlest level of consciousness; it exists at the root of all consciousnesses. Similarly, all of us have some level of compassion, despite differences of vastness, and all of us have a faculty of intelligence that distinguishes good and bad. Though small, these serve as positive fundamental conditions. Let us now return to our main topic.

ATTRIBUTES OF THE FOUR NOBLE TRUTHS

True Sufferings

Sixteen attributes of the four noble truths are posited in relation to sixteen misconceptions about them. The four attributes of true sufferings are impermanence, suffering, emptiness, and selflessness. Realization of these four counters four misconceptions about what are actually instances of suffering, misery, but which we conceive to be otherwise. These are misconceptions that true sufferings are pure or clean, that they are blissful, that they are permanent, and that they are self.

Through the fact that the mental and physical aggregates have a changeable nature, it is established that they are *impermanent*. Also, because they are under the influence of another power, namely, the force of contaminated actions[4] and afflictive emotions,[5] they are entities of *suffering*. Thus the meaning of "suffering" here is to be under the influence of what is other.

Because the mental and physical aggregates are without a self that has its own separate entity, it is established that they are *empty* of a permanent self that is devoid of production and disintegration. Since there is no self that has its own factual basis separate from the mental and physical aggregates, when the mental and physical aggregates are produced and disintegrate, the self also must be produced and disintegrate. Hence, there is an emptiness of a permanent self. Also, the mental and physical aggregates are *selfless* in the sense that they are not established as a self that is under its own power.

Except for certain qualms with respect to the Sammitīya subschool of the Great Exposition School, which asserts an inexpressible self, all Buddhist schools assert these four attributes of sufferings. Also, since we are speaking about a type of selflessness that all Buddhist schools assert, the selflessness that is described in these four attributes is merely the absence of an independent self and does not refer to the *subtle* types of selflessness that the higher schools of tenets assert. Hence, the selflessness and emptiness that are attributes of true sufferings are coarse compared to the selflessness and emptiness asserted by the higher schools, such as the Consequence School. In Shāntideva's *Engaging in the Bodhisattva Deeds* someone makes the objection:[6]

> One is liberated through seeing the truths,
> What then is the use of seeing emptiness?

Since one can be liberated from cyclic existence through seeing the sixteen attributes of the four truths and cultivating that realization in meditation, what is the use of meditation on some other emptiness? Shāntideva responds with many proofs showing that liberation from cyclic existence cannot be attained through realization of the coarse selflessness and the coarse emptiness set forth in the sixteen attributes of the four truths and can be attained only through realization of the subtlest emptiness.

True Sources

The four attributes of true sources are cause, source, condition, and strong production. The four corresponding misconceptions are that suffering is causeless, that the source of suffering is comprised of only one cause, that suffering is created only within the context of supervision by a deity, and that the states of suffering are impermanent but their nature is permanent. The four attributes of true sources are set as antidotes to these four misconceptions.

Attachment is the origin, the root of suffering; hence, it is a *cause* of suffering. Also, because attachment, for instance, again and again produces suffering as its own effect, it is the *source*; the reference here is too many causes producing suffering, not just one.

Also, attachment strongly produces suffering as its own effect; hence, it is *strong production*. Moreover, attachment to cyclic existence acts as a cooperative condition for the production of suffering, and, therefore, it is a *condition*.

True Cessations

The four attributes of true cessations are cessation, pacification, high auspiciousness, and definite emergence. The four respective misconceptions are that liberation does not exist at all, that some contaminated state is liberation, that what is actually a state of suffering is a state of liberation, and that although liberation exists, one can fall from it. As antidotes to these misconceptions, one needs to realize that true cessations actually are *cessations* in the sense that whatever portion of suffering has been alleviated has been removed forever. True cessations are also to be understood as being *pacifications* because that portion of the afflictive emotions has been pacified forever. True cessations are said to be *highly auspicious* because they are states of separation from afflictive emotions, these states being entities that bring help and happiness. Moreover, true cessations are cases of *definite emergence* from suffering because one has overcome a level of suffering such that it will not return.

True Paths

The four attributes of true paths are path, suitability, achievement, and deliverance. The four corresponding misconceptions are that a path of liberation does not exist at all, that the wisdom realizing selflessness is not a path of liberation, that a certain type of concentrative state is a path of liberation, and that no path removes suffering forever. How does realization of the four attributes of true paths serve to counteract these four misconceptions? Because the wisdom realizing selflessness has the capacity of achieving liberation, it is a *path*. Because the afflictive emotions are indeed unsuitable, the path that generates a wisdom consciousness realizing emptiness is *suitable,* fitting. Because this path directly realizes the actual mode of being of things without error, it is an *achiever.* Also, because the wisdom realizing selflessness definitely eradicates the root of cyclic existence, it is *definite deliverance.* Those, in brief, are the sixteen attributes of the four noble truths.

THE WORLD

Let us consider true sufferings in some detail. As Asaṅga says in his *Compendium of Manifest Knowledge,*[7] there are two types of true sufferings—environments and the beings within them. The varieties of suffering within cyclic existence are included within the three realms of cyclic existence—Desire Realm, Form Realm, and Formless Realm. The three realms are rough groupings of levels of cyclic existence in terms of the fruits of three levels of consciousness, these being determined by levels of conceptuality. Rebirth in the Formless Realm is an effect of the subtlest level of meditative stabilization; rebirth in the Form Realm is an effect of lower levels of meditative stabilization, and rebirth in the Desire Realm, our realm, is an effect of a lower level of consciousness that has not reached such concentration.

Within the Formless Realm, there are four levels that themselves proceed from the gross to the subtle. These are called Limitless Space,[8] Limitless Consciousness,[9] Nothingness,[10] and Peak of Cyclic Existence.[11] Within the Form Realm, there are, briefly, four levels of cyclic existence called the First, Second, Third, and Fourth Concentrations. In a more extensive presentation, there are either sixteen or seventeen levels of the Form Realm. All types of Form and Formless Realm beings are considered to be happy transmigrations, relative to lower states, and are all included within the classification of gods.

Within the Desire Realm, there are basically two types of beings—those in happy and those in bad transmigrations. The happy transmigrations are those of gods, demigods, and humans. Gods of the Desire Realm, in turn, are of six types—the Four Great

Royal Lineages,[12] the Heaven of the Thirty-Three,[13] the Land Without Combat,[14] the Joyous Land,[15] Those Who Enjoy Emanations,[16] and Those Who Make Use of Others' Emanations.[17] The bad transmigrations are animals, hungry ghosts, and hell-beings.[18]

In terms of the number of worlds, we can speak of a unit of worlds composed of one billion world systems that are roughly like our own. The formation and destruction of all these billion world systems are said to be roughly simultaneous. This is the explanation found in Vasubandhu's *Treasury of Manifest Knowledge*.[19] In addition, the *Vajrapāṇi Initiation Tantra*[20] says that a billion such world systems of a billion worlds is called an "endless ocean," a billion of those is called "one continuum of endless oceans," a billion of those is called a "middling continuum of endless oceans, and a billion of those is called a "third continuum of endless oceans." The last is the largest number; from then on, they are merely called "endless." Despite having created a huge set of numbers, the text says that the whole scope of it is nevertheless endless. Similar to this type of teaching, science fiction often depicts beings traveling far into outer space. Still, some science fiction depicts the beings of outer space as being just ugly and frightful; I doubt that this is necessarily so.

In any case, you can see that Buddhists believe that the world is endless and that sentient beings are infinite in number. Therefore, some people ask, "If there is an endless number of sentient beings, isn't the generation of an intention to become enlightened for the sake of all sentient beings rather senseless?" The answer to this is that the intention is very important. When one generates a good intention, whether one can actually achieve it or not is another matter. For instance, if a doctor generates great determination to rid the world of a certain illness and, due to that, engages in research, this would be good, would it not? In terms of determination, willpower, there is no limit. Whether practical or not, your decision—with strong determination right from the beginning—will carry weight. Whether it is achieved or not is a different question.

These one billion worlds within one world system are formed, abide, undergo destruction, and remain in a state of vacuity over a period of eighty intermediate eons. Formation takes twenty eons as do the periods of abiding, destruction, and vacuity. Though Vasubandhu's *Treasury of Manifest Knowledge* gives the size, shape, and so forth of the world system, it does not agree with modern scientific findings and thus is very difficult to accept as literally true. As already explained earlier, Buddhists must accept reasoning, and thus it is said that it is not suitable for Buddhists to accept a tenet that is contradicted by reasoning; even more so, it is unsuitable to accept a position that is contradicted by direct perception. Also, a further reason why Vasubandhu's description of the cosmos need not be accepted literally is that Buddhist scriptures themselves give many different descriptions of the cosmos.

Earlier it was explained that by way of levels of grossness and subtlety of mind, there are three realms and six types of transmigrating beings. However, it is not the case, according to Buddhism, that beings achieve liberation by progressing higher and higher within these levels. For when one arrives at the Peak of Cyclic Existence, it is not as if one is at the threshold of liberation; it is still easy to fall back into lower states. Therefore, it is said that there is no definiteness with respect to states of rebirth.

How does one pass from one birth state to another? First, we must discuss rebirth. The main reason establishing rebirth is the continuation of mind. There are basically two types of phenomena, internal consciousness and external matter. Matter can serve as a cooperative cause for the generation of a consciousness such as when a material, visible object serves as a cause of a consciousness's being produced in the aspect of that particular object, this being called an "observed object condition."[21] However, matter cannot serve as the substantial cause[22] of a consciousness. To explain this, let us consider the three causal conditions that generate, for example, an eye consciousness. The three are an empowering condition,[23] an observed object condition, and an immediately preceding condition.[24] Each of the three conditions has a unique function. For instance, that an eye consciousness is able to perceive a visible form and not a sound is due to the eye sense power (a type of subtle, clear matter located in the organ of the eye) that is its empowering condition. That an eye consciousness is generated as having an aspect of, for example, blue and not yellow is due to the patch of blue itself which is its observed object condition. Also, that an eye consciousness is generated as an entity of luminosity and knowing is due to an immediately preceding moment of consciousness that serves as its immediately preceding condition.

Without a former continuum of consciousness, there is no way that it could be produced as an entity of luminosity and knowing. Therefore, it is established that without a preceding mind a later mind cannot be produced. In this way, it is also established that there is no beginning to consciousness, and in the same way there is no end to the continuum of a person's consciousness.

According to the Great Exposition School, however, when Buddha passed into the great nirvana,[25] the continuum of his consciousness ended. Nāgārjuna refuted this position with reasoning, saying that if the followers of that school take nirvana to be severance of the continuum of the mental and physical aggregates, then when a nirvana is actualized, there would be no person to actualize it and that, conversely, when the person still existed, there could be no nirvana—the import being that a person's attainment of nirvana would be impossible. Therefore, Nāgārjuna posited the meaning of nirvana differently. The point here is that the continuum of the mind never stops.

The quality of one's rebirth in the next life is determined by the quality of one's mental activity in this one. Generally speaking, we have no power to choose how we are born; it is dependent on karmic forces. However, the period near the time of death is very influential in terms of activating one from among the many karmas that a person has already accumulated, and, therefore, if one makes particular effort at generating a virtuous attitude at that time, there is an opportunity to strengthen and activate a virtuous karma. Moreover, when one has developed high realization and has gained control over how one will be reborn, it is possible to take what is called "reincarnation" rather than mere rebirth. Again, there are many types of reincarnations,[26] but let us return to our topic.

How does one go from lifetime to lifetime? When one dies from either the Desire Realm or the Form Realm to be reborn in the Formless Realm, there is no intermediate state; otherwise, whenever one takes rebirth, there is an intermediate state between this life and the next life. What is the mode of procedure of death and what is the nature of the intermediate state? First, dying can take place upon the exhaustion of the life span, or upon the exhaustion of merit, or from an accident. According to the very coarse explanation of death in Vasubandhu's *Treasury of Manifest Knowledge,* the mind of death itself can be virtuous as can even the first moment of conception. In this case, a virtuous mind of death can act as an immediately preceding condition causing a virtuous mind of conception of the next life. However, Asaṅga's *Compendium of Manifest Knowledge* sets forth a more subtle presentation in which the mind of death is necessarily neutral, as is the mind of the first moment of rebirth. In addition, in Highest Yoga Mantra, there is a presentation of far subtler levels of consciousness which can be utilized such that a person who has practiced Highest Yoga Mantra well can transform even the subtlest mind of clear light of death into a virtuous consciousness.

In general, those who have strongly practiced virtue over their lifetime have an easier and more peaceful death, whereas those who have engaged in many non-virtuous activities have a more difficult and more agitated death. However, a nurse from Europe told me that those who believe in religion die with much more fright! Still, if over most of your life you have a good motivation sincerely seeking to help other people as much as you can, then when the last day comes, you will have no regrets. You will feel that you have done whatever you could, that you have spent your life meaningfully and fruitfully. This is one of the best safeguards for avoiding fright near the time of death. However, people who spend most of their time cheating, deceiving, and bullying others tend to develop a deep feeling of guilt, a guilty conscience. Even your own friends may not know your inner feelings, but when the last day comes, your own deep-seated feelings of uneasiness will emerge.

During the process of death, the warmth of the body withdraws from parts of the body in different ways for different types of people. For those who have accumulated a great deal of virtuous karma, the warmth of the body initially withdraws from the lower portions of the body, whereas for those who have accumulated a great deal of non-virtuous karma, the warmth initially withdraws from the upper portions of the body. Then, stage by stage, the outer breath ceases, and the warmth gathers at the heart.

According to the system of Highest Yoga Mantra, the process of death is presented in terms of the four or five elements. In this explanation, the capacities of the elements to serve as bases of consciousness gradually diminish, thereby producing a series of mental appearances. When the capacity of the earth element to serve as a basis of consciousness deteriorates, as an external sign the body becomes thinner, and so forth. As an internal sign, in accordance with the explanation of the Guhyasamāja system, you have a sense of seeing a mirage. Then, when the capacity of the water element to serve as a basis of consciousness deteriorates, your tongue dries, and your eyes sink into your head. As an internal sign, you have a sense of seeing smoke. Then, when the capacity of the fire element to serve as a basis of consciousness deteriorates, the warmth of the body gathers, as explained above. As an internal sign, you have a sense of seeing fireflies. Then, when the capacity of the wind or air element to serve as a basis of consciousness deteriorates, your breath ceases, and as an internal sign, you have a sense of seeing a burning butter lamp in space in front of you. Earlier there was an appearance of fireflies or of sparks from a fire; this now disappears, and a reddish-type appearance occurs.

Then, the subtler levels of the winds, or inner airs, that serve as the mounts of consciousness begin to dissolve. First, the winds that serve as the mounts of the eighty conceptions dissolve into a mind called "appearance," during which there is a vivid white appearance; this is the first of four states called the four empties. Then, when the mind of vivid white appearance—as well as the wind or inner energy that serves as its mount—dissolves into the mind called "increase of appearance," there is a vivid red or orange appearance. Then, when the mind of vivid red increase of appearance, as well as the wind that serves as its mount, dissolves into the mind called "near-attainment," there is an appearance of blackness. If doctors happened to be present at this time, they would probably have already declared you to be dead; however, in terms of this explanation, a person has not died but is dying. Then, after the vivid black near-attainment, the mind of clear light of death dawns. This consciousness is the innermost subtle mind. We call it the Buddha nature, the real source of all consciousness. The continuum of this mind lasts even through Buddhahood.

While the clear light of death is manifesting, the consciousness is still inside the body. Then, simultaneous with the cessation of the mind of clear light of death, mind and body separate. This is the final farewell!

Simultaneous with the separation of mind and body, one passes through the same set of eight appearances in reverse order. If there is to be an intermediate state, it begins with the re-appearance of the mind of vivid black near-attainment.

What is the nature of an intermediate state? A being of the intermediate state does not have a gross physical body like ours, but a subtle body. It is achieved just from the winds (inner airs) and mind. Hence, wherever the intermediate state being feels to go, the body of that person immediately arrives there; thus, it must be faster than light because it is just by thought. If it were not faster than light, then since from one end of a galaxy to another there are so many light-years—even several millions—one would have to travel an absurdly long time between some lives.

What is the physical shape of a being in the intermediate states? About this, there are two discordant presentations. According to Vasubandhu and certain mantric texts, the body of an intermediate state being resembles that of the being as whom he or she will be reborn. With respect to how long one spends in the intermediate state, a single life span in the intermediate state is, at maximum, seven days, at the end of which there is a small death, and the longest period one can stay in such a series of intermediate states is seven weeks—forty-nine days. However, there are two different ways of calculating how long a day is; one system posits them in terms of human days, and the other, in terms of the type of life into which one will be reborn.

What kinds of perceptions does an intermediate state being have? In accordance with the good and bad karma (deeds) of the person, various favorable and unfavorable appearances occur. Also, one can see other beings of one's own level. Moreover, Vasubandhu's *Treasury of Manifest Knowledge* says that persons who have achieved through effort the clairvoyance of the divine eye can see beings in the intermediate state.

Just after one leaves one's old body and emerges into an intermediate state, one can indeed see that old body; however, in general, one has no wish to enter back into it. Still, in cases when persons have re-entered the old body, it is possible—if the karmic circumstances are present—to revive the old body. In Tibetan, this is called *day lok*,[27] "returning from having passed away." I think that among those who have "returned from having passed away," there must be many different types—those who, from within the process of dying, return from the mind of vivid white appearance, from the mind of vivid red increase, from the mind of black near-attainment, or even from the intermediate state after the mind of clear light of death.

During the intermediate state, many different appearances occur, and thus practices are described for persons so that they can recognize that they are in the intermediate state, whereupon advancement in the path can be achieved. *The Tibetan Book of the Dead*[28] sets forth such practices for persons who are practicing the forty-eight peaceful and the fifty-eight wrathful deities. Similarly, for persons who practice deity yoga and have advanced to the point of decisively viewing all phenomena of cyclic existence and nirvana as the sport of the mind—as appearances of the fecundity of the mind—many practices are described to be performed within such a view. Most of these teachings come from Highest Yoga Mantra. (The Kālachakra system of Highest Yoga Mantra does not speak of attaining Buddhahood in the intermediate state; according to that system, Buddhahood must be achieved either in this lifetime or over the course of lifetimes. This points back to the fact that in the Kālachakra system there is a unique presentation of the substantial cause of a Buddha's Form Body.)

The intermediate state being makes connection to a new birth, and, in general, four types of birth are described—spontaneous birth, birth from a womb, birth from an egg, and birth from heat and moisture. An intermediate state being is a case of spontaneous birth. Also, it is said that when this world system first formed, beings were born here spontaneously, fully developed. If the rebirth is to be from heat and moisture, one sees a pleasant, warm place to which one becomes attached such that one has a wish to stay there. If one is to be reborn by way of womb-birth, one sees the father and mother in copulation. Those to be reborn as males are attracted to and desire the mother; those to be reborn as females are attracted to and desire the father; within such desire, the intermediate state stops and the birth state begins.

Cessation of the intermediate state and conception in the mother's womb are simultaneous. In the process of the cessation of the intermediate state, one passes through the eight signs beginning with a sense of mirage, as explained earlier, at the end of which the mind of clear light dawns. Because the body of an intermediate state being is subtle, these eight signs are not clear and occur quickly, whereas because our type of body is gross, the eight signs are clear and last a longer period of time. Due to this fact, it is said that for a person who wishes to practice Highest Yoga Tantra, a human birth is very favorable.

This is the way we travel, seemingly endlessly, in cyclic existence. As long as we are in such cyclic existence, we undergo many different types of suffering. In brief, these are comprised by the three forms of suffering—pain itself, the suffering of change, and the suffering of pervasive conditioning. Beings in the bad transmigrations of hell-beings, hungry ghosts, and animals, as well as those in happy transmigrations as humans, demigods, and gods of the Desire Realm, undergo all three types of suffering. Then, within the Form Realm, gods in the First, Second, and Third Concentrations have only blissful feeling, and thus there is no suffering of pain, but there is still the suffering of change. From the Fourth Concentration up through the four levels of the Formless Realm, there is only neutral feeling, and thus there is only the suffering of pervasive conditioning. Therefore, it is said that as long as one is in cyclic existence, one is in the grip of some form of suffering.

That finishes a rough explanation of the truth of suffering.

3. THE PSYCHOLOGY OF CYCLIC EXISTENCE

Tuesday Morning

QUESTION AND ANSWER PERIOD

QUESTION: If phenomena are selfless but suffering is real, who suffers?

ANSWER: This question comes from not understanding that self-lessness does not mean non-existence but refers to the absence of *inherent existence*. This point will be explained later when discussing the debates between the Mind Only School and the Middle Way School and debates within the Middle Way School. Other schools accuse the Consequence School of being nihilistic, but the Consequentialists do not accept this; they point out that they differentiate between existence and inherent existence and that they are not nihilists because, although they refute inherent existence, they assert that all phenomena are dependent-arisings and thus existent.

QUESTION: Would you please define consciousness?

ANSWER: The definition of consciousness is that which is luminous and knowing, but this is not easy to understand. In any case, consciousness is not something physical; it does not have any shape or color. Like space which is a mere absence of obstructive contact, it is open. Its nature is luminous, clear, and capable of knowing any object through reflecting the aspect of that with which it comes into contact. Still, it has its own measure of being beyond expression. If you withdraw the mind inside and gradually get some feeling of the nature of consciousness, becoming familiar with it, your sense of consciousness will become clearer and dearer.

When a consciousness has not met with an object, its capacity to comprehend that object is non-manifest. For instance, when a consciousness has not yet come into contact with these flowers that are in front me, a consciousness that apprehends these flowers has not been generated, but it has the capacity of knowing them. When objects are contacted, consciousness comes to know them through the force of their casting their own aspect toward the consciousness. The Great Exposition School asserts that consciousnesses know their objects nakedly without being generated in the aspect of those objects, but the higher systems of tenets maintain that consciousnesses know their objects within being generated in the aspect of those objects. Thus, when we say that our mental consciousness sees a flower, it should be analyzed whether it sees the external flower or an aspect, a reflection, of the flower. When one thinks about it in this way, one comes close to the view of the Mind Only School. In that school, the perception of objects is produced through activation of predispositions that are within consciousness, and thus the objects of consciousness are not a different substantial entity from the mind that perceives them. It is as if everyone has his or her own individual world. Nowadays, scientists are similarly investigating whether the mental consciousness sees an actual external object or whether it sees an image reflected in the rods and cones inside the eye. Also, it is interesting to consider color blindness in which, due to certain nerves being deficient, the perception of the object changes.

When one has just contacted the object, but the conceptuality of considering the object to be good, bad, and so forth has not yet started, the mere luminous and knowing nature of the mind is more obvious. At that time, it is beyond the state of being non-manifest but has not yet arrived at the point of conceptual apprehension. It is a time of mere luminosity and knowing. In the system of the Great

Completeness,[1] this is said to be the identification of the nature of the mind. When first accomplishing this in one's own experience, one can do it only briefly.

When we speak of knowing the real nature of phenomena, in terms of the ascertainment factor of the consciousness, the mode of apprehension of one's mind is merely ascertaining the absence of inherent existence. However, when we speak of being in meditative equipoise, a beginner is probably remaining concentrated on the luminous and knowing nature of the mind that is realizing the real nature of phenomena. One's mindfulness is being held on mind itself. We will discuss this more later.

QUESTION: How can we perceive or know the fact of the cyclic round of existence?

ANSWER: This is difficult. There is a continuum of mental and physical aggregates that are under the influence of contaminated actions and afflictive emotions and that serve as a basis of suffering. This is cyclic existence. In order to establish its existence, one first has to understand how these mental and physical aggregates come to be a basis of suffering by way of former actions. To do this, one must understand how contaminated actions and afflictive emotions come to be. One must understand how an unbroken continuum of such exists. If one were logically proving the existence of cyclic existence, one would state these reasons which then would have to be established individually—that contaminated actions and afflictive emotions exist in general, that these have a connection with our mind and with our experience of pleasurable and painful effects, that there is an unbroken and beginningless continuum of consciousness between lives, that the mental and physical aggregates that are impelled by contaminated actions and afflictive emotions, the continuum of which has existed unbrokenly from lifetime to lifetime, have a nature of suffering and serve as a basis of suffering, and that the root of all this meets back to a mistaken awareness which perceives the nature of phenomena wrongly.

Once it is established that these thoroughly afflicted phenomena are generated with a mistaken consciousness as their root, it can be understood that when this mistaken consciousness is removed, the afflictive emotions generated in dependence upon it are also removed, whereby the contaminated actions generated in dependence upon them are also removed. Through that, birth in cyclic existence that is produced in dependence upon contaminated actions is overcome. In this way, the twelve branches of the dependent-arising of cyclic existence[2] are overcome. It is through such a combination of understandings that one can gain ascertainment with respect to the process of cyclic existence; it is not something that can be explained all in one piece.

QUESTION: As long as one can live a mindful life of kindness and compassion for all beings, is it necessary to know all or even any of these seemingly endlessly complex divisions and amplifications of concepts?

ANSWER: Sentient beings have an endlessly different number and types of dispositions and interests, and there are basically two types of teachings for these trainees. One is the type of teaching that was given to the public by Buddha himself as well as by the Six Ornaments of the World in their general teaching. Since among the listeners there were persons of a great variety of dispositions and interests, these teachings are of great variety and complexity. However, there also are direct modes of teaching by great adepts to particular people in particular situations without such complexity.

There is a story that a philosopher was debating with the great yogi Milarepa about logic and epistemology, considering such topics as logical signs, contradiction, relation, and appearance without ascertainment. Milarepa said, "I do not know logic and epistemology. But I know that the fact that this philosopher's mind is mixed with afflictive emotions is an effect-sign; that its contradiction with the Buddhist religion is a sign of contradiction; and that the fact that externally you appear to be a practitioner but internally are not necessarily a practitioner is a case of appearance without ascertainment." People like Milarepa have internalized all of the real teachings—the thought definitely to leave cyclic existence, altruism, and the wisdom that realizes the emptiness of inherent existence according to the Consequence School.

There was a time when an evil force was attempting to get at Milarepa. After talking back and forth with the spirit, Milarepa finally answered, "In terms of the ultimate, never mind an obstructor like you, even a Buddha does not inherently exist. The Buddha's doctrine does not inherently exist. The Spiritual Community does not inherently exist. That is said to be the ultimate truth. However, the omniscient Buddha, in consideration of the thoughts of students, said that everything exists, this being in terms of a conventional valid consciousness." This is an exact presentation of the view of the Consequence School. Therefore, people like Milarepa did not need to know complicated metaphysics but knew the essential meaning. Such is sufficient.

For instance, even if you go to a small country store, it might not have a great variety, but it has all the basic necessities. If you go to a huge supermarket in New York City, there is a great variety but in terms of the basic necessities, it is the same as the country store. Still, there is a difference; in the big store there are many choices.

QUESTION: Can liberation be achieved without acceptance of this specific worldview including the different realms, rebirth, and so forth?

ANSWER: I usually say that if one spends one's life wisely, even if one does not pay much attention to rebirth, there will be a good effect. It will accumulate into a good development, a good force; thus, there is no question that it will help.

Even if one does not know everything, one can progress on the path. Roughly speaking, it is impossible to know everything that is knowable until one becomes omniscient. Thus, if it were the case that one could not progress on the path without knowing everything, then it would be impossible to become a Buddha.

QUESTION: What is a path consciousness?

ANSWER: A path, or vehicle, has the sense of a means of progressing. When we speak of a path consciousness, it is not like a superhighway that might take one to Buddhahood. Buddhahood is achieved through mental development; therefore, a path consciousness refers to mental qualities. Still, in terms of high paths, there are some that are physical, but this means that they have a connection with the inner winds; it does not mean that one is going from one place to another.

QUESTION: What is meant by dualism with respect to an exalted non-dual consciousness?

ANSWER: There are many types of dualistic appearance. One is the appearance of conventional phenomena. Another is the appearance of subject and object as if distant and cut off. Another is the appearance of a conceptual image. Another is the appearance of inherent existence. In deep meditative equipoise on emptiness, there is neither appearance of conventional phenomena, nor appearance of subject and object as if distant and cut off, nor appearance of conceptual images, nor appearance of inherent existence. However, for a Buddha's omniscient consciousness in its aspect of knowing the varieties of phenomena, there is the dualistic appearance of conventional phenomena. From a Buddha's own point of view, a Buddha has no sense of objects as being distant and cut off through the force of any mistakenness; however, in those systems in which external objects are asserted, it may be that a Buddha has some sense of objects as distant and cut off. In any case, a Buddha does not have any sense of dualistic appearance of objects due to defilements that make it impossible to directly perceive the two truths, conventional truths and ultimate truths, simultaneously.

Among the assertions of scholars, there are many disagreements regarding a Buddha's omniscient consciousness in terms of its aspect of knowing conventional phenomena. A Buddha's mode of knowing must be differentiated into two types, one that is from a Buddha's own point of view and another that is only by way of appearances to other beings. For example, if someone who is color-blind explained his or her perceptions to those of us who are not color-blind, it would not be from our own viewpoint that we could speak of their perceptions but from the viewpoint of how things appear to a color-blind person. This is not known through one's own force, but through the force of appearing that way to the other person. Similarly, in general, there is an appearance of inherent existence, and since a Buddha must know everything that exists, a Buddha must know the appearance of inherent existence. However, because a Buddha has overcome and eradicated the appearance of inherent existence, a Buddha's knowing of the appearance of inherent existence is only from the viewpoint of that appearance to persons who have not overcome it.

Also, it is explained in both sūtra and tantra that whatever appears to a Buddha appears as the sport of bliss. Then, one could ask whether the sufferings of sentient beings appear as the sport of bliss to a Buddha? If the sufferings of sentient beings appeared to a Buddha to be the sport of bliss, then the Buddha's consciousness would be a mistaken consciousness. Also, if the sufferings of sentient beings do not appear to a Buddha, then a Buddha would not be omniscient. So, how does such appear? They appear as the sport of bliss from a Buddha's own point of view; however, they also appear as suffering, but only from the point of view of, only through the force of, their appearing to other beings as sufferings.

QUESTION: What are the distinctions between enlightenment, nirvana, and *parinirvāṇa*?

ANSWER: These will be discussed later, but I will say just a little here. There are differences between the way that nirvana is said to be actualized according to the Hearer Schools (the Great Exposition and the Sūtra Schools) and the higher schools (the Mind Only and the Middle Way Schools). In the Hearer Schools, it is explained that when Shākyamuni Buddha achieved enlightenment under the bodhi tree in Bodhgayā, he actually did become enlightened at that time and before that actually was an ordinary sentient being. Therefore, according to these schools, he did not overcome all four demons when he became enlightened in Bodhgayā.

To discuss this, we must identify the four demons. The first is the demon of aggregates, which are the mental and physical aggregates that are appropriated through contaminated actions and afflictive emotions. The reason why such mental and physical aggregates are called demons is that they serve as a basis of suffering and thus are unwanted. The second set of demons are the afflictive emotions themselves, which are called demons because they are what issue forth suffering. The third demon is the Lord of Death, powerless death, which is called a demon because the chief suffering and the root suffering is that of death. The fourth set of demons is comprised of those beings who deliberately make obstacles for persons who want to overcome the other three demons; these are called *devaputra* demons [that is to say, demons who are children of gods]. Probably, devils with horns on their heads would be in this class!

Buddha became enlightened under the bodhi tree at dawn. The night before, he overcame the *devaputra* demons; at dawn, when he became enlightened, he overcame the demons of the afflictive emotions. However, according to the Hearer Schools, he had not overcome the demon of the mental and physical aggregates and the demon of the Lord of Death, which he only overcame at Kushinagara when he passed away. Therefore, Shākyamuni Buddha's physical body is considered by these systems to be a true suffering.

According to these lower systems, when Buddha actualized the nirvana without remainder[3] which is the great parinirvāṇa, the continuum of his mental and physical aggregates was severed. According to their assertions, the Buddha's mind at that point was completely enlightened but had completely ceased. It was no longer conscious. It would seem that such a tenet could make one more discouraged; it seems to me to be far better to have a living consciousness than to disappear completely, but that is the explanation according to the Hearer systems.

According to the texts of Maitreya, however, from the time when Shākyamuni Buddha left the Joyous Pure Land[4] just before his birth in this world, he was performing the activities of a Buddha, of someone who had already become enlightened, and was *displaying* how to become enlightened; actually he had become enlightened many eons ago. Thus, the display of the twelve deeds of a Buddha in India were for the sake of disciples, so that they might know how someone newly becomes enlightened. In this way, Shākyamuni Buddha is in the category of a Supreme Emanation Body,[5] and the emanator of that emanation is a Complete Enjoyment Body,[6] the continuum of which lasts forever. The distinction should be made that the *entity* of a Complete Enjoyment Body is impermanent but its *continuum* is permanent. That from which a Complete Enjoyment Body comes is a Buddha's Truth Body.[7] Those are the Three Bodies of a Buddha described in the Great Vehicle.

Therefore, according to the Great Vehicle systems, when Shākyamuni Buddha became enlightened many eons ago, he completely overcame the four demons in both their coarse and subtle forms. Nirvana will be discussed in more detail later.

THE SOURCES OF SUFFERING

Yesterday, we discussed true sufferings; today, let us discuss true sources of suffering. The fact that sufferings are not *always* produced but are produced in *some* places at *some* times and cease at *some* times and in *some* places indicates that they are caused. Logically, it can be said that sufferings are caused because of being produced occasionally. If sufferings were produced causelessly, either they would never exist or they would always exist.

Since sufferings are caused, one needs to look into what their causes are. In the Buddhist systems, the causes are explained to be contaminated actions and afflictive emotions. In the non-Buddhist systems of India, there are many different presentations of what the causes of suffering are. In general, there are many non-Buddhist systems, which are condensed into five main systems; among them, the chief seem to be the Sāṃkhyas and the Jainas. The Sāṃkhyas enumerate twenty-five categories of objects of knowledge—of existents; according to them, the basic cause of both pleasure and pain is the fundamental nature,[8] also called the general principal,[9] and the experiencer of pleasure and pain is the person.[10] They say that through understanding that the varieties of pleasure and pain are created by the general principal, the general principal is, so to speak, flushed with shame and ceases its transformations with respect to that person, whereby the person attains liberation.

The Jainas, on the other hand, posit a state of liberation that is like an upside down umbrella on top of the world system. There are many such systems of explanation, which engage in critical discussion with each other. In the Buddhist systems, once the effects— true sufferings—are compounded phenomena, their causes must be compounded, impermanent phenomena and could not be permanent factors.

For instance, if I had an angry feeling, this could serve as a motivating force that would lead to a harsh attitude, harsh speech, and harsh physical gestures. Since the anger that serves as the motivating factor is a defilement—an afflictive emotion—the physical and verbal actions done through that motivating force are negative karmas, negative actions. Through them, the atmosphere immediately changes into one of tension. Right away, I might not feel the effects of those actions, perhaps even feeling that I had gained a victory over someone, even shouting, "I have won." However, later I will feel very sorry and shy, deep down experiencing a guilty conscience. Similarly, those around me would immediately lose their tranquility and peace. These are painful results of actions impelled by a bad motivation. This is the law of karma—motivation, action, result.

Conversely, a good, open, sincere motivation such as compassion with a deep respect for others impels verbal and physical actions that immediately create a peaceful, harmonious, enjoyable atmosphere. Due to that, I feel happy and calm, enjoying that atmosphere, and others around me also enjoy the same. Therefore, bad motivation creates problems, suffering, and pain, whereas good motivation creates happiness and peacefulness—something good.

This is the general explanation. On a deeper level, right at the time of an action, predisposing potencies are instilled in the consciousness. The performance of an action establishes a predisposing potency in the mind that, in the future, will serve as the causal condition for one's experiencing a good or bad effect.

Karma

With respect to actions, karma, there are two types—actions of intention[11] and intended actions,[12] that is to say, motivations and actions motivated. With respect to intended actions, the Proponents of the Great Exposition and the Consequentialists posit physical, verbal, and mental actions, whereas the Proponents of Sūtra and Proponents of Mind Only hold that all intended actions are only mental since physical and verbal actions are, for them, the mental factor of intention[13] at the time of the performance of these actions.

In terms of the avenues by which actions are displayed, there are actions of body, speech, and mind. In terms of their effects, there are two types, virtuous and non-virtuous actions. Within the virtuous, there are again two types, actions of merit that impel rebirth in happy transmigrations in the Desire Realm and non-fluctuating[14] actions that impel rebirth in the Form and the Formless Realms.

In terms of the experience or non-experience of the effect, there are two types—those of which the effect is definite to be experienced and those of which the effect is not definite to be experienced. These can be understood through discussing another division into four types by way of motivation and accomplishment—those done deliberately, those deliberated but not done, those done but not deliberately, and those neither deliberated nor done. An example of the first would be to deliberately kill a mosquito. Then, let us suppose that an insect was bothering you, and you wanted very much to kill it, but someone distracts you. In this case, you have karmically accumulated the motivation but you did not carry out the action; this is an action deliberated but not done. An example of an action done but without deliberation would be to kill a mosquito by just moving one's hand without having intended to do so; you killed it, but not deliberately. The fourth type is when one neither has the motivation nor carries out the action.

Of these four types, the first two—those done deliberately and those deliberated but not done—are actions the effects of which are definite to be experienced. The other two—those done without deliberation and those neither deliberated nor done—are actions the effects of which are not definite to be experienced. For instance, if a person who does want to kill is inducted into an army and ordered to kill, even when that person kills someone, as long as he or she has an immediate sense of very strong regret, that action is one of which the experience of its effect is indefinite.

From this, one can see that the action is not as important as the motivation. Thus, a big general or leader of a country, who, out of a motivation to destroy all the opposing forces, actually orders that war be made accumulates all the sins of killings that occur during the war, even if his physical body is not involved in carrying out the action that he orders. Similarly, if ten persons make plans for a feast that involve buying an animal and slaughtering it, only one animal is killed, but since all ten have the motivation to kill and eat the animal, each of the ten persons accumulate the complete sin of killing that sentient being.

Again, with respect to those actions of which the effects are definite to be experienced, there are different divisions from the viewpoint of the time when the effect is experienced. With some actions, their effects are begun to be experienced in this very lifetime. For others, their effects are begun to be experienced in the next lifetime. Again, there are others of which the effects are begun to be experienced in lifetimes after the next lifetime.

Also, with respect to virtues, there are many types. A true cessation of a level of suffering, for instance, is an *ultimate virtue*. Faith and compassion, for instance, are *virtues by way of their own nature*. Mental factors such as mindfulness and introspection that accompany a virtuous consciousness are *virtues by way of association*. If, with a helpful motivation, one walked from one area to another, although the walking itself is not a virtuous activity, each step would be a *virtue by way of motivation*. Also, the virtuous predispositions established by virtuous minds and mental factors are *virtues through subsequent relation*.

That concludes a short discussion of karma. For a Buddhist practitioner, the basis of the various types of ethical practices is the abandonment of the ten non-virtues, many of which are like the ten commandments.

Buddhist Psychology

Because these actions, or karmas, are driven by afflictive emotions, what are afflictive emotions? First, since the principal factor involved in actions is the mental factor of intention, which is a type of consciousness, and because the afflictive emotions are also types of consciousness, it is important to have an understanding of Buddhist psychology.

As was explained earlier during the question period, the definition of consciousness is that which is luminous and knowing. In order to promote a variety of insights and realizations with respect to consciousness, it is divided from many different points of view. First, consciousnesses are divided into those that realize their objects and those that do not. Realizational consciousnesses, in turn, are divided into those that explicitly realize their objects and those that implicitly realize their objects. In the case of those consciousnesses that explicitly realize their objects, the aspect of their object actually appears to the consciousness, whereas in the case of implicit realization, the aspect of the object does not appear to the consciousness.

There is also a division into conceptual and non-conceptual consciousnesses. Conceptual consciousnesses are those that apprehend their objects through the medium of a conceptual image, technically called a "sound-generality"[15] or a "meaning-generality."[16] Non-conceptual consciousnesses apprehend their objects directly, without the medium of a conceptual image.

Again, there is a division into valid and non-valid consciousnesses as well as a division into what are called the seven types of knowledge and awareness—direct perception, inference, subsequent cognition, correctly assuming consciousness, a consciousness to which an object appears but is not noticed, doubt, and wrong consciousness. Let us start with a correctly assuming consciousness. For instance, when, from hearing correct information about the four noble truths, one merely thinks about them as one has been taught, this consciousness is a correctly assuming consciousness. Such a consciousness has not developed into an entity which is a valid cognition that ascertains the four noble truths incontrovertibly, but it properly or correctly holds them to be as they are. Correctly assuming consciousnesses also have many subdivisions that I will not explain.

Another of the seven types of knowledge and awareness is a consciousness to which an object appears but is not ascertained. For instance, when the eye consciousness is particularly absorbed in a visible form, even though the ear consciousness hears a sound, it is not ascertained. That ear consciousness is one to which an object appears but is not ascertained. From the point of view of the Sūtra School and the Mind Only School, such consciousnesses can occur among sense direct perceptions, mental direct perceptions, and self-knowing consciousnesses. Thus, among the four types of direct perceptions, consciousness to which an object appears but is not ascertained cannot occur among yogic direct perceptions, since these necessarily ascertain their objects.

The next is a subsequent cognition—a consciousness that realizes an object that has already been realized. In the Consequence School, a subsequent cognition can be a prime cognition,[17] whereas in the other systems, such is impossible because, in the Mind Only School, for instance, "prime cognition" is interpreted as a *new* incontrovertible knower and thus a subsequent cognition cannot be a *prime* cognition. However, in the Consequence School, the term "prime"[18] in "prime cognition" is not taken as meaning "new" but is taken as meaning "main," and thus they consider "prime cognition" to be a consciousness that is incontrovertible with respect to its *main* object. The reason behind the other schools' taking "prime cognition" to mean a *new* incontrovertible knower is that they assert that all phenomena inherently exist and thus, when the object designated as "prime cognition" is sought analytically, it must be found as being incontrovertible with respect to such inherent existence. In the system of the Consequence School, however, it is maintained that when objects designated are sought analytically, they cannot be found, and thus phenomena, including prime cognitions, are not posited within the context of being found under such analysis. Hence, they posit "prime cognition" in accordance with how it is widely used in the world, for the world does not use the term "prime cognition" [or "valid cognition"] in the context of *new* incontrovertible cognition and instead only uses it in reference to incontrovertible cognition, valid cognition. Hence, since subsequent cognitions and their several subdivisions are incontrovertible and valid, they are *prime* or *valid* cognitions in the Consequence School.

Then, the next is a *wrong consciousness*, which apprehends its object perversely. There are two subdivisions, conceptual and non-conceptual wrong consciousnesses. Then, there is *doubt,* which is a mental factor that has qualms in two directions with respect to its object.

The remaining two types of knowledge and awareness are *direct perception* and *inference*. In the Sūtra School, a direct perception is an awareness that takes a specifically characterized phenomenon[19] as its appearing object, and a conceptual consciousness is an awareness that takes a generally characterized phenomenon[20] as its appearing object. There are several interpretations of this topic that need not be explained here.

Basically, a directly perceiving consciousness—for instance, an eye consciousness apprehending a flower—is such that all attributes that are of one substantial entity with the flower appear to the eye consciousness, but it does not necessarily ascertain all of them. The impermanence of the flower as well as its productness, its momentary disintegration, its being made by causes and conditions, and so forth appear to that eye consciousness, but it does not necessarily notice or ascertain them. Thus, a direct perception engages its object holistically. However, conceptual consciousnesses and terms engage their object in a partial manner. For instance, when a conceptual consciousness apprehends a flower, it puts aside these many attributes and just zeros in on one factor and apprehends the flower in this exclusive and partial way. When a non-conceptual consciousness has transmitted its information, a conceptual consciousness can, one by one, look into those attributes, distinguishing them.

To understand the difference between a non-conceptual consciousness and a conceptual consciousness, it is helpful to differentiate between the objects of those consciousnesses. One has to differentiate between the appearing object[21] and the object of operation.[22] In the Consequence School, to an eye consciousness apprehending a form, the form appears as well as a seeming inherent existence of the form. The eye consciousness apprehending the form is a valid cognition with respect to the form, and it is a valid cognition with respect to the *appearance* of the form as inherently existent,[23] but it is not a valid cognition with respect to the inherent existence of the form, since the form does not, in fact, inherently exist.

From the point of view that its object falsely appears to exist inherently, this eye consciousness is said to be a mistaken consciousness, but this does not mean that it must be mistaken in all respects. For, in relation to its apprehending or realizing the form, it is non-mistaken and thus can be posited as a valid cognition that certifies [the existence of] the form. Thus, it is both a mistaken consciousness and a valid cognition, these two being explained with regard to different objects. A consciousness cannot be both mistaken and valid with respect to the same object, but with respect to two objects, one consciousness can be described as a mistaken consciousness and a valid cognition; it is mistaken with respect to its appearing object and a valid cognition with respect to its object of operation.

This is a unique tenet of the Consequence School, which stems from the fact that the proponents of this school do not accept that phenomena, even conventionally, exist by way of their own character. In the other subdivision of the Middle Way School, the Autonomy School, it is said that the object of negation in the view of selflessness does not appear to a sense consciousness, but in the Consequence School, the object of negation, inherent existence, appears even to sense consciousnesses. Thus, in this system, even a valid cognition can be said to be mistaken relative to the factor of the appearance of its object as if it exists in its own right. Therefore, all consciousnesses except for a wisdom consciousness directly realizing emptiness in meditative equipoise are mistaken with respect to their appearing objects.

Then, someone might object that a mistaken consciousness could not certify [the existence of] conventional phenomena such as forms. It indeed is the case that if a truly established form were to be certified, it would have to be certified by a consciousness that is unmistaken relative to the appearance of form as inherently existent. However, since truly established forms are not asserted even conventionally, forms are posited as falsities—appearing to be truly established but not actually so, and once this is the case, a mistaken consciousness is more appropriate as a certifier of a falsity. This is a very important point for ascertaining the view of emptiness. The basic tenet is that, except for a Superior's meditative equipoise directly realizing emptiness, all consciousnesses are necessarily mistaken.

Also, a consciousness is posited through the force of an appearance of an object, whether the appearance of that object is right or wrong. For instance, an appearance of inherent existence occurs to a consciousness conceiving inherent existence, and it is by way of that appearance of inherent existence that the consciousness conceives of inherent existence. Since that appearance appears to the consciousness, it is held that the consciousness is valid with respect to that appearance and is even a direct valid cognition with respect to that appearance. Hence, even a wrong consciousness conceiving inherent existence is valid relative to the appearance of inherent existence and is a direct valid cognition relative to the appearance of inherent existence since it is valid with respect to the mere fact that inherent existence appears to it. Nevertheless, since inherent existence never has nor will occur, it is wrong.

4. More about Consciousness and Karma

Tuesday Afternoon

Question and Answer Period

QUESTION: Those who have been denied a sense of self-worth seem to benefit from gaining self-identity through therapy, support groups, and self-assertiveness training. Are such therapeutic approaches to self-validation increasing illusion and suffering even though they seem to do the opposite? How can the need for individual integrity and power be reconciled with the spiritual principle of selflessness? In our practice, how can we avoid the state of pride from accomplishment and depression caused by disintegration of the ego?

ANSWER: This question meets back to not understanding well the fact that the self, the person, is indeed asserted to exist conventionally. There are two types of elevated attitudes. One is an elevated or confident attitude that is well reasoned—has a reasonable foundation; this is a state of courage and is definitely needed. Another type is an elevated or proud attitude, which is actually based on misconception; it is pride. However, if one engages in a practice and experiences the true imprint or result of that practice, it is suitable to be proud of this in the sense of taking delight in it.

Shāntideva speaks of various types of elevated attitudes in his *Engaging in the Bodhisattva Deeds*. One type is to have the courage of thinking that you can do what others cannot do; this is strength of will, not pride, and is not contradictory with taking a humble or lower position when meeting with others. For instance, the second of the *Eight Stanzas on Training the Mind* speaks of the need to take the lowest position when meeting with any others:[1]

> Whenever I associate with others, I will learn
> To think of myself as the lowest among all
> And respectfully hold others to be supreme
> From the very depths of my heart.

The modes of thought in pride and in courageous thought are entirely different.

Depression caused by disintegration of the ego probably comes from not being able to posit a conventionally existent I. Still, when some understanding of emptiness develops, you have a different feeling of I than that to which you previously were accustomed. Our usual feeling is that the I is something solid, really independent, and very forceful. Such no longer remains, but at the same time there is a sense of a mere I that accumulates karma and performs actions. Such a sense of self is not at all a source of depression.

If you have difficulty positing a merely nominal I as well as a merely nominal cause and effect of actions—if you get to the point where if you assert selflessness, you cannot posit dependent-arising—then it would be better to assert dependent-arising and give up selflessness. Indeed, there are many levels of understanding selflessness, and Buddha, out of great skillfulness in method, taught many different schools of tenets that posit coarser levels of selflessness for those temporarily unable to understand the more subtle levels. It is not the case that only if the most profound level is immediately accessible, it is suitable, and if it is not accessible, the whole endeavor should be thrown away. You have to proceed step by step with whatever accords with your level of mind. Between emptiness and dependent-arising, you should value dependent-arising more highly.

QUESTION: Yesterday you said that some objects of knowledge, such as those for which you would need inference by belief, are not comprehensible through usual investigation. How can it be determined that the self for which one searches analytically is not an object that really does exist but simply is not findable by usual analysis, perhaps because it is too subtle?

ANSWER: Yesterday we were talking about the three types of inference—inference by the power of the fact, inference through renown, and inference through believability. With regard to these, one needs to know about the three types of objects of comprehension[2]—the manifest,[3] the slightly hidden,[4] and the very hidden.[5] Logical proofs are not needed for manifest phenomena, such as the color of the walls in this room, which can be experienced in direct perception, but slightly hidden, or slightly non-obvious, phenomena need to be inferred in dependence upon reasoning that works through the power of the fact. For instance, emptiness is a slightly hidden object that is accessible to reasoned analysis. The self, or person, however, is something that is in the class of manifest objects. For instance, when you think, "I am hot," or, "I am sick," it is not necessary to use reasoned analysis to infer the existence of the I, and thus it is a manifest phenomenon.

The division of objects into these three types of objects of comprehension is within the context of conventional valid cognition. For, when one analyzes with the reasoning analyzing the ultimate, just as the person or self is not found, so all other phenomena are not found either. Emptiness itself is not found. This has nothing to do with whether the object being analyzed is manifest, slightly hidden, or very hidden, but has to do with the mode of analysis. One is analyzing whether the object is ultimately established or not, whether it is truly established or not, whether it is inherently established or not.

With regard to very hidden objects, these are phenomena such as very subtle presentations of particular actions and their exact effects. How can very hidden phenomena be realized? Here, one must rely on another, third factor. For instance, the people in this room are all manifest phenomena; it is not necessary to use any reasoning to realize their existence. However, if we considered whether there are any persons on the other side of that wall, we would look for a sign of a person's being there, such as whether anyone is speaking or cars are moving, since there would not be any of these unless a person is there. Even further, if we wondered whether a flower is growing outside the wall on the eastern side of this room, there is no way that we could look into the matter from here. Thus, as a technique, we have to depend on the speech of someone who has seen whether there are flowers there or not. Now, if we are to rely on someone's speech, we have to look into whether that person usually lies or not, or whether there is a reason why the person might lie on this occasion. If, having done such analysis, we determine that the person would not lie and would speak the truth, then what that person says about the matter would be reliable. Through such a route, we can come to the conclusion that the person's speech is valid about this topic, whereupon we can rely on what the person reports.

One has to examine whether that person's speech can be considered to be valid or not. If yesterday the person said that there was a flower outside the wall but today says that there is not, there would be a contradiction between what was said earlier and later. Similarly, a topic such as a subtle presentation of the exact effects of a particular action (*karma*) is not something that we can determine through our usual reasoning; we have to rely on a person who has experience with these facts. Thus, we need to examine whether that person has a reason to lie about such things and whether there are explicit or implicit contradictions in the person's earlier and later statements on this topic. Through such examination, it can be determined that what this person says about this is reliable. For example, our knowledge of our own birthdate and birthplace is not from reasoning but depends upon our mother's word; based on what she said, we speak of our birthdate and birthplace. I can figure out that I am less than sixty years old by looking at others who are sixty years old and comparing their faces with my own face as reflected in a mirror. I can see that I do not quite look like someone who is sixty, but there is no possibility for me to know the exact time, date, month, and year of my birth. I could never calculate this by myself and instead must rely on some other factor. Such a situation of having to rely on another's word occurs frequently in ordinary life.

Among the three types of objects of comprehension, the manifest are those objects that are known without depending on any reasoning but are ascertained through direct perception. The slightly hidden are those objects that are known through inference by way of the power of facts—usual logical reasoning. The very hidden cannot be known through the usual process of proofs but can only be known through a process that involves depending on someone else's word, this being called inference through believability.

To realize an object that is very hidden to us, inaccessible to our direct perception and usual inference, we have to rely on scripture, but it is not sufficient merely to value scriptures highly. Rather, as explained earlier, the scripture itself has to be established as valid through a great deal of analysis.

In this vein, Dharmakīrti explains in detail the import of the expression of worship to Buddha at the beginning of Dignāga's *Compendium on Valid Cognition*. In the second chapter of his *Commentary on (Dignāga's) "Compendium on Valid Cognition,"*[6] Dharmakīrti establishes that Buddha is a valid, or reliable, person through establishing that Buddha's sayings, his scriptures, are incontrovertible. This mode of procedure accords with the first reliance, to rely not on the person but on the doctrine. With respect to the scriptures, some are concerned with means for achieving a high type of life, called high status,[7] within cyclic existence and some are concerned with attaining liberation from cyclic existence and attaining omniscience, these being called definite goodness.[8] As Dharmakīrti's *Commentary on (Dignāga's) "Compendium on Valid Cognition"* says:[9]

> Because [it is established by inference from the power of the fact that Buddha's word] is not mistaken with regard to the principal meaning [the four noble truths],

[Due to similarity, Buddha's word] can be inferred [to be unmistaken] with regard to others [i.e., very hidden topics, as well].

That Buddha's teachings are incontrovertible with respect to definite goodness and the means of achieving it can be established by inference that, through the power of facts, one realizes that his teaching of the four noble truths is incontrovertible. Based on that, it can be inferred that his word is also incontrovertible with respect to other, less accessible topics. Similarly, Āryadeva's *Four Hundred Stanzas on the Yogic Deeds of Bodhisattvas* says:[10]

> Whoever has generated doubt
> Towards [statements] in Buddha's word concerning hidden
> [ie., obscure] topics
> Will believe that only Buddha [is omniscient]
> Based on [his profound teaching of] emptiness.

A person who has doubt with respect to Buddha's teachings on non-manifest, hidden topics, should—in dependence upon on looking into Buddha's teaching on emptiness—gain conviction with respect to these other teachings that are not accessible to such inference. Through this kind of analysis, scriptures on very obscure topics are proved to be valid; such analytical realization is called "inference through believability," which therefore is not a matter of immediately accepting a scripture. Rather, one has to analyze with reasoning.

QUESTION: In sleep or the dream state, where is the consciousness?

ANSWER: During sleep, the five sense consciousnesses are withdrawn, but not totally, because if someone scratched your hand, for instance, you would wake up. In any case, the sense consciousnesses become more subtle. In general, the main location where consciousness dwells is said to be the heart, not this organ that is pumping, but a nerve or channel center at the heart region. In mantric[11] texts, the nerve centers are described as being in the center of the body, but these descriptions are for the sake of meditation and do not have to correspond to the actual fact in terms of exact location. However, when one meditates in accordance with these instructions, there definitely are effects, such as generating heat and stopping conceptuality.

Just that place where the consciousness enters into the fertilized egg in the womb is the place where the heart center forms, and later when one dies, it is from there that the innermost subtle consciousness leaves the body. The *Kālachakra Tantra* sets forth a system of four drops that serve as bases of subtle consciousnesses into which various types of predispositions are infused. In this presentation, the drop at the forehead generates the waking state; the drop at the throat generates the dream state; the drop at the heart generates the deep sleep state; and the drop at the navel generates the state of bliss, called the fourth state.[12] Thus, it is explained that when one is sleeping deeply, the inner energies (or winds) and consciousness predominantly gather at the heart center, and when one is dreaming, the inner energies (or winds) and consciousness gather at the throat center.

Therefore, if a yogi who is a practitioner of Mantra wants to cause the clear light of the dream state to dawn, the yogi imagines that the winds and consciousnesses gather at the heart center of the dream body, whereby it becomes possible to stop dreams and manifest the clear light. Thus, with regard to sleep and dream, there is a connection with the heart center and the throat center.

QUESTION: Are the Buddhist teachings on the intermediate state between lives and on rebirth to be understood literally or metaphorically?

ANSWER: They are asserted literally.

QUESTION: Is experience of death influenced in any way by its nature, such as when death comes about by way of illness, suicide, murder, or old age?

ANSWER: If one dies by accident such as in an auto accident, the eight levels of dissolution of consciousness occur, but they take place very quickly. If a person dies after a prolonged, severe illness in which the constituents of the body have been consumed and the body has become extremely weak, the stages of dissolution occur but not clearly—they are vague. This is the reason why one implements the practice of transference of consciousness—if one is capable of it—at a point when the body has not become very weak. However, the practice of the transference of consciousness is to be done only when definite signs of death have been perceived and when one has tried techniques to reverse the process of dying but these have not succeeded. Otherwise, there would be the fault of committing suicide.

Let us return to our ongoing topic.

MINDS AND MENTAL FACTORS

Consciousness can also be divided into main minds and mental factors. Some scholars explain that main minds distinguish the general entity of the object, and mental factors distinguish particular features of the object.

The various Buddhist systems have different interpretations of the number of consciousnesses. One system asserts only one consciousness, a mental consciousness. They give a nice example of this: a monkey inside a house goes from window to window, and thus, to someone outside, there appear to be many monkeys. Similarly, the single consciousness operates through the various sense organs and thus seems to be many but is only one. However, this is an extreme position that posits too few consciousnesses.

Another system, the Mind Only School Following Scripture, posits, in addition to the standard six consciousnesses—eye, ear, nose, tongue, body, and mental consciousnesses—two more, a mind-basis-of-all[13] and an afflicted mind.[14] The root reason for their positing a mind-basis-of-all is that they want to posit something findable as the person when the person is sought analytically among its bases of designation. Any system that asserts a mind-basis-of-all does not accept external objects; apprehended objects appear to be external entities, separate from the consciousnesses perceiving them, but are actually not so, being within the entity or nature of the mind.

Again, in the system of the Indian scholar Paramārtha, there is an additional ninth consciousness, called the stainless mind. These assertions of eight and nine consciousnesses are extremes of too many, whereas the assertion of six is in the middle, neither too few nor too many. These six are the five consciousnesses of the five senses and a mental consciousness.

Mental Factors

Mental factors, as explicitly identified in Asaṅga's *Compendium of Manifest Knowledge*, are fifty-one in number. These are five omnipresent factors,[15] five determining factors,[16] eleven virtuous factors,[17] six root afflictions,[18] twenty secondary afflictions,[19] and four changeable factors.[20] Five factors accompany any consciousness and thus are called omnipresent mental factors. These are:

1. *Feeling*,[21] comprised of the feelings of pleasure, pain, and neutrality. In this context, feeling is not the object felt, but the consciousness that feels.

2. *Discrimination*,[22] which is discrimination of objects as "this is such and such; that is such and such."

3. *Intention*,[23] or attention, which moves the mind to the object.

4. *Mental engagement*,[24] which is the factor that takes the object to mind.

5. *Contact*,[25] which distinguishes the object as attractive, unattractive, or neutral.

When the five mental and physical aggregates are posited, out of the fifty-one mental factors only two of them—feelings and discriminations—are treated as separate aggregates. As is said in

Vasubandhu's *Treasury of Manifest Knowledge*,[26] the reasons for this are that, out of wanting pleasant feeling and not wanting pain, we quarrel, and also discriminations—"This is such and such, not that," "That is mine, not yours"—serve as the basis for all debates among systems. For these reasons, feelings and discriminations are counted separately among the five mental and physical aggregates. Vasubandhu's *Treasury of Manifest Knowledge*[27] has very clear presentations of the five aggregates, the twelve sense spheres, and the eighteen constituents.

The next group of mental factors are called determining mental factors because they deal with specifics of the object. These are:

1. *Aspiration*,[28] which is a seeking of the object.
2. *Belief*,[29] which is the factor of holding an object to be as it was ascertained.
3. *Mindfulness*,[30] which is to hold the object in mind.
4. *Stabilization*,[31] which is one-pointedness of mind. This does not refer to great meditative stabilization but to the slight factor of one-pointedness, or stability of mind, that we have now.
5. *Knowledge*,[32] which analyzes the object.

The next group are the eleven virtuous mental factors:

1. *Faith*.[33]
2. *Conscience*,[34] which brings about avoidance of improper behavior from thinking that it would not be suitable from one's own viewpoint to do it.
3. *Embarrassment*,[35] which brings about avoidance of improper behavior out of concern for what others might think.
4. *Non-attachment*,[36] which views desire as faulty, thereby deliberately restraining desire.
5. *Non-hatred*,[37] which views hatred as faulty, thereby deliberately restraining hatred.
6. *Non-ignorance*,[38] which views ignorance as faulty, thereby deliberately restraining ignorance.

7. *Effort*,[39] which is enthusiasm for virtue.
8. *Pliancy*,[40] which is physical and mental serviceability induced by developing meditative stabilization.
9. *Conscientiousness*,[41] which is self-examination, self-checking; this is very important in daily practice.
10. *Equanimity*.[42]
11. *Non-harmfulness*.[43]

These eleven are virtuous mental factors, since they are virtuous by way of their own entities.

Then, there are the six root afflictions:

1. *Desire*,[44] which is attachment to internal or external objects.
2. *Anger*,[45] which is hatred upon observing any of the nine sources of generating harmful intent. What are these nine? Someone who has harmed oneself, is harming oneself, or will harm oneself, or someone who has harmed one's friend, is harming one's friend, or will harm one's friend, or someone who has helped one's enemy, is helping one's enemy, or will help one's enemy. The sources of developing an angry attitude are these nine.
3. *Pride*,[46] of which there are seven types. One is the pride of thinking of an [inherently existent] I. Another is a puffing up of the mind within thinking that oneself is superior to lower persons, whereas in a different version one fancies that one is superior to those who are actually equal. Another is the pride of thinking that oneself is slightly inferior to others, who are actually considerably superior, as in pretending, "Oh, I know almost as much as so and so does." Then, there is pride beyond pride, which is a case of conceiving oneself to be even greater than superior people. Again, there is a type of pride in which one fancies that one has powers such as clairvoyance not actually attained; in another variety, one thinks that one has attained special powers whereas one has actually been carried away by a spirit, for instance.

4. *Ignorance*,[47] which, in this context, is a non-realizing consciousness that obstructs one from seeing the actual mode of subsistence of objects. According to Asaṅga, from between consciousnesses that misconceive the truth and those that just do not know the truth, this is a consciousness that simply does not know the truth. However, according to Dharmakīrti and Chandrakīrti, ignorance is a consciousness misconceiving the nature of things.

5. *Doubt*.[48] One interpretation holds that all doubt is necessarily afflictive, whereas another holds that it is not necessarily afflictive.

6. *Afflictive view*,[49] which is a mind of analysis that has reached a wrong conclusion and thus is an afflictive knower. Since afflictive views are divided into five types, the root afflictions can be considered to be of ten types—the five nonviews and the five afflictive views. The latter are:

1. *View of the transitory collection as inherently existent I and mine*,[50] which is an afflictive cognition that, upon observing the disintegrating collection of the mental and physical aggregates, conceives of an inherently existent I and inherently existent mine.

2. *View holding to an extreme*,[51] which is an afflictive cognition that, upon observing the I that is conceived by the view of the transitory collection, views it either as permanent, stable, and unchanging or as not connecting to a future life. These two, respectively, are views of permanence and annihilation.

3. *Conception of a bad view as supreme*,[52] which is an afflictive cognition that, upon observing either the view of the transitory collection as inherently existent I and mine, a view holding an extreme, a wrong view, or the mental and physical aggregates in dependence upon which these views arise, considers it to be supreme.

4. *Conception of bad ethics and modes of conduct as supreme*,[53] which is an afflictive cognition that—upon observing either faulty systems of ethics or modes of conduct such as those that call for behaving like dogs or other animals—or the mental and physical aggregates in dependence upon which these arise, considers such to be supreme.

5. *Wrong view*,[54] which is an afflictive cognition that denies what actually does exist or superimposes existence on what does not exist. In the list of ten non-virtues, wrong view refers only to the former, but here in the context of the five views it is both.

Those are the five afflictive views, which, together with the five non-view afflictions, comprise what are called the ten subtle increasers of afflictive states.[55] When the five afflictive views are treated as just one category, there are *six* subtle increasers of afflictive states.

Then, there are the twenty secondary afflictive emotions:

1. *Belligerence*,[56] which is caused by anger.

2. *Resentment*.[57]

3. *Concealment of faults*.[58]

4. *Verbal spite*,[59] which is like belligerence but involved with speech.

5. *Jealousy*.[60]

6. *Miserliness*.[61]

7. *Deceit*,[62] which is to pretend to have good qualities one does not.

8. *Dissimulation*,[63] which is to hide one's faults.

9. *Haughtiness*,[64] which is a case of the mind's being puffed up.

10. *Harmfulness*.[65]

11. *Non-shame*,[66] which is lack of conscience.

12. *Non-embarrassment*,[67] which is lack of concern for others' opinion.

13. *Lethargy,*[68] which is to stay beclouded in darkness, without thinking about anything.
14. *Excitement,*[69] which is a scattering of the mind to an object of desire.
15. *Non-faith.*[70]
16. *Laziness.*[71]
17. *Non-conscientiousness.*[72]
18. *Forgetfulness.*[73]
19. *Non-introspection.*[74]
20. *Distraction.*[75]

The next group is that of changeable mental factors, which change due to their context:

1. *Sleep.*[76] If, prior to sleeping, your mind is virtuous, the factor of sleep also will be virtuous, but if, prior to sleeping, your mind is non-virtuous, involved with an afflictive activity, then the factor of sleep will also be non-virtuous.
2. *Contrition,*[77] which is a factor of regret. If one regrets having done a virtuous action, such contrition is non-virtuous, whereas if one regrets having done a non-virtuous action, such is virtuous.
3. *Investigation,*[78] which is to look into objects in a rough way.
4. *Analysis,*[79] which is to look into objects in a detailed fashion. Investigation and analysis are changeable in the sense that if they occur within the context of objects of desire and hatred, for instance, they are non-virtuous, but if they are done within the context of virtuous objects, they themselves are virtuous.

That concludes discussion of the fifty-one mental factors as explicitly described in the system of Asaṅga's *Compendium of Manifest Knowledge*; they do not include all mental factors, there being many more. All of these are similar in having the nature of consciousness but are designated separately from the viewpoint of their various functions.

LEVELS OF CONSCIOUSNESS

In addition, in the Mantra system, consciousnesses are set forth in terms of the grossness or subtlety of their entities themselves. According to the Mantra system, the five sense consciousnesses are gross; the eighty conceptual consciousnesses are subtler. Among the entities of the eighty conceptual consciousnesses, there are many varieties in terms of virtue and non-virtue and many levels of subtlety within that category. What are the eighty conceptual consciousnesses? Thirty-three have the nature of the mind of vivid white appearance; forty have the nature of the mind of vivid red increase, and seven have the nature of the mind of vivid black near-attainment.[80] These three minds—of vivid white appearance, vivid red increase, and vivid black near-attainment—as well as the mind of clear light are the subtlest consciousnesses. These four are also called the four empties.

Thus, three levels of consciousness are distinguished—gross (the sense consciousnesses), subtle (the eighty conceptual consciousnesses), and subtlest (the four empties). Among the latter, the most subtle is the mind of clear light. This presentation is not in terms of function, as was the case with the mental factors, but in terms of the grossness or subtlety of their own entities.

That concludes the discussion of consciousness. The main consciousness is like a president or prime minister, and the others are like secretaries or ministers. Our main mind itself is very honest and pure, like a very honest president, but on the secondary level there are many good and bad thoughts such as desire, haughtiness, deceit, and dissimulation that, like cabinet ministers or cabinet secretaries, give bad advice to the main consciousness. Now, what is our responsibility? First, we must identify these various factors and then distinguish which are good advisers and which can be used but are not so reliable. Gradually, we should get more advice, more suggestions, more influence from the good side, whereby our whole mental attitude will improve.

Thus, a practitioner is a real combat soldier, not combatting an external enemy but the enemy forces that are within ourselves—anger, hatred, attachment, and so forth. These are the real enemies. Once we are ruled by these thoughts, we will accumulate bad karma and, as a result, suffering. Therefore, we must organize the good side of our mind and engage in combat, really fight, using wisdom as the ammunition and one-pointed meditation as the weapon—a rocket launcher! We cannot throw a rocket by hand, without a launch vehicle. Similarly, without one-pointed mindfulness, we cannot use wisdom properly. So, we need wisdom as well as focused meditation. All of these, in turn, are based on good daily conduct—proper ethics—as their ground.

KARMA

How is karma accumulated through the force of afflictive emotions? In brief, non-virtuous karmas are accumulated through the force of desire and hatred. The root of desire and hatred is ignorance. Since the Consequence School is identified as chief because of its many reasonings, I will speak about ignorance from its point of view.

Due to conditioning from beginningless time, we have remained conceiving that the mental and physical aggregates inherently exist. For, no matter what phenomenon appears, we adhere to it as inherently established—established from its own side. The mental and physical aggregates appear to be inherently existent, and we adhere to this appearance.

Within the division of phenomena into persons and other phenomena, the conception of the mental and physical aggregates as being truly established is called a conception of a self of phenomena. The mental and physical aggregates are objects of use, and the user of these is the I that is designated in dependence upon the mental and physical aggregates. Just as we conceive that the mental and physical aggregates, in dependence upon which the I is designated, are inherently existent, so we also conceive that the I that is designated in dependence upon them is inherently existent.

Then, as Dharmakīrti says in his *Commentary on (Dignāga's) "Compendium on Valid Cognition"*:[81]

> When a self exists, other is discriminated.
> When self and other have formed, there is attachment and hatred.

Once there is a sense of a solidly existent, palpable, reliable I, there is a discrimination of other—once there is "I" there also is "you"—whereupon, there is attachment to one's own side and anger toward the other side. As Chandrakīrti says in his *Supplement to (Nāgārjuna's) "Treatise on the Middle"*:[82]

> Homage to that compassion for transmigrating beings
> Who are powerless like a bucket traveling in a well
> Through initially adhering to a self, "I,"
> And then generating attachment for things, "This is mine."

Transmigrating beings first conceive of a truly existent I and then, in dependence upon that, conceive of truly existent mine. Through the force of such, beings wander in cyclic existence, like a bucket powerlessly traveling up and down in a well.

Since this is the case, as long as one has not seen the nature of phenomena, one conceives phenomena to exist from their own side, inherently, due to which desire and hatred are generated, and karmas are accumulated. However, once one has directly perceived the truth of the absence of inherent existence, from that time on, even though one might accumulate non-virtuous karmas, one would not accumulate any new karma that impels a lifetime in cyclic existence. Therefore, those persons who newly accumulate karmas that impel them into cyclic existence are common beings, ranging from Bodhisattvas on the supreme mundane qualities[83] level of the path of preparation on down to all other common beings.

Regarding the mode of accumulating karmas that impel lifetimes in cyclic existence, there are basically two types—accumulating karmas for the sake of pleasurable feeling and for the sake of neutral feeling. The first, in turn, is of two types—(1) accumulating karmas for the sake of pleasurable feelings that arise from externally oriented involvement with the attractive qualities of the Desire Realm, such as pleasant forms, sounds, odors, tastes, and objects of touch and (2) accumulating karmas for the sake of pleasurable feelings that arise from having overcome attraction for external pleasures and having become attracted to the internal pleasurable feelings of meditative stabilization. The first—the accumulation of karma for the sake of externally directed pleasures—is, in turn, of two types, (1) accumulating karmas mainly for the sake of pleasures during this lifetime until one's death, these being non-meritorious karmas, and (2) accumulating karmas that are mainly directed toward pleasures in future lifetimes, these being meritorious karmas.

Karmas that are accumulated for the sake of internal pleasure, upon having overcome attraction for external pleasure and having become attached to the pleasure that arises with internal meditative stabilization, are involved with the first three concentrations. These are called unfluctuating karmas in that they bear their fruit only in those concentrations. Then, karmas that are accumulated upon having turned away even from such pleasure of internal meditative stabilization and within seeking just neutral feeling are unfluctuating karmas associated with the fourth concentration and the four formless absorptions. However, if, through understanding this presentation, you develop renunciation of all types of such cyclic existence, and accumulate karmas for the sake of permanent bliss, these karmas will bring about liberation from cyclic existence.

TWELVE BRANCHES OF DEPENDENT-ARISING

One accumulates these karmas through the force of ignorance and, due to having accumulated them, is drawn into further rounds of cyclic existence. What are the stages of production of the afflictive emotions, the karmas that are influenced by them, and a life in cyclic existence? This brings us to the topic of the twelve branches of dependent-arising.

In the *Rice Seedling Sutra*,[84] Buddha set forth the twelve-branched dependent-arising of cyclic existence both in its forward and reverse processes. In the forward process, one enters into cyclic existence; in the reverse process, one attains liberation from it. As my source, I will use the twenty-sixth chapter of Nāgārjuna's *Treatise on the Middle*.[85] To begin, let us enumerate the twelve branches of dependent-arising. The first is beginningless *ignorance,* which is what I have just been explaining—a consciousness conceiving inherent existence. As a student of Nāgārjuna and Chandrakīrti, I must explain it this way. In the systems of the Proponents of Sūtra and the Proponents of Mind Only, the ignorance that is the first branch of dependent-arising is explained as misconceiving the nature of the person as being substantially existent in the sense of being self-sufficient. The schools ranging from the Autonomy School down to the Great Exposition School similarly describe the selflessness of persons as a person's emptiness of being substantially existent in the sense of being self-sufficient. However, the Consequentialists, despite using similar terminology, set forth a different meaning for the selflessness of persons. In the other systems, there is a difference of grossness and subtlety between the selflessness of persons and the selflessness of phenomena, whereas in the Consequence School there is no difference in subtlety between the two.

Thus, the first branch in the twelve-branched dependent-arising, beginningless ignorance, is a consciousness conceiving inherent existence. However, as a secondary type, there is the ignorance that is an obscuration with respect to actions, or karmas, and their effects.

The second branch is *compositional action,* of which there are three types—meritorious, non-meritorious, and nonfluctuating. These were described earlier. Basically, the second branch refers to actions.

Next is *consciousness,* which, in its causal aspect, refers to the consciousness that serves as the basis for the infusion of the potencies of karmas. The Mind Only School Following Scripture identifies this consciousness as the mind-basis-of-all; the Consequence School, on the other hand, speaks of two bases of infusion of karmic potencies—temporary and continual. The temporary is the continuum of consciousness; the continual is the mere I.

When, motivated by ignorance, one accumulates a non-virtuous karma, the causal motivator is ignorance with respect to the reality of the absence of inherent existence, and the motivator at the actual time of the action is an ignorance with respect to the effects of actions. With such ignorance, one engages in an action, which, in turn, infuses a potency in the consciousness. However, in the case of a virtuous karma, the causal motivator is ignorance with respect to the reality of the absence of inherent existence, and within that context one engages in a virtuous action that infuses a potency in the consciousness. This consciousness into which these potencies are infused is called a "causal consciousness." The "effect consciousness" is the first moment of consciousness of the new lifetime.

Through these three—ignorance, an activity motivated by it, and the consciousness into which the karmic potency is infused— the *name and form* of a new lifetime arise. Therefore, the fourth branch of dependent-arising is name and form. "Form" refers to the form aggregate, and "name" refers to the other four, mental aggregates—feelings, discriminations, compositional factors, and consciousnesses.

In dependence upon the production of the dependent-arising of name and form, the *six sense spheres*—the sense powers of the eye, ear, and so forth—arise. Then, in dependence upon the dependent-arising of the six sense spheres, *contact*—which distinguishes objects as attractive, unattractive, or neutral—arises upon the coming together of the sense power, consciousness, and respective object. This is the sixth branch.

Due to the condition of having developed contact—the sense of an object as being attractive, unattractive, or neutral upon the coming together of the sense power, consciousness, and respective object—*feelings* of pleasure, pain, or neutrality arise. Due to such feelings, *attachment* develops, this being the attachment of not wanting to separate from pleasure and the attachment of wanting to separate from suffering. This is the eighth branch.

Then, due to the condition of attachment to the four types of objects, grasping of four types is produced:

1. Desirous grasping, which is desire involving strong attachment to visible forms, sounds, odors, tastes, and tangible objects.
2. Grasping at bad views, which is desire involving strong attachment to afflictive views, except for the false view of the transitory collection as inherently existent I and mine.
3. Grasping at bad ethics and mode of conduct, which is desire involving strong attachment to a bad system of ethics or mode of conduct which one considers to be supreme.
4. Grasping at propounding self, which is desire involving strong attachment to the false view of the transitory collection as inherently existent I and mine.

Thus, due to the condition of attachment, there is grasping, and through the force of the production of any of these four types of grasping, the potency that was established in the causal consciousness by an action is nourished. Thereby, that karma becomes potentialized such that it can project the next lifetime.

This fully potentialized karma is called the tenth branch of dependent-arising, *existence*. This is a case of calling the cause—the fully potentialized karma—with the name of its effect—the "existence" of the next lifetime. In this way, grasping nourishes, or enhances, a karma such that it is ready to impel the next lifetime. Then, after death, an intermediate state between lifetimes is produced, after which there is *birth*, or conception, this being the eleventh branch of dependent-arising. Due to the condition of birth, the dependent-arising of aging and death is established. As Nāgārjuna's *Treatise on the Middle* says:[86]

> In this way arise what are
> Just aggregates of suffering.

The stopping of the latter branches from among these twelve depends upon stopping the former ones; thus, if you want to stop the suffering of aging and death, you have to stop ignorance. As a summary, Nāgārjuna says that since the stopping of the latter branches depends upon stopping the former, the stopping of the former branches serves as a condition for stopping the latter branches. He says:[87]

> Through the cessation of this and that [earlier branch]
> This and that [later branch] do not arise.
> What are just aggregates of suffering
> Thoroughly cease in this way.

These aggregates—appropriated through contaminated actions and afflictive emotions and having a nature of just suffering—stop through overcoming ignorance.

This layout of the twelve branches is an enumeration in temporal order in the sense that the earlier branches induce the latter. However, the twelve can be condensed into four groups—projecting branches, projected branches, actualizing branches, and actualized branches. In this way, there are two sets of causes and effects. Why are the twelve set forth in these two groups of causes and effects? It is to indicate the nature of suffering by way of two different approaches, one being effects that are true sufferings *projected* by projecting causes and the other being effects that are true sufferings *actualized* by actualizing causes. The true sufferings that are effects projected by projecting causes—name and form, the six sense spheres, contact, and feeling—are the *bases* of suffering, ready to give rise to suffering. The true sufferings that are effects actualized by actualizing causes—birth and aging/death—are *entities* of suffering at the time of fruition.

In how many lifetimes does one pass through this cycle of twelve? At the fastest, two lifetimes. In the first lifetime, motivated by *ignorance*, one engages in an *action*, thereby accumulating that karma, the potency being infused in the *consciousness*, and near the time of death *attachment* and *grasping* nourish that karmic potency, which, when fully potentialized, is called *existence*. Then, in the next lifetime one undergoes the effects of those—*name and form*, the *six sense spheres, contact*, and *feeling* as well as *birth* and *aging/death*.

At the longest, one cycle of the twelve takes three lifetimes. In one lifetime a person engages in an *action* motivated by *ignorance*, thereby depositing a potency in *consciousness*—these being the first three branches. Then, during a later lifetime (there could be one lifetime or many lifetimes intervening), when *name and form* through to *feeling* occur, the person's *attachment* and *grasping*—the eighth and ninth branches—serve to nourish the particular potency established by that action done in the earlier lifetime, thereby actualizing the tenth branch—*existence*. Then, in the very next lifetime, the remaining dependent-arisings—*birth* and *aging/death*—are actualized. In this mode of reckoning, there are at least three lifetimes for one cycle of the twelve.

Thus, nowadays when we generate a manifest consciousness conceiving inherent existence and, within such a motivational context, engage in an action, a karma is immediately accumulated. Even if we do not know how to identify ignorance—a consciousness conceiving inherent existence—clearly in our own continuums, whenever we generate desire or hatred, ignorance acts to assist its production. Without assistance from ignorance, desire and hatred cannot be generated. We all recognize that we generate desire and hatred, do we not? At the very moment we generate them, we accumulate a karma—an imprint is established in consciousness right at that time. Even though our type of consciousnesses changes, these predisposing potencies stay in the mental consciousness as potential energies such that when the proper conditions are encountered, they are activated.

The very next moment after the time of an action, the action has ceased, but a predisposing potency remains. The various Buddhist systems give different interpretations of what these potencies are. In the Consequence School, objects of the three times are asserted to be functioning things, and similarly the state of an action's having ceased also is asserted to be a functioning thing. Thus, it is held that the destructiveness of an action is capable of producing an effect.

If we take as an example an action the effect of which is to be experienced in the next lifetime, the attachment and grasping that one has near the time of death nourish the karmic potency that this action established in the mind. Most likely, attachment and grasping would not be just one instance but types of attachment and grasping that occurred over and over during the lifetime, just as, in order to be reborn in a Pure Land, one must take to mind again and again the features of a Pure Land and aspire to be reborn there. In this way, just near the time of death, the tenth branch of dependent-arising, "existence," is actualized. Then, in the next lifetime the dependent-arising of birth and aging/death are produced. This is the way that the twelve branches of dependent-arising that stem from *one* action motivated by ignorance occur; thus, it can be seen that while one cycle of dependent-arising from the time of the initial cause to the full production of its effects is occurring, many other cycles of dependent-arising revolving around other actions motivated by ignorance are occurring. This is like committing a crime, being put in jail, and committing more crimes while in jail. Thus, until ignorance is removed, it is as if endless—there does not seem to be any way to end it.

This is how one travels in cyclic existence by way of the twelve branches of dependent-arising. Yesterday, I spoke about true sufferings; today, the topic was the true sources of suffering, contaminated actions and afflictive emotions—the twelve branches of dependent-arising being the manner in which the sources of suffering bring about suffering. Tomorrow, I will speak about the methods to get out of this cycle—liberation.

5. CESSATION AND BUDDHA NATURE

Wednesday Morning

QUESTION AND ANSWER PERIOD

QUESTION: How do Buddhists feel about abortion?

ANSWER: Abortion is considered an ill deed of killing a living being. With respect to monks and nuns, there are four types of ill deeds that bring about a defeat of the vow itself; one of them is to kill a human being or something forming as a human being.

Birth control that does not involve abortion, however, is to be considered relative to the situation. We have to be concerned about overpopulation in general and each family's situation in particular; all of these factors must be considered. It depends upon the circumstances.

QUESTION: I have the strong wish to be reborn in any of the realms in a position to truly help other sentient beings in that realm. Is it wrong for me in these circumstances not to have the strong wish to leave the wheel of cyclic existence?

ANSWER: Your wish to stay in order to help is certainly right. One of Shāntideva's prayers, roughly translated is,[1] "As long as there is space, I will remain with sentient beings, to serve and help them." Therefore, I also am trying to practice this. Helping others is the real purpose of life; it will bring the most satisfaction. The one action of helping others out of a sincere motivation brings two results— satisfaction for yourself and benefit to others. It is most beautiful.

One might ask whether there is a contradiction between a Bodhisattva's developing a determination to leave cyclic existence by viewing it as faulty and a Bodhisattva's wishing to remain in cyclic existence in order to help others. An answer to this is given in Bhāvaviveka's *Heart of the Middle Way*:[2] He says that, upon seeing the faults of cyclic existence, one does not have any wish to stay in such a life and has a strong wish to be freed from the cyclic round of birth, aging, sickness, and death—and, in a similar fashion, Asaṅga's *Bodhisattva Grounds*[3] sets forth many varieties of meditations on the sufferings of cyclic existence. Nevertheless, as Bhāvaviveka says, because of being under the influence of love and compassion, one is not captivated by the idea of retreating into solitary peace and, with an attitude of seeking to bring about the welfare of other sentient beings, remains in cyclic existence. This attitude is really marvelous. Though you are really fed up with cyclic existence, still because of a willingness and a determination to serve others, you voluntarily accept to remain.

However, as is indicated by the frequently cited example of a lotus that is produced from mud but not polluted by it, a Bodhisattva stays in cyclic existence but is not affected by its faults. It would indeed be hypocritical to claim from one's mouth that one had taken up the practice of a Bodhisattva but actually to be happily stuck in cyclic existence with great attachment.

QUESTION: Would you explain about how a high lama works on the consciousness of a dying or a dead person, to guide that person to a better rebirth?

ANSWER: If the lama has the capacity, it is possible to bring about a transference of the consciousness of the dying person so that the person is reborn in a better state. Otherwise, it is helpful for an acquaintance to stimulate mindfulness of the dying person's usual practices by slowly and gently repeating important points of that practice into the person's ear as long as the ear consciousness still functions. This will have the same effect.

It is important to recognize that the time near death is the last opportunity, so that we help in such a way that we avoid any object or attitude that would cause the dying person to feel anger or to experience attachment and thereby make it more difficult for the person to depart. Therefore, children or companions should not remind the dying person of these feelings. It is better for a courageous companion to remain with her or him, trying to influence the dying person's mind to become peaceful and restful as much as possible. Even religious persons who have not practiced much can make great use of this period, if they remember to practice. It is very helpful to die within concentrating on a virtuous topic.

QUESTION: As ordinary beings die, do they recognize that they are dying?

ANSWER: Until the subtler consciousnesses are generated, even ordinary persons could know that they are dying, but when the consciousness becomes quite subtle, one tends to lose awareness. The third of the four subtler consciousnesses that appear in series during the process of death has two periods, one in which the person is still conscious and another in which the person is no longer conscious.

QUESTION: In the case of massive stroke and total loss of bodily functions, which can last for years, what can be done to help? What effect does this have on the intermediate state?

ANSWER: A person who has had a stroke but still has a clear mind and is able to think is in a comparatively better situation since the techniques just mentioned can be used. When the power of thought is also damaged, the situation is difficult. However, I doubt that a prolonged stroke would have much effect on the intermediate state since at that point one has the form of the being as whom one will be reborn. Technically speaking, the intermediate state belongs to the next life. Still, there would be a degree of influence because the intermediate state is a continuation of the earlier mind of the stroke victim.

QUESTION: What is the rainbow body?

ANSWER: In the sūtra system, it is explained that on the three pure Bodhisattva grounds—the eighth, ninth, and tenth—a Bodhisattva achieves a mental body. It has a mental nature and has arisen in dependence upon the predispositions of ignorance and uncontaminated karma. It is not a solid physical body but is like a rainbow. In the sūtra system, this body remains right up to Buddhahood; it even serves as the immediate cause of a Buddha's physical body.

The tantric system criticizes this view, saying that despite that body's being a light, rainbow body, it is generated within the confines of the level of the predispositions of ignorance. Thus, they say that there is no way that a physical body generated from an impure cause could be of one undifferentiable entity with a Buddha's exalted mind that is utterly separate from all defilements. Hence, in Highest Yoga Tantra it is said that a Buddha's physical body must be achieved in dependence upon the very subtle wind and mind. As I explained the other day, these have a very pure nature, and thus they can serve as the source of a Buddha's physical body. In general, a body created from subtle wind and mind is called an illusory body.

Production of a pure body from subtle wind and mind is the system of the *Guhyasamāja Tantra*.[4] Most of the tantric teachings— the *Heruka Tantra*,[5] the *Hevajra Tantra*,[6] and so forth—present such a combination of body and mind, but the mother tantras have a different, unique explanation of the achievement of a rainbow body. Also, in the texts of the Old Translation School of Mantra in the Ñying-ma tradition, there is a teaching of a rainbow body of great transference. Again, there is a teaching of the body's being released as a rainbow body, in which the old body completely dissolves into a rainbow body; this is for someone who is practicing the leap-over system in Ñying-ma. In the Kālachakra system, there is an explanation of an empty body—a body empty of material particles—which is not an illusory body achieved from wind but is achieved in the context of the mind of clear light. Thus, there are many different types of rainbow bodies.

QUESTION: If the root of all suffering is attachment, are the desire to have a family and the desire for liberation from suffering contradictory?

ANSWER: I think that a distinction should be made between desires that are due to ignorance and desires that are reasoned. In Tibetan, a difference can be made between "wish"[7] and "desire";[8] for instance, a Bodhisattva is reborn through his or her own wishes, not out of desire. Similarly, it is suitable to aspire toward liberation. Also, persons, such as Foe Destroyers, who have completely overcome all of the afflictive emotions, have thoughts such as, "Such and such is good; I need it." Merely such thoughts are not afflictive consciousnesses. Similarly, if we consider the desire for a family, there are persons practicing the Bodhisattva path who have families; also, in the scriptures of discipline, Buddha himself set forth vows for laypersons and vows for monks. Hence, there is no general prohibition of the wish to have a family.

QUESTION: Is freedom from cyclic existence the same as complete Buddhahood?

ANSWER: No. There are two types of nirvana, which will be explained later.

QUESTION: Can objective experiments be performed on subtle matter or subtle mind, such that they might be convincing to a scientific materialist?

ANSWER: It would be good to do this. Try it!

QUESTION: If the nature of consciousness is luminous, is the nature of ignorance dark?

ANSWER: This is a difficult point. As is said in the Great Completeness[9] system of Ñying-ma, all consciousnesses are pervaded by the nature of mere luminosity and knowing. This is indeed true; it is really something to be contemplated. Even though a consciousness such as ignorance or anger has a perverse mode of apprehension, its very nature—its mere entity of luminosity and knowing—is not polluted by any sort of defilement. We need to realize this.

Because consciousness is not something physical, it is not that the main mind is one lump and the mental factors that accompany it are other things tacked onto it. Therefore, it seems that the explanation that, when anger is generated, there is a main mind and a mental factor of anger means that there is a factor that is the mere entity of luminosity and knowing and another factor that at the same time is a misapprehension. Thus, the one consciousness, though mistaken in terms of its mode of apprehension, has a nature of mere luminosity and knowing. Simultaneously, the five omnipresent mental factors—from among the fifty-one mental factors— have to be present.

Therefore, we certainly must say that the luminous and knowing nature of even ignorance is luminous.

QUESTION: Why are women the main object of criticism in so many Buddhist texts?

ANSWER: In, for example, Nāgārjuna's *Precious Garland*[10] and Shāntideva's *Engaging in the Bodhisattva Deeds*[11] the faults of the bodies of women are discussed; however, these were not written out of discriminating women to be lower. Rather, the majority of the people who had assumed vows of the clergy were males; thus, such explanations of meditation on the faults of the female body were made for the sake of mainly assisting men in overcoming generation of desire for the female body. In just the same way, a nun has to apply the same faults to the male body for the sake of overcoming generation of desire for the male body.

QUESTION: Can you suggest ways in which Buddha's teachings might help in alleviating severe depression?

ANSWER: This is difficult to say. It is explained that once a karma has ripened, it cannot be reversed. This means that if your ear organ, for instance, is deformed due to past karma, nothing much could be done about it. However, before that result has manifestly ripened, there are means to overcome the force of the karma that otherwise would produce this result. One technique is to engage in disclosure, confession of that deed, and to develop a sense of regret for having done it as well as to develop an intention to restrain from it in the future.

I think that once you have become severely depressed, it is difficult to reverse it, but still there could be exceptions. Nevertheless, in the early stages of depression, there are many types of mental training to stop it. According to my own experience, when you face many difficulties, many problems, tragedy, there are certain teachings that help. Realization of impermanence is useful, as is realization that this type of life has a nature of suffering. Also, understanding that such an event is occurring due to one's own karma is very helpful. When you experience tremendous difficulties and suffering, it is important to realize that it is basically due to your own past mistakes, past faults; such an attitude lessens anxiety, uneasiness. Then, look into the problem itself; it has a nature of impermanence—it has come, and it will go. This also is helpful.

In addition, we are, after all, in cyclic existence; so, sooner or later these problems are bound to arise. This perspective gives you more strength. Again, as Shāntideva says,[12] if it is something that can be fixed, there is no need to worry about it, and if it something that cannot be fixed, what help would it be to worry! It is really nice to think along these lines.

Also, one very helpful piece of advice is to reason that it is better to face this small amount of tragedy during a human lifetime because we have better equipment, as humans, to face problems. If the same problem were to occur during a different type of lifetime—for instance, as an animal—it would most likely be hopeless. Thus, from this point of view it is fortunate that the problem is being faced during this period.

Also, it is helpful to think:

> From my own experience, I know that I have anger, I have desire, I have jealousy, I have pride; all these things are in my mind. From immemorial time, I have been too accustomed to such attitudes. Now, since the causes are clearly there, bad results are bound to come. This is why I must face such and such a problem, this suffering.

Then, it is helpful to think:

> May the suffering that I am undergoing now, function as the actualization of many bad karmas that I have accumulated in the past.

Again, it is helpful to consider a Bodhisattva's way of thinking, emphasizing the welfare of the majority—everyone else—over one's own benefit. I am a human, a monk, and in my case, the Dalai Lama, whom quite a number of people respect, but when the welfare of others and my own welfare are compared, I am just a single person and thus not worthy of my primary concern. Others' welfare is far more important. Then, within such an attitude, it is helpful to think, "May the pain that I am experiencing serve as a substitute for the suffering that others have to undergo." This is called the practice of taking others' suffering and giving them your own happiness. It gives you real inner strength.

Through thinking along these lines, you will look on your own pain as not unfortunate but a fortunate opportunity to practice these teachings. You will even think, "Even more problems *should* come; then, I will have more opportunities to practice." This gives you inner determination—a Bodhisattva's determination, like steel.

These teachings are very useful. Mental determination and will-power are among the best methods for overcoming mental suffering. We have to train in such attitudes so that when something happens, we are already prepared. Usually, we just forget to practice; then, when something happens, it is difficult at that time suddenly to try to practice a technique to which we are not accustomed. This is why practitioners choose to think on death. In my own daily practice, I think of my death and the stages of the process of dying more than six times a day. Practice, practice, practice—thinking, thinking, thinking. This means that even though I am not actually dying, I am preparing for it. Still, when it actually comes, I do not know whether I will be successful, but in any case I am preparing. I suppose that it is also possible that one could spend one's whole life preparing and yet completely fail!

Thus, mental preparation—not external, but internal—right from the beginning is important and useful. Usually, whether I am speaking with Tibetans or other friends, I say that my strategy is to hope for the best but prepare for the worst. This is my usual outlook.

QUESTION: How does one develop the will to do what is good and virtuous?

ANSWER: This topic is also connected with ways to develop inner strength. Another technique is to investigate, "What is the meaning of life? What is the meaning of money? What is the meaning of body?" Investigate more; think more. Then, you will develop conviction that all these physical things, as well as your life, have an end. There is a point at which they give you sadness. Money, wealth, or fame—if you think deeply—ultimately do not afford permanent happiness and thus are not worthy of being sought as the final object of attainment.

Nirvana may be the final object of attainment, but at the moment, it is difficult to reach. Thus, the practical and realistic aim is compassion, a warm heart, serving other people, helping others, respecting others, being less selfish. By practicing these, you can gain benefit and happiness that remain longer. If you investigate the purpose of life and, with the motivation that results from this inquiry, develop a good heart—compassion and love—using your whole life this way, then each day will become useful and meaningful. I think that this is the main method to develop will.

Now let us return to our subject, which may seem unrelated to daily practice, but to get a picture of the whole system—the structure—of Buddhism, it is necessary to know these topics. Though one does not need to know some of these points for daily practice, still, in order to know the background and direction of Buddhism, one needs to know these points.

CESSATION OF SUFFERING

The day before yesterday, we talked about the nature of suffering, the first of the four noble truths. Yesterday, mainly about the sources or causes of suffering. Today, we will talk about the cessation of suffering and its causes.

First, as was explained earlier, that sufferings are produced occasionally indicates that they are caused. It is necessary to ascertain that ignorance is the root of cyclic existence, the basic source of suffering. It also is helpful to identify in more detail how anger and attachment develop; thus, in order to get at the topic of the cessation of suffering, let us discuss this.

When we feel anger with someone, how does the object appear right at that time? You are getting angry because the person has harmed, is harming, or will harm you—what is this I that is being harmed? At that very moment, we have a feeling that both the subject, I myself, and the object, the enemy, are very solid and independent. It is due to this appearance of the object as inherently established and oneself as inherently established and then one's assenting to these appearances that anger is generated. However, if right at that time you make use of reasonings as they are found in Middle Way treatises—examining "Who am I? Who is this one who is being hurt? What is the enemy? Is the enemy body? Is the enemy mind?"—this solidly existent enemy who previously seemed to be self-instituted as something to get angry at and this self-instituting I who was hurt seem to disappear. Due to this, the anger is as if broken apart. Is this true or not? Think about it yourself. Even if you do not understand this well, you can get some sense that when desire or anger are generated strongly, these attitudes are assisted by a conception that the object and oneself are self-established.

That the mode of subsistence of phenomena is an emptiness of inherent existence will be explained later. Let us just posit here that desire, hatred, and so forth are consciousnesses produced with the assistance of a wrong consciousness misconceiving things to be inherently existent.

If these bad thoughts were inseparable from our main mind, then as long as our main mind functions, these bad thoughts— anger and so forth—would have to be there, but this is clearly not the case. At just this moment in this room, it seems that nobody feels anger. My main mind is functioning to think and to speak, and your main minds are functioning to listen and to concentrate, and at the present moment anger is not present. This shows that secondary thoughts such as anger and attachment can be separated from the main mind.

In our minds, there are two classes of attitudes—anger and attachment on the one hand and detachment, contentment, love, and compassion on the other. However, at exactly the same time, toward one object, a person cannot simultaneously have desire and hatred. These can manifest in former and later moments, and similarly, today's enemy can become tomorrow's best friend. Even in international politics this often happens; on the private level it often happens too. However, in the very same moment it is impossible to have both desire and hatred toward one object; this shows that these two attitudes have contradictory modes of apprehension. Thus, when one of them increases in strength, the other decreases. For example, after someone enters the military and participates in warfare, due to becoming used to hatred and thoughts of killing—how to kill, how to sabotage, and so forth—when this person returns to civilian life, others notice something uncomfortably rough about the person, that the former soldier is easily agitated, and so on. This is because the person has become conditioned to the class of angry thoughts. However, when that person is in situations where there are no sources of anger and gradually becomes strongly accustomed to a loving attitude, the angry side of thought becomes weaker. In this way the two attitudes harm each other.

Love and compassion have the support of valid cognition; their production does not need assistance from ignorance that misconceives objects to be inherently existent. However, for the majority of people who do not have an understanding of emptiness, when they generate compassion, the misconception of inherent existence most likely is involved as a contributing factor. However, in general, virtuous consciousnesses do not require such misconception. Non-virtuous attitudes, such as hatred, pride, and so forth—no matter how strong they are—are generated *only* with the assistance and support of a conception of inherent existence. Therefore, without such misconception, there is no way that desire and hatred can operate, but consciousnesses that are the opposites of desire and hatred can operate even when there is no misconception of inherent existence.

As mentioned earlier, a consciousness conceiving inherent existence is erroneous; its conceived object does not exist even conventionally. A wisdom consciousness realizing emptiness, within observing the very same object which such ignorance observes in its misconception of inherent existence, has a mode of apprehension exactly opposite to ignorance—it apprehends the object to be devoid of inherent existence. The absence of inherent existence has a valid foundation; thus, when it is investigated, it becomes clearer and clearer. However, inherent existence, except for our stupidly persisting to believe in it due to former conditioning, is without a reasoned foundation; thus, the more you look into it, the more it disappears.

To repeat: A consciousness misconceiving inherent existence and a consciousness that realizes the emptiness of inherent existence harm each other, and, in addition, the wisdom realizing the absence of inherent existence has a valid foundation; therefore, through the force of accustoming oneself to the wisdom realizing emptiness, the consciousnesses conceiving its opposite weaken in strength. Also, because a consciousness realizing selflessness—as well as a compassionate consciousness—are qualities that depend on the mind, and because the mind exists continually, their basis is stable or continuous. Due to this, once one has trained in them, one does not need to rely on repeated exertion to regenerate them, and thus they can become stronger and stronger. Consequently, they can be developed to a limitless degree. For instance, when you carry a pack on your back, because your body is a coarse basis, you can carry only a limited amount—you cannot carry a limitless amount. As Dharmakīrti[13] says, you can train in jumping only to a certain limit; there is a point beyond which you cannot go; similarly, with boiling water, from boiling it too much, it itself is used up. However, even with regard to ordinary study, except for the fact that there is a limit to our lifetime, it is not that you arrive at a point where there is no more room in your brain. No matter how much you study, even if you study a hundred thousand million words, the mind can still retain them. This indicates that the basis of these qualities, consciousness, is stable and continuous.

The other day, I made a joke to someone who was asking about the brain. I said that if, like a computer, you needed a cell for each moment of memory, then as you become more and more educated, your head would have to get bigger and bigger!

Because of these reasons—that compassion, wisdom, and so forth are qualities that depend on the mind, and the mind is stable and continuous—they can be developed to a limitless degree. It is from this point of view that it is said that the conception of inherent existence can be extinguished. When one removes the conception of inherent existence, one thereby also ceases the afflictive emotions generated in dependence upon that ignorance. Also, since the ignorance that drives contaminated actions has ceased, this class of actions ceases. Once the motivator of the action and the actions cease, the results of those actions will cease. That is how the third noble truth—true cessation—comes to be.

Buddha Nature

What is nirvana? The basis due to which it is possible to attain nirvana is called the Buddha nature, or the naturally abiding lineage.[14] The individual systems of Buddhist tenets have different interpretations of what the Buddha nature is; thus, there come to be many Buddha natures in terms of their level of subtlety. The Hearer Schools do not speak of a *Buddha* nature because they assert that there are three final vehicles. Due to this, they speak of a *Superior's* nature, or *Superior's* lineage.[15] They hold that when Hearers or Solitary Realizers have attained their respective enlightenment as Foe Destroyers, then upon the actualization of the nirvana without remainder, their continuum of mind is severed, due to which there can be no further training, such as in the Bodhisattva path. Therefore, they maintain that there are three final vehicles.

Although even in certain Great Vehicle sūtras Buddha speaks of three final vehicles, these statements are shown to require interpretation by way of indicating the thought behind Buddha's statement, his purpose in stating that there are three final vehicles, and reasonings that damage the literal reading of such scriptures. What is posited as the basis in Buddha's thought when he taught three final vehicles? It is that *temporarily* people have a definiteness of lineage as, for instance, a Hearer, a Solitary Realizer, or Bodhisattva.

The Hearer Schools, as mentioned just earlier, identify a Superior's nature, or Superior's lineage, as the four lineages of Superiors. The first three are for a practitioner to be satisfied with mediocre food, clothing, and shelter. The fourth is, in dependence upon these, to make effort at removing faulty states and at attaining advantageous qualities. These are called the four lineages—causal lineages—of Superiors in that they are what cause one to attain the level of a Superior.

In the system of the Mind Only School Following Scripture, this being the branch that, following Asaṅga, asserts a mind-basis-of-all, the Buddha nature is identified as a seed of uncontaminated exalted wisdom, which is in the mind-basis-of-all. As long as it has not been activated by conditions such as hearing doctrines and thinking on their meaning, it is called the naturally abiding lineage. Then, when it has been activated, it is called the developmental lineage.[16]

In the system of the Mind Only School Following Reasoning, this being the branch that, following Dignāga and Dharmakīrti, does not assert a mind-basis-of-all, they speak of the Buddha nature as a seed of uncontaminated exalted wisdom that is with the internal sense spheres. When the appropriate conditions of hearing, thinking, and so forth are encountered, it is capable of generating realizations of the three vehicles. This is the naturally abiding lineage.

In the system of the Middle Way School, the Buddha lineage, in general, is identified as that which, when transformation takes place, is suitable to transform into a Buddha Body. It is divided into that which is suitable to transform into a Buddha's Truth Body and that which is suitable to transform into a Buddha's Form Body— the first being the naturally abiding lineage and the second being the developmental lineage. Based on this teaching of a Buddha nature present in all beings, the Middle Way School explains that there is only one final vehicle.

What is the nirvana that is attained in dependence upon the Buddha nature, the Buddha lineage? If we consider nirvana in general, let us first consider the natural nirvana,[17] which is the final nature of phenomena. It, in itself, is naturally pure, and also—due to this pure sphere that is the nature of phenomena—defilements are suitable to be removed and liberation can be attained. Furthermore, the entity of liberation is just this pure nature. Hence, from these points of view, the pure nature of phenomena is called the natural nirvana.

With regard to nirvanas that are attained, the lesser nirvana is of two types, with remainder and without remainder. The meaning of a nirvana without remainder is that, according to the systems of the Hearers, one has actualized nirvana but still has a remainder of mental and physical aggregates that are impelled by earlier contaminated actions and afflictive emotions. A nirvana without remainder, on the other hand, occurs when nirvana has been actualized but there is no longer any remainder of mental and physical aggregates that are impelled by earlier contaminated actions and afflictive emotions. The reason why these are called *lesser* forms of nirvana is that, from between the two types of obstructions, only the afflictive obstructions to liberation from cyclic existence have been extinguished; the obstructions to omniscience have not.

The highest type of nirvana occurs at the level of Buddhahood. It is called a non-abiding nirvana because one is not abiding either in the extreme of cyclic existence or in the extreme of a solitary peace. Rather, one has brought to perfection one's own development as well as the capacity to effect the welfare of others. One not only has completely overcome the afflictive obstructions to liberation from cyclic existence but also has utterly overcome the obstructions to omniscience.

The obstructions to liberation from cyclic existence cause suffering for persons who have them in their continuums, and the obstructions to omniscience, since they prevent one from knowing all objects of knowledge, cause one to be unable to know the constitutions, thoughts, interests, and predispositions of trainees, and thereby prevent one from bringing about the welfare of others on a vast scale. Therefore, when one overcomes just the afflictive obstructions, one is liberated from cyclic existence, but when, in addition, one overcomes the obstructions to all that is knowable, one attains the state of omniscience.

Where are such nirvanas included within the two truths, ultimate and conventional? Chandrakīrti says that a nirvana is an ultimate truth; this is because a nirvana is a true cessation, which itself is identified as an emptiness. How is this? Through the power of the antidote, that is to say, the wisdom realizing self-lessness, or the absence of inherent existence, the defilements are extinguished in the sphere of the final nature of phenomena; such a pure sphere of reality is called a true cessation. This is how a nirvana is an ultimate truth.

Even though true cessations are all of the same general type, there are many different levels, beginning with the true cessation that is the abandonment of what is to be abandoned by the path of seeing. A discussion of the five paths will come later, but for the time being, these are the paths of accumulation, preparation, seeing, meditation, and no more learning. There are five each for Hearers, Solitary Realizers, and Bodhisattvas—making fifteen, three sets of five. At the time of the first two paths—accumulation and preparation—one does not have direct realization of the truth of emptiness; hence, a true cessation has not yet been attained. However, at the time of the path of seeing, one has direct realization of emptiness, and thus has a true cessation that is a state of having separated from those objects to be abandoned by the path of seeing—these being the artificial or learned version of the afflictive obstructions. On the path of meditation, one abandons the innate afflictive obstructions. In both cases, these obstructions are removed by way of their antidotes such that they will never return.

In general, cessations are of two types, analytical and non-analytical. A non-analytical cessation is a case of an absence of something due to the non-aggregation of the causes and conditions that would have produced it, whereas an analytical cessation is a cessation of something that has been overcome forever through its antidote.

On both the paths of seeing and of meditation, there are uninterrupted paths and paths of release. An uninterrupted path serves as the actual antidote to a level of obstructions. A meditative equipoise that then has the attribute of having been separated, or released, from that particular level of obstruction is called a path of release.

Also, there are many divisions of the factors that are abandoned by the paths of seeing and of meditation, these being made in reference to the three realms—Desire, Form, and Formless Realms. A great many of these are set forth in Vasubandhu's *Treasury of Manifest Knowledge* and in Asaṅga's *Compendium of Manifest Knowledge,* but I will not go into them here. However, a root point is that the Consequence School considers consciousnesses that conceive inherent existence to be afflictive obstructions, due to which they consider the obstructions to omniscience to be the predispositions established by the conception of inherent existence. However, the Autonomy School considers a consciousness conceiving true existence to be an obstruction to omniscience; therefore, the Autonomists are put in the difficult position of asserting that even though practitioners have not overcome the *final* root of cyclic existence which is the conception of true existence, they can be liberated from cyclic existence through abandoning the conception of a self of persons, which is the conception that persons are substantially established in the sense of being self-sufficient. Therefore, the Autonomists hold that even though practitioners have not abandoned the conception of a self of phenomena, which is the *final* root of cyclic existence, it is possible for them to be liberated from cyclic existence. The Consequentialists, however, posit the conception of true or inherent existence as the root of cyclic existence and thus the basic afflictive obstruction; hence, they do not have this problem.

The Autonomy School divides the obstructions to omniscience into nine cycles and explains that these are abandoned from the second through the tenth Bodhisattva grounds. However, because the Consequence School posits the conception of true or inherent existence itself as the chief afflictive obstruction and posits the predispositions established by that misconception as the obstructions to omniscience, it is not possible to begin generating an actual antidote to the obstructions to omniscience without first having completely abandoned the afflictive obstructions. Gung-tang Gön-chok-den-bay-drönmay[18] gives an example that makes this very easy to understand. If you put garlic in a vessel, it deposits some of its odor in the vessel itself; thus, when you seek to clean the vessel, it is necessary first to remove the garlic. Similarly, a consciousness conceiving inherent existence, like garlic, deposits predispositions in the mind that produce the *appearance* of inherent existence; thus, there is no way to cleanse the mind of those predispositions, which are like the flavor of garlic left in the vessel of the mind, until one removes all consciousnesses conceiving inherent existence from the mind. First, the garlic must be removed; then, its odor can be removed.

For this reason, according to the Consequence School, until one has utterly removed all of the afflictive obstructions, one cannot begin to overcome the obstructions to omniscience. Since this is the case, a practitioner cannot begin overcoming the obstructions to omniscience on any of the first seven Bodhisattva grounds, which are called "impure" because one still has afflictive obstructions to be abandoned. Rather, one begins abandoning the obstructions to omniscience on the eighth Bodhisattva ground, and continues to do so on the ninth and tenth grounds, these being called the "three pure grounds" because the afflictive obstructions have been abandoned.

As explained earlier, the non-Consequentialist schools posit a selflessness of phenomena that is subtler than the selflessness of persons. These other systems also posit afflictive emotions as generated from a consciousness conceiving a self of persons, which they identify as conceiving persons to be substantially established in the sense of being self-sufficient.[19] The Consequence School, however, holds that the conception of a self of persons and the conception of a self of phenomena are equally subtle. Thus, the Consequentialists say that the other schools' presentations of the process by which afflictive emotions are generated are not complete in that they do not take account of all levels of afflictive emotions. Therefore, the

Consequentialists explain that a Foe Destroyer who has overcome the foe of such afflictive emotions as explained by these systems is not a fully qualified Foe Destroyer. Thus, among our afflictive emotions, there are two levels—those induced by the subtle conception of inherent existence and those induced by a coarser conception of persons as being substantially existent in the sense of being self-sufficient.

LEVELS OF EMPTINESS

All of these points revolve around the fact that there are many different levels of emptiness, coarser and more subtle. One is the emptiness that is the non-establishment of a person as substantially established in the sense of being self-sufficient. Another is the emptiness of duality of subject and object or a form's not being established by way of its own character as the referent of words or of a conceptual consciousness. Another is the emptiness of true establishment or the emptiness of an object's being established by way of its own uncommon mode of subsistence such that the object is not posited through appearing to a non-defective consciousness. Another is the emptiness of inherent existence even on the conventional level.

How is the difference of profundity among these to be determined? Which are true? Which are not?

The emptiness of a difference of entity between subject and object that is asserted in the Mind Only School cannot be accepted by the Consequentialists because they assert external objects. However, the Consequentialists accept the other types of emptiness, but not as the most subtle emptiness. How is this? While the understanding of one of the coarser types of emptiness is still functioning, it is possible for an awareness conceiving the opposite of a more subtle type of emptiness to be produced, but when one generates an understanding of a subtler type of emptiness and that understanding has not deteriorated in its functioning, it is impossible to generate any of the misconceptions associated with the opposite of the coarser types of emptiness.

Thus, if you ascertain the subtlest emptiness, all of the coarser modes of misapprehension are completely overcome. For instance, even if you have ascertained that the person is not substantially established in the sense of being self-sufficient, you could still generate the misconception that the person is truly established. Similarly, even though a Proponent of Mind Only realizes that a form is not established by way of its own character as the referent of words and of a conceptual consciousness thinking about the form and even though that realization is still functioning without any deterioration, this does not prevent the person's conceiving that the form is established by way of its own character and that its being the referent of a word or a conceptual consciousness is established in its own right.

Similarly, even though Middle Way Autonomists have decided from the very depths that objects are not established by way of their own uncommon mode of subsistence—such establishment requiring that objects are not posited through appearing to a non-defective consciousness—the conception that objects are established from their own side still remains.

However, when one has ascertained that phenomena, except for being merely nominally posited, are not established inherently, that is to say, objectively in their own right, then, as long as the functioning of that realization has not deteriorated, there is no way for any of the coarser types of misconceptions to be generated. Therefore, the view as it is set forth by the Consequence School can act as an antidote to all types of misconceptions that are reifications of the status of phenomena.

However, if one negates more than what is described as the object of negation by the Consequentialists—something more than inherent existence—then, one has fallen to an extreme of nihilism. This is the reason why it is said that the emptiness described by the Consequentialists is the unmistaken view of the Middle Way School.

6. Paths and the Utilization of Bliss

Wednesday Afternoon

Question and Answer Period

QUESTION: It seems that sometimes good motivation and good intentions result in bad karmic effects, as in a situation when you love someone and try to help but in fact do the opposite. It would appear that to say good motivation produces good results is an oversimplification.

ANSWER: If, motivated by concern for others, one engaged in an action that did not help but harmed, then because from one's side one had a good motivation, there would be no fault to oneself, and the karmic effect for oneself would be good. The harm that was temporarily brought to the other person is due to one's having been obscured with respect to the appropriate method to help that person. This is the reason why altruistic motivation and wisdom are required in union. Therefore, it is said that even a Bodhisattva on the path of preparation has only a facsimile of bringing about the welfare of others. However, when one has attained the path of seeing and the path of meditation and has the five clairvoyances, one knows others' mental dispositions and thoughts just as they are; through such knowledge, the capacity to help others improves better and better.

QUESTION: Could you please talk about healing through using psychic energy?

ANSWER: I do not have much to offer on this. In Mantric rituals, there are means for curing illnesses and so forth. These are done by way of a combination of the forces in substances, mantra, and meditative stabilization. Also, in a simpler way, one can make prayer-wishes or can make expressions of the power of the truth—that if such and such that I have done is true, may it help. There are also cases of persons who are gifted with the power to heal due to actions in former lifetimes.

QUESTION: Does suicide necessarily create greater suffering in subsequent rebirths?

ANSWER: Suicide is described as being extremely harmful. In particular, it is said that for someone who has taken the tantric vows upon receiving initiation in either Yoga Tantra or Highest Yoga Tantra, killing oneself incurs the fault of killing a deity.

QUESTION: Science and logic have demonstrated that sense consciousnesses are brain phenomena; if, as you said yesterday, the grosser consciousnesses are dependent upon bodily functioning, then when the brain ceases to function at death, the sense consciousnesses likewise cease to function. Their basis for functioning gone, the sense consciousnesses cannot continue as part of mind in a process of rebirth. Yet, we are born with all sense consciousnesses intact because we see, hear, smell, etc. Furthermore, the entire mind, both the gross and subtler levels, must take rebirth, not just the subtler levels. Therefore, the doctrine of rebirth is damaged.

ANSWER: For example, at the moment we are experiencing a certain level of consciousness; again, when we are dreaming, it is another, deeper level. Then, in dreamless deep sleep, we experience another, deeper level of consciousness. In fainting, when even breathing has stopped, an even deeper level of consciousness is experienced; you may regard it as semiconscious or unconscious, but according to the tantric system there is still consciousness. Now, the deepest level occurs when we are dying; it is the most subtle consciousness. The progression of these levels shows that the subtler levels are more isolated from the physical body.

The subtlest consciousness is something that has the subtlest capacity to generate consciousnesses into being entities of luminosity and cognition. Scientific experiments about the human brain are very interesting, and it is very important to know these findings, but it is difficult to speak about these topics with full knowledge now because the science of mind is not known in its completeness. It is still developing, progressing. For Buddhists, if through valid scientific experiment it were determined that besides the brain there is no mind—if this were actually proved, it not just being the case that the mind was not found—then we would have to accept it.

With respect to your question, this subtlest consciousness is what transmigrates; the grosser consciousnesses do not. However, seeds of the grosser consciousnesses are contained within the subtlest mind.

QUESTION: If someone has committed the act of murder through abortion without fully realizing what it actually means, what can one do now?

ANSWER: We are all persons who have accumulated sins in the past. This is indicated by the fact that at present bad thoughts constantly rise up in our minds, thereby showing that in the past for a long period we have become excessively used to these bad thoughts. In this way, it is said that you can tell what you were doing in the past by examining your body now and that you can tell what will come in the future by looking at what you are doing with your mind now.

In any case, with regard to whatever misdeeds have been done in the past, you should engage in disclosure of them and in developing an intention to restrain from them in the future. For a Buddhist practitioner, the usual practices include prostration and recitation of certain mantras such as the one hundred syllable mantra. One of the best methods is to make gifts to poor and sick persons. The giving of donations for education as well as in the medical field is very great work, one of the best ways to gain merit.

QUESTION: In this country there are many groups and books dealing with sex and tantra—sex as a spiritual path, sex as a means to nirvana. In the traditional tantric teaching, what is the role of sex in attaining realization? What is the role of celibacy?

ANSWER: There is a great danger of misunderstanding here. As I mentioned earlier, there are different levels of consciousness, and when a subtler consciousness is used in the path, it is more forceful. Usually, when we experience subtler levels of mind, it is due to a natural stoppage of the grosser levels of consciousness, and thus we are unaware, unconscious, unable actively to make use of their force. However, if through a specific technique a practitioner deliberately controls and ceases the grosser levels of consciousness, the subtler levels become active, manifest. When this happens, not only does a subtler mind become active but also it is alert, very sharp, very clear. This level of consciousness can then be transformed into a wisdom that understands emptiness, selflessness. In order to do this, first the practitioner has to try to stop the grosser levels of consciousness, and to do that, it is necessary to bring about a change in the movement of the white and red basic constituents.

This is where sex becomes involved. Actually, union here is not in the ordinary sexual sense. Rather, the human body is composed of the six constituents—these being, in one interpretation, three "treasuries" obtained from the father and three from the mother. The three from the father are bone, marrow, and regenerative fluid, and the three from the mother are flesh, skin, and blood. In another interpretation, the six constituents are earth, water, fire, wind, channels, and drops of essential fluid. In any case, due to the special condition of the physical body of a human on this planet, certain changes in the elements inside the body bring about changes in the level of subtlety of consciousness. For instance, such changes take place very briefly when we sneeze as well as when yawning, falling to sleep, and during sex. It is due to our physical nature that these changes in the level of consciousness take place, among which the strongest that can be utilized by a practitioner occur during sex. Because of this fact, sex is used as a technique in the tantric path.

A tantric yogi in the Desire Realm, who has not yet abandoned desire, generates a mind of desire intentionally as part of practice, and then during the period when the essential constituents are undergoing change and when the gross levels of mind are supplanted by subtler minds, the yogi uses the subtlest level of consciousness, switching it to realization of emptiness. Since one consciousness cannot have two discordant modes of apprehension at the same time, the mind of desire has completely disappeared when this consciousness realizes emptiness.

The mind of attachment and desire that induces changes in the channels, winds, and essential physical drops is assisted in its generation by the conception of inherent existence, but the subtle mind that is manifested due to such desire acts as an antidote—when it realizes emptiness—to the consciousness conceiving inherent existence that assists in the generation of desire. This is illustrated with the ancient example of a worm that is generated from wood and then eats that very wood.

Therefore, first of all, a person who engages in such practices should have at least some experience or understanding of the theory of emptiness, selflessness, and, secondly, since these practices must be meant for Buddhahood, the practitioner must have some experience of the altruistic intention to become enlightened. Without these two qualifications, such techniques cannot be implemented properly. Certain practices in Highest Yoga Tantra can also be dangerous; one has to employ techniques to cause the inner winds to enter the central channel because the physical changes to which I have been referring are mainly results of the winds entering, remaining, and dissolving in the central channel. For instance, a forceful technique is to squeeze the channels at the neck, and if someone knows how to do this properly, it can succeed, but if one does not know how to do it well, death can be the result. Several such methods are mentioned in the tantric systems, but they are dangerous; this is why the whole system is called a secret doctrine. Without a properly trained, experienced teacher and unless the student is well qualified and all the groundwork has been done, it is impossible.

QUESTION: Would you comment on the existence, validity, and nature of clairvoyance?

ANSWER: Ways of achieving clairvoyance are set forth in the sūtra system and in the tantra system. In the sūtra system, initially a practitioner must achieve the meditative stabilization of calm abiding;[1] without this, it is impossible to achieve clairvoyance. After calm abiding has been achieved, the practitioner takes to mind again and again the aspect of the object that he or she wants to know and causes the mind to remain steadily on that object, whereby, over time, the object becomes clearer and clearer. In tantra, whether clairvoyance is intentionally practiced or not, at a certain point it will be achieved naturally. In any case, when one arrives at the point where an exalted wisdom of non-dual bliss and emptiness realizes emptiness directly, clairvoyances are subsequently induced through its force. Otherwise, prior to that level, clairvoyance can be achieved in dependence upon wind yoga. There are five basic and five secondary winds; the clairvoyances are achieved through the practice of vajra repetition utilizing the five secondary winds.

QUESTION: How and by what signs can one, in one's own experience, recognize a valid cognition?

ANSWER: With respect to realizing impermanence or selflessness, for instance, if one gains ascertainment of such through, on the positive side, having reasons for their correctness and, on the negative side, having reasons for refuting the opposite, then the awareness that ascertains the topic can be posited as valid. However, there are indeed cases in which a certain idea has been generated, but you cannot know whether it is right or wrong until the event actually takes place. Still, in general, it is said that once a person has determined something to be a certain way, then if upon analyzing with other reasoning, there is no contradiction, it can be posited as a valid cognition.

Topics concerning consciousness can be very complicated. However, if one does not accept any sort of internal consciousness, there are still many questionable points, such as the formation of this world. If you ask *how* this happened, there probably are explanations—this coming from that, and so forth. But, if you ask *why,* it is immediately difficult. When you consider galaxy on galaxy forming and dissolving, it is, in fact, just their nature to be like that. But, if their forming and dissolving is just an accident without specific causes and conditions, it is very difficult. In our daily life, we often use the words "lucky" and "unlucky." Something happens, and we say, "Oh, today I am very lucky!" Or, "Oh, today I am very unlucky." We do not know the real cause, and we are satisfied simply with the explanation that it is luck or the lack of it. However, there must be a reason, a cause, for being lucky or unlucky.

It is understandable that, in general, pleasure and pain depend on causes and conditions, and it would be difficult to posit that some are caused but that others are mere accidents—you would have to give a reason for making such a distinction. When you look into things this way, there are many mysteries. This being the case, the various religions and philosophies have different explanations—a creator god, the cause and effect of karma, and so forth.

TRUE PATHS

We have spoken about nirvana. In the eighteenth chapter of his *Treatise on the Middle* Nāgārjuna says:[2]

Once the self does not exist,
How could the mine exist?

When the self does not inherently exist, the mine could not possibly inherently exist. He also says:[3]

When thoughts of self and mine are extinguished
With regard to the internal and the external,
Appropriation [of new mental and physical aggregates]
ceases.
Through the extinction of this, rebirth is extinguished.

When, with respect to internal and external phenomena, one extinguishes the conception of inherently existent I and mine, the appropriation of mental and physical aggregates is extinguished. Due to this, rebirth is extinguished.

In brief, when the accumulation of new karma is extinguished and there are no afflictive emotions to nourish the remaining old karma, at that time there is liberation from cyclic existence. Contaminated karmas are produced from afflictive emotions, and afflictive emotions are generated from improper conceptuality. Improper conceptuality, in turn, is generated from the elaborations of the conception of inherent existence. Consciousnesses conceiving inherent existence are ceased by emptiness. This is how Nāgārjuna explains the process of achieving liberation.

This brings us to the fourth noble truth, paths that lead to the end of suffering. Those which directly induce true cessations are true paths directly realizing emptiness. According to the Consequence School, a Superior of any of the three vehicles—Hearer, Solitary Realizer, or Bodhisattva—has necessarily realized emptiness directly. Even direct perception of the four noble truths cannot harm the conception of inherent existence.

In order to generate in one's continuum such an actual true path of direct realization of emptiness in which all dualistic appearance has vanished, one needs the wisdom arisen from meditation that realizes emptiness within dualistic appearance. To generate this, one first needs to form an understanding of emptiness—ascertaining its meaning with the wisdoms arisen from hearing and from thinking.

As one advances over the five paths as either a Hearer, Solitary Realizer, or Bodhisattva, one proceeds from a lower path to a higher—from a lower realization to higher—within meditative equipoise realizing emptiness. Thus, the five paths are set forth in terms of the ever-increasing profundity of the practice of emptiness. The path of accumulation is a period when one has wisdoms arisen from hearing and thinking. Then, the path of preparation begins with the attainment of wisdom arisen from meditation that realizes emptiness. After that, the path of seeing begins with the initial direct perception of emptiness. Then, the path of meditation is a period of repeated familiarizing with the direct perception of emptiness. The fifth and last path is the period when one has completed training in the respective series of paths, and thus it is called the path of no more learning. It is the object one is seeking to attain; for the two lower paths of Hearers and Solitary Realizers, it is a *temporary* attainment, leading to entry into the Great Vehicle.

Mere realization of emptiness is not sufficient; it must be conjoined with method. The chief scriptures of the Great Vehicle, the Perfection of Wisdom Sūtras, teach in an explicit way about emptiness but, in a hidden way, also teach about the types of method that assist the various levels of realization of emptiness as well as the levels of clear realization[4] that are generated. These sūtras were set forth mainly for disciples who are Bodhisattvas, but Bodhisattvas—in order to bring about others' welfare—must know the many and various paths of Hearers, Solitary Realizers, and Bodhisattvas; they must know all paths, and this is why these sūtras speak about all of these paths.

What is the mode of procedure of the paths of Hearers and Solitary Realizers for actualizing nirvana? These are the paths of the thirty-seven harmonies with enlightenment.[5] When these are condensed in terms of practice, there come to be the three trainings.

The first is the training in higher ethics. In the scriptures of the Hearers, eight types of vows of individual liberation are described. The first three are for householders, and the latter five are for those who have left the householder life. If one looks at it superficially, it seems that the celibacy required in some vows of individual liberation and the use of sex in the path in Highest Yoga Mantra would be contradictory, but they are not. This is because these practices are set forth appropriate to the level of realization and capacity of individual persons; at the beginning level of training, celibacy is very important, but when one develops to the point where one can realistically have the confidence that other practices can be utilized properly, then the situation is different.

The union that is described in Highest Yoga Tantra is not a matter of engaging in sexual union from being afflicted with the pangs of desire. Rather, within perceiving the disadvantages of desire, the practitioner understands that another, higher level of the path can be induced through sexual union. It is within such a context of perceiving the faults of desire and a special purpose in union that practices utilizing union are set forth.

The root of all the vows for laypersons and for monks and nuns is the ethics of the abandonment of the non-virtues. Three physical actions (killing, stealing, and sexual misconduct), four verbal actions (lying, divisive talk, harsh speech, and senseless chatter), and three mental actions (covetousness, harmful intent, and wrong views) are to be abandoned. I will not elaborate on these here.

When one restrains ill deeds of body and speech, coarse mental distractions are also restrained, and from this viewpoint the mind becomes a little withdrawn inside. A second factor is that one has to use constant introspection, built on conscientiousness, to determine whether physical and verbal ill deeds are arising or not, and thereby the power of mindfulness and introspection is generated. These two—the withdrawal of the mind inside and the generation of the power of mindfulness and introspection—are indispensable factors in the development of meditative stabilization. This is the relationship between ethics and meditative stabilization.

When practicing the ethics of individual liberation, the main point is to refrain from harming others. When practicing the Bodhisattva ethics, the main point is to refrain from self-centeredness. Again, in the mantric system of ethics, the main point is to refrain from ordinary appearances and the conception of being ordinary.

For all the vehicles, higher and lower, the procedure of the three trainings is similar. One reason why there are just three trainings is in terms of taming the mind: the training in ethics is for the sake of causing the distracted mind not to be distracted; the training in meditative stabilization is for the sake of causing the unequipoised mind to be set in meditative equipoise; and the training in wisdom is for the sake of freeing the unfreed mind. Another reason why there are just three trainings is in terms of their respective effects: an effect of not letting ethics degenerate is the attainment of rebirths in happy transmigrations within the Desire Realms as humans and gods; an effect of the training in meditative stabilization is the attainment of rebirths in happy transmigrations within the Form and Formless Realms; and an effect of training in wisdom is the attainment of liberation.

Another reason why there are just three trainings is in terms of the afflictive emotions that they cause to be abandoned: ethics suppress afflictive emotions; for example, when one gets angry at someone and thinks to harm that person, the memory that one formerly decided to refrain from harming others stops such behavior. Meditative stabilization suppresses the manifest form of afflictive emotions, and the training in wisdom removes afflictive emotions down to the level of their seeds.

The Buddhist teachings repeatedly indicate that we must control ourselves, but nowadays some people say that when one generates a mind of desire or hatred, one should not hold it in but instead should let it out, display it. I feel that, for instance, in cases of depression that are due to trauma, it indeed is very helpful to express openly one's feelings, but with consciousnesses such as desire and hatred, if you express them as soon as they are generated, the expression does not clear them away; they will be produced again and again.

From your own experience, you can understand that if you try to control your mind with self-discipline and self-awareness, even though at the beginning you may still be very short-tempered, over time as years pass, it will improve—the amount of anger will decrease. However, if you leave your irritableness without paying attention to it and without taking care, it will increase. Now, after all, nobody wants anger. Once anger comes, you go mad; you will even break your own beautiful possessions. Again, afterwards, you will really feel sorry, at least about your broken articles. Therefore, no one loves anger; it is far better to control it. Of course, in the beginning, it is not at all easy, but through determination, realization, and willpower, gradually the situation will change, if you work at it wisely and not just with stubbornness. The mind is such that if we make a plan—that in the next five years I should reach such and such a stage—and carry it out with strong determination, the mind definitely will change.

Thirty-Seven Harmonies with Enlightenment

Four establishments in mindfulness
The thirty-seven harmonies with enlightenment are essential ingredients of the path. They are divided into seven sets, the first of which is comprised of the four establishments in mindfulness. These are the establishments in mindfulness of body, feeling, mind, and phenomena. One observes body, feeling, mind, and phenomena and investigates their specific and general characters.

For a practitioner, there is much to think about with respect to the body—the faults and the nature of the body—so that attachment to it can be overcome. I will not explain the faults of the body in detail; someone who wants to meditate on this can understand how to reflect on the body based on the many descriptions of its faults in Nāgārjuna's *Precious Garland*[6] and Shāntideva's *Engaging in the Bodhisattva Deeds*.[7]

In the establishment in mindfulness of the body, one reflects on the body as having a nature of ugliness in order to perceive it as having the nature of a true suffering. This serves as a technique for overcoming attachment to the body and for generating a wish to separate from a body that has such a nature.

Then, in the establishment in mindfulness of feeling, one reflects on the nature of pleasurable, painful, and neutral feelings. One pays special attention to the fact that, due to the condition of feeling, attachment is generated—painful feeling giving rise to the attachment of wanting to separate from it and pleasurable feeling giving rise to the attachment of wanting not to separate from it. Thinking this, one comes to understand the disadvantages of attachment, the main cause of the true sources of suffering.

Then, in the establishment in mindfulness of the mind, one investigates the specific character of the mind—that it disintegrates moment by moment but in terms of its continuum remains forever. Through this reflection, one realizes that there is no self that is isolatable separate from the mind, whereby one becomes able to ascertain selflessness—the non-existence of a self-sufficient, permanent person. Through meditating on this, one comes to understand the peace of selflessness, nirvana.

Then, in the establishment in mindfulness of phenomena, one investigates the character of what phenomena are to be adopted and what are to be discarded. Reflecting this way, one comes to understand true paths.

Having reflected on the specific characters of body, feeling, mind, and phenomena, one reflects on their general character, which are identified as the four seals that testify to a doctrine's being Buddhist. As were mentioned earlier, these are that:

1. All compound things are impermanent.
2. All contaminated things are miserable.
3. All phenomena are empty and selfless.
4. Nirvana is peace.

When one sees that compounded things are impermanent, one realizes that they are under the influence of other factors—causes and conditions—due to which suffering is suitable to be stopped and happiness is suitable to be generated in dependence upon their respective causal conditions. Through this, one finds courage in knowing that suffering can be removed and that happiness can be achieved.

Then, through investigating the second seal, that is to say, that all contaminated phenomena are miserable, one determines the root of suffering. This is done by understanding that the phenomena of cyclic existence are contaminated, that is to say, that because they are under the influence of other factors—specifically, contaminated actions and afflictive emotions—they do not pass beyond a nature of suffering. One thereby develops a wish to overcome not just temporary suffering but the very root of suffering. Here, in the term "contaminated phenomena"[8] the contaminations are actions, or karma, and afflictive emotions, and "contaminated phenomena" are those produced through their influence. There are many different interpretations of the meaning of being contaminated and uncontaminated according to context.

Then, through investigating the third seal—that all phenomena are empty and selfless—one realizes that the root of suffering is a distorted consciousness misconceiving inherent existence, and one perceives that the conception of inherent existence can be extinguished and thus that liberation can be attained. If one can see that the conception of inherent existence which drives cyclic existence can be pacified, one gains understanding of the fourth seal—that nirvana is the final, everlasting peace, that nirvana is the aim to be attained.

Through the establishments in mindfulness of body, feeling, mind, and phenomena in terms of their specific and general characters, one understands that these have a nature of impermanence and of suffering. Through this, one's mind turns away from overemphasis on the appearances of this lifetime and from unidirectional adherence to the prosperity of future lifetimes of high status within cyclic existence as the aim to be attained. Overcoming such overemphasis on the appearances of this and future lifetimes, one generates an awareness that is directed toward liberation from cyclic existence in all of its forms.

What is the reason for meditating on suffering? As Āryadeva's *Four Hundred* says:[9]

> How could whoever is not discouraged about this
> Be intent on pacification of it?

If a person has not become discouraged with respect to cyclic existence, how could that person generate an attitude aspiring to liberation from it? Cyclic existence has a nature of suffering, does it not? You do not want suffering, do you? Thus, it is important in the beginning to recognize what is actually a state of suffering as suffering and to develop a revulsion from it, thereby engendering an attitude seeking liberation.

Through thinking in this way on the manner in which we suffer, one develops an attitude seeking liberation, nirvana, thinking, "If I could only attain liberation!" When this attitude is generated in a decisive way, one attains the path of accumulation of a Hearer or Solitary Realizer.

That completes our discussion of the four establishments in mindfulness.

Four thorough abandonings

The second set from among the thirty-seven harmonies with enlightenment is the four thorough abandonings which have a nature of effort. The four are to generate virtues not yet generated, to increase those already generated, not to generate non-virtues that have not yet been generated, and to abandon non-virtues already generated.

Four legs of emanation

The third set is comprised by the four legs of emanation. In dependence upon the magical emanations of meditative stabilization, one can go to pure lands of Buddhas and so forth, and, therefore, the factors that accomplish this are like legs; thus these are called *legs* of manifestation.

The path of accumulation is divided into three levels—small, middling, and great. At the very point when one generates in one's mental continuum the intention to leave cyclic existence in the manner just described, one has generated the small level of the path of accumulation. To proceed further to the middling and great levels of the path of accumulation, one needs meditative stabilization; otherwise, it is impossible—effort alone is not sufficient. This is the reason why the four legs of emanation are set forth at this point.

In connection with this, I will explain, in a rough way, how to achieve the level of meditative stabilization called "calm abiding."[10] Nowadays meditation is popular; so, let us treat the topic in a little detail. In general, there are two types of meditation, stabilizing and analytical. These are also called the cultivation of calm abiding and the cultivation of special insight. They are the roots of all the good qualities of all the Buddhist vehicles, mundane and supramundane.

What are the entities, or natures, of calm abiding and special insight? Using the *Sūtra Unravelling the Thought*[11] as our source, we can say that calm abiding occurs when, within the mind's abiding one-pointedly on its object of observation without any laxity or excitement, the power of such stability generates the bliss of physical and mental pliancy and such pliancy has become stable. What is special insight? Within the context of having attained the factor of stability, when the bliss of mental and physical pliancy is induced through the force of one-pointed analysis of the object of observation, at that point one has attained special insight.

In order to attain the bliss of mental and physical pliancy of special insight that is induced through the power of analysis, it is necessary first to attain the bliss of mental and physical pliancy of calm abiding that is induced through the power of the factor of stability; otherwise, it is impossible. Since this is the case, Shāntideva's *Engaging in the Bodhisattva Deeds* speaks of the special insight that destroys the afflictive emotions as thoroughly depending upon calm abiding:[12]

> Having understood that the afflictive emotions
> Are overcome through special insight
> Thoroughly endowed with calm abiding,
> One should first seeking calm abiding.

One who has the steadiness of calm abiding is to engage in the development of analytical special insight.

The entity of calm abiding is stabilizing meditation, and the entity of special insight is analytical meditation, but this does not entail that all stabilizing meditation is calm abiding or that all analytical meditation is special insight. Also, special insight is not necessarily just meditation that realizes emptiness, the final mode of existence of phenomena, and calm abiding is not necessarily meditation on something from within the varieties of phenomena rather than the final mode of existence of phenomena. Calm abiding and special insight are types of meditation distinguished from the viewpoint of the *mode* of meditation, not from the viewpoint of their objects of observation. Hence, calm abiding can observe emptiness or something from within the varieties of phenomena; similarly, the object of special insight does not have to be emptiness—it can be something from among the many varieties of phenomena.

What is the reason why a union of calm abiding and special insight is needed? As already explained, it is only *in addition* to having steadiness of mind that one can develop the power of analysis of special insight. For example, if one wants to look at something in the dark, a lamp is needed, and, furthermore, the lamp has to be bright and hence cannot be fluctuating due to wind. Similarly, one needs a consciousness that is not fluctuating due to conceptuality or due to laxity and excitement—that is endowed with the factor of stability—and, in addition, has the capacity to analyze.

In Highest Yoga Tantra, it is explained that calm abiding and special insight can be achieved simultaneously in dependence upon a special technique. Also, in Highest Yoga Tantra, it is explained that special insight can be achieved in a practice that proceeds not by way of analytical meditation but by way of stabilizing meditation. Again, this meets back to techniques that I mentioned earlier, which, if properly practiced, can lead to speedy simultaneous achievement of calm abiding and special insight within a few months.

HOW TO ACHIEVE CALM ABIDING

Now, let us turn to the actual practice of calm abiding. The first topic is that of prerequisites, for which the practice of ethics is basic. You need a completely isolated place with silence and tranquility—this is highly necessary. The place should be free from undue noises of the elements; it is said that the thorn of concentration is sound. Thus, you need a place that is not under the path of airplanes! And no sound of flowing water. Then, from your own side, you must be contented, and all worldly business must stop during this period. Also, your diet has some connection—overeating is not good. When we eat too much, our minds become dark, and it can even make it difficult to sit straight, requiring us to bend to one side or the other. Therefore, less eating is useful. Also, the amount of sleep must be proper. There is no question of drinking alcohol.

Once you have fulfilled these conditions, the posture that you assume is important. You should sit in the vajra cross-legged posture, but this can be difficult for some people because, due to the very difficulties of the posture, all of your concentration will go to the pain that is in your legs. In that case, it would probably be all right to sit on a chair. Place your left hand under the right with both palms upward and with the two thumbs together—the hands being four finger-widths below the navel. If you sit in the vajra cross-legged posture, your rear should be slightly higher. Your back should be straight like an arrow; the two shoulders should be set naturally, and you should put your arms out a little because if they are too close to your sides, it will create too much warmth. Then, bend your head down just a little; touch the tip of the tongue to the palate—this keeps too much breath from passing through the mouth and keeps you from becoming thirsty. Leave your teeth and lips as usual. If you have no teeth, you can purse your lips together! Aim your eyes at the point of your nose. If your nose is too small, it can cause considerable pain to aim them there. Thus, it is not necessary to look at the tip of the nose; you can look over the tip of the nose. However, given the size of your noses, Westerners would not have a problem with this!

With respect to whether to close your eyes or not, while you are not used to meditation, it is helpful to close your eyes, but real meditation and concentration comes with the mental consciousness, not with the eye consciousness. Thus, once you really become accustomed to meditation, the eyes are not very important, it not being necessary to close them. Also, it can make your mind clearer to wear your glasses, but this seems to make less stability, whereas if you take them off, you will have more stability but slightly less clarity. This is due to the fact that there is a great connection between the mental consciousness and the eye consciousness. Also, if you face the wall, as is done in Zen, it is truly helpful.

Tomorrow I will talk about the objects of meditation.

7. Techniques for Meditation
Thursday Morning

Question and Answer Period

QUESTION: If desire and hatred cannot be experienced together, how do you explain the love-hate relationships we witness between two people who are very close to each other?

ANSWER: I was speaking about these occurring simultaneously, right in one second. During just the time when generating the mode of apprehension of desire, at that very time it is impossible to generate the mode of apprehension of hatred. But, in terms of a series of moments, in our own experience we know cases of very good friends or couples who alternate between fighting and being friendly.

QUESTION: Is it useful or advisable to be brought under hypnosis into one's former lifetime and intermediate state in order to understand better one's actual life?

ANSWER: I think that this depends on the situation of the particular person. For some people, it could help in that they would remember virtuous activities in former lifetimes and thereby be drawn into more in this lifetime. Also, there could be cases of people who would remember an awful event in the past which might cause them great anxiety.

QUESTION: What are the spiritual responsibilities of parents to their children?

ANSWER: This is very important. The future of children is very much related with their early period when they are with their parents. Education is gained from various schools, but education alone is just an instrument; the being or person, whether called "soul" or "self," is what uses that instrument, and a person's healthy development very much depends on family influence, the family atmosphere. In this respect, whether the parents are believers in religion or non-believers, the child's becoming a good human being is their responsibility. This is not just a religious matter; it concerns helping children to become good and wholesome.

QUESTION: Since a Hearer does not set out to realize the emptiness of inherent existence but rather is attempting to realize a coarser emptiness, how can it be the case that Hearers actually become Foe Destroyers, Arhats?

ANSWER: A distinction has to be made between *proponents* of Hearer tenet systems and Hearer *practitioners.* Similarly, a distinction needs to be made between *proponents* of Great Vehicle tenets and Great Vehicle *practitioners.* For instance, there could be a person who, by school of philosophy, is a Proponent of the Great Exposition, a Hearer school, but, in terms of motivation, is a person of the Great Vehicle; in other words, there could be a Bodhisattva who, by school of philosophy, is a Proponent of the Great Exposition. Also, there could be a person who is a Consequentialist—a proponent of a Great Vehicle school—but, in terms of motivation, is a Hearer.

Nevertheless, whoever has reached the level of a Superior—someone who has directly realized emptiness—must be a Consequentialist. Still, this does not mean that anyone who accepts or knows the view of the Consequence School is necessarily a Consequentialist, just as all Buddhists do not have to be proponents of a philosophical school. In order for someone to be posited as a proponent of a particular system, the person must study the texts of that system, become trained in it, and be able to present it by way of reasoning. It seems that to be a *proponent* of a system of tenets you would have to be facile with words! So, those who know the essential meaning but stay off by themselves would not be posited as proponents of that system in accordance with the general usage of this term in the world.

QUESTION: Western religions use the term "God," and Buddhism does not. Could emptiness or nirvana be considered God? If the afflictive obstruction that is the conception of inherent existence is eliminated, does one realize that everything is God?

ANSWER: If God is interpreted as an ultimate reality or truth, then selflessness may be considered as God and even as a creator in the sense that within the nature of emptiness things appear and disappear. In this sense, emptiness is the basis of everything; because of emptiness, things can change, and things can appear and disappear. Thus, voidness—emptiness, selflessness—is this kind of basis.

With respect to the doctrine of the two truths, ultimate truths and conventional truths [or truths-for-a-concealing-consciousness], some people mistakenly think that just one phenomenon is posited as an ultimate truth or a conventional truth through the force of two levels of consciousness—that as long as one has the ignorance of the conception of inherent existence, it is a conventional truth for that person, whereas when one no longer has such ignorance, it is an ultimate truth. This is not the case, however.

In the term for conventional truth [or truth-for-a-concealing-consciousness], *saṃvṛtisatya*, the word *saṃvṛti* in general is used to mean worldly conventions, interdependence, and concealer—the latter referring to the ignorance that conceals reality. However, the predominant meaning in this context is "concealer," as Chandrakīrti says in his *Supplement to (Nāgārjuna's) "Treatise on the Middle"*:[1]

The Subduer said that obscuration[2] is the "concealer"
Because it obstructs the nature.

An ignorant consciousness conceiving inherent existence conceals the reality of selflessness; therefore, it is called a concealer (*kun rdzob, saṃvṛti*). Those which are true for this concealing ignorance are called truths-for-a-concealing-consciousness (*kun rdzob bden pa, saṃvṛtisatya*). Because this is the case, Chandrakīrti says that since Hearers and Solitary Realizers who have reached the end of their particular path as Foe Destroyers, as well as Bodhisattvas on the eighth ground and above, no longer have the ignorance that conceives of inherent existence, for them these phenomena are mere conventionalities and are not truths-for-a-concealing-consciousness (*kun rdzob bden pa, saṃvṛtisatya*). Thus, the word "truth" in the term "truth-for-a-concealing-consciousness" does not mean truth in fact but "truth" for a particular awareness.

Because these conventional objects can be truths only for an obscured ignorant consciousness that misconceives phenomena to be inherently existent, there is no other consciousness that can posit them to be truths, that is to say, to be objects that exist the way they appear. This is why conventional phenomena are called "truths-for-a-concealing-consciousness," things that are truths for an obscuring consciousness conceiving inherent existence. Then, is it the case that these conventional phenomena only *exist* for an ignorant consciousness? No. Since these conventional phenomena are validly established as existent, that which certifies or posits their existence cannot be an ignorant mistaken consciousness, but must be valid cognition. Therefore, we must make a distinction between the ignorant consciousnesses with respect to which these conventional phenomena are posited as "truths" and the validly cognizing consciousnesses that posit them as existing.

With respect to the term "ultimate truth" (*don dam bden pa, paramārthasatya*), the Consequentialists explain, etymologically, that since an emptiness is an object (*don, artha*), the highest (*dam, parama*), and a truth (*bden pa, satya*), it is an ultimate truth. However, in the Autonomy School, "object" and "highest" are treated in different ways—emptiness being a truth that is the object of the highest wisdom or a truth for the highest object, that is to say, the highest wisdom.

QUESTION: Could you say something about the loss of self in mental illness?

ANSWER: There are many levels of mental illness, and as I mentioned earlier about depression, some of them are probably untreatable for the time being. In general, as is said in Shāntideva's *Engaging in the Bodhisattva Deeds,* one has to be cautious when one is very successful since at that time there is danger of becoming prideful and becoming involved in the non-religious, and one has to be cautious also when one has undergone lack of success and so forth since there is a danger of becoming discouraged—the life of the mind, so to speak, dying—due to which harm to one's practice could be incurred. These two times of inflation and deflation are contrary circumstances, and thus it is necessary to employ antidotes to them individually. I think that these antidotes may have some relation to your question.

Specifically, in situations of low self-esteem, Shāntideva recommends reflection this way:[3]

> Even very tiny bugs and worms have the Buddha nature and thus, when they encounter certain conditions, through the power of effort they can achieve the non-abiding nirvana of a Buddha. Now, I have been born as a human with the capacity to understand what is to be adopted in practice and what is to be discarded; thus, there is no reason for me to be discouraged. The great saints and so forth of the past who achieved a high level were people with a life-basis such as I have, not something separate.

Through such reflection, a resurgence of will can be generated.

QUESTION: What is the nature of the developmental lineage, and how is it transformed into the Form Body of a Buddha?

ANSWER: In our continuums now we have a capacity such that, when we meet with certain conditions, in the future we will manifest uncontaminated qualities. The developmental lineage refers to a time when that capacity has been nourished, or activated.

QUESTION: The theory of evolution describes development of higher forms of life out of lower forms, such as humans out of the animals, whereas Buddhism depicts cyclic existence as going up and down in cycles. Can Your Holiness reconcile these two views?

ANSWER: The explanation of evolution and the Buddhist explanation that our own series of rebirths are indefinite in terms of type have different contexts. Evolution has to do with the development of this particular world, whereas the indefiniteness of birth is concerned with *one* person's births in many possible worlds. Thus, the point of controversy does not come here. However, one problem is found in different explanations of how this world system first formed. In Vasubandhu's *Treasury of Manifest Knowledge,* it is explained that when beings first formed in this world system, their life span was "immeasurable" and that their bodies were like that of a deity, something like a spiritual body, it not being necessary for them to partake of coarse food—their sustenance was the food of meditative stabilization. Also, there were not any males and females. But then, gradually things got worse and worse; the average life span became shorter and shorter, and it will continue shortening down to a minimum of ten years. Thus, it is quite complicated to put *this* together with Darwin's theory of evolution. So, how can we make a compromise? Frankly, I do not know. Perhaps, we are again to poke some fun at Vasubandhu!

Still, it may be possible that there are two levels happening at once. Some of you may be interested in an account of a mystery; in Tibet there were several occurrences of children of gods even in this generation. Among my parents' generation there was a person in the Hor area of northern Tibet, called Gagya-dam-nga, who was known to be a child of a god. His mother slept with a god of her area and gave birth to him. He himself was a very powerful and clever bandit—no one could get the better of him. This story illustrates how there can be a relationship between a human and a non-human. So, perhaps the best compromise is to say that there is one level of being that is undergoing the type of process that Vasubandhu describes—proceeding downwards—and there are other types of beings on the same planet that are evolving in the manner described by Darwin.

In our own indigenous history, the Tibetan race is said to have come from a male monkey who mated with a female ogress. Perhaps, from the viewpoint of the mother, this is like Vasubandhu's theory, and from the viewpoint of the father, like Darwin's theory!

It is also explained that Tibetans are descended from a race of Indians; there are many theories, many explanations. A pluralistic approach seems best. In any case, investigation and analysis are important, as in archaeology—making digs, testing, and performing experiments. Such analysis is very important. For instance, there is a great deal of controversy concerning how many years have passed since Shākyamuni Buddha's death. In one system, it is said that more than three thousand years have passed; in another, approximately two thousand eight hundred; in another, approximately two thousand five hundred, and so on. Now, the actual fact cannot be all of them; it has to be one of them. It is preferable to decide that this is a matter best pursued not by calculation based on old records but, instead, by investigating actual relics.

In a scripture, Buddha, while living in India, said that after a certain length of time beings would appear in a snowy land upon the subsiding of a lake. Around 1947 or 1948, as some as you may know, two Europeans, Peter Aufschnaiter and Heinrich Harrer, who were prisoners of war, escaped from India and came to Tibet. They were employed by the Tibetan government; Aufschnaiter did construction work toward building a hydroelectric facility.

While making a channel, he came upon a covered square chest, inside of which he found a complete skeleton along with some articles including things hung on the neck and small iron knives. He sent the skeleton and artifacts to Europe for examination where it was found that the skeleton was over four thousand years old. This obviously means that when Buddha was in India, there were already human beings in Tibet. Therefore, the scripture that speaks of beings appearing in the snowy land upon the subsiding of a lake after Buddha's time must refer, not to the whole of Tibet, but to the Lhasa area, which would then have to have been a lake during Buddha's time.

There is another scientific reason why the Lhasa area was a lake at that time. Around 1953, a Chinese team of archaeologists and geologists came to do research near the northern range of mountains in Lhasa Valley. In the foothills, the team found a very large fossil leaf, which a member of the team said confirmed a Tibetan historical account that in ancient time the Lhasa area was a lake. The fossil is a clear sign that where Lhasa presently is there used to be a great lake that was surrounded by a forest. Through combining these sources, we can see that the particular Lhasa area itself was a lake but that there were already human beings in the surrounding region. So, it is interesting to use a combination of scriptural sources and actual findings—very useful and helpful.

QUESTION: Do women have the potential to become Bodhisattva Superiors, Foe Destroyers, lamas, reincarnations, and other such venerable members of the spiritual community?

ANSWER: There is no difference at all between men and women in this regard. Still, one problem is that it is said that in order to take the vows of a fully ordained nun, the ceremony requires the presence of a combination of monks and nuns, but no fully ordained Indian nuns ever came to Tibet such that an ordination ceremony could be conducted. Thus, in the past in Tibet novice nuns could not take the vows of a fully ordained nun. However, at present, among the Chinese Great Vehicle tradition, there are fully ordained nuns.

In terms of the transmission of the vows, one needs to know that there are eighteen subschools of the Great Exposition School, which are divided among four basic schools—Sthaviravāda (or Theravāda), Mahāsaṃghika, Sammitīya, and Sarvāstivāda. The vows of fully ordained monks in Thailand, Sri Lanka, and so forth are of the Theravāda transmission. Those of the Tibetan tradition are of the Sarvāstivāda transmission. The vows of a fully ordained monk according to the Theravāda school are 227 in number whereas according to the Sarvāstivāda school, they are 253. Upon examination, however, the differences are very minor; the main points are exactly the same. According to the Sarvāstivāda school, in order to conduct the vow ceremony of a fully ordained nun, it is necessary to have both monks and nuns, and our research has determined that there is no current transmission of the vows of a fully ordained nun according to this school. Though the *Aphorisms on Discipline* speak of the rules for nuns, they have not continued in practice. Perhaps, however, the situation is different in the tradition that exists in China, and thus we are currently investigating this.

According to the *Aphorisms on Discipline,* the lineage of the vows of monks and nuns must meet back to Shākyamuni Buddha. For tantric vows, such is not necessary; a qualified lama can, from his or her own visionary experience, receive certain tantric practices, but for the discipline of monks and nuns the lineage of the vows must strictly stem from Buddha and not just from the visions of those with pure perception.

Thus, if the tradition in China is authentic, it will be very useful. This is a problem within the Buddhist community as yet unsolved.

Let us return to our central topic.

CULTIVATION OF CALM ABIDING

After having assumed properly the posture of meditation, one first needs to watch the inhalation and exhalation of breath. One should leave the breath in a natural manner moving gently in and out, without forcing it strongly or making it extremely weak.

With respect to achieving meditative stabilization, this is to be achieved by way of getting rid of five faults through eight antidotes. As Maitreya's *Differentiation of the Middle and the Extremes* says:[4]

> It arises from the cause of utilizing the eight
> Activities [of antidotes] abandoning the five faults.

What are the five faults?

1. Laziness.
2. Forgetting the advice, which means to forget the object.
3. Laxity and excitement—if these are taken separately, there are then six faults.
4. Non-application of the antidotes when laxity or excitement arises.
5. Over-application of the antidotes when laxity and excitement are no longer present.

In order to abandon these five faults, eight antidotes are prescribed. The antidotes to laziness are fourfold—faith, aspiration, exertion, and pliancy. The last, pliancy, is impossible in the beginning, for it is a state in which one is devoid of the assumption of bad physical and mental states such that one's mind is serviceable in a virtuous direction, and thus, pliancy can only be achieved after a great deal of meditation. Still, in the beginning it is helpful to reflect on its value. The first antidote, therefore, is the *faith* of seeing the advantages of meditative stabilization. In dependence upon this, one generates *aspiration* seeking meditative stabilization. In dependence upon it, one has *exertion* toward achieving meditative stabilization. These four are the antidotes to laziness.

As an antidote to the fault of forgetting the object, one needs *mindfulness*. Even though mindfulness also acts as an antidote to laxity and excitement, the main antidote to these is *introspection*. Then, as an antidote to not applying antidotes to laxity or excitement when they occur, one needs *application*—the mental factor of intention that applies the antidotes. Finally, as an antidote to overapplication of the antidotes when laxity and excitement have already been removed, one needs the *equanimity* of forsaking application of those antidotes.

What kinds of objects of observation can be used? In sūtra, the Supramundane Victor Buddha spoke of four types—pervasive objects, objects for purifying behavior, skillful objects, and objects for purifying afflictive emotions.

Pervasive objects

Pervasive objects are so called because they apply to all objects of calm abiding, from the viewpoint of both the observing consciousness and the objects. There are four types of pervasive objects of observation, the first two being from the viewpoint of the observing consciousness and the latter two from the viewpoint of the object:

1. Non-analytical images, which are objects within the context of stabilizing meditation without analysis.
2. Analytical images, which are objects within the context of analysis.
3. The limits of phenomena, these being the two categories of the varieties of phenomena and the final mode of being of phenomena.
4. Thorough achievement of the purpose, which is not objects meditated upon but the purposes for which one is meditating—all the fruits of meditative stabilization from liberation up to the omniscience of Buddhahood.

Objects for purifying behavior

In accordance with the type of afflictive emotion to which one is most accustomed, one meditates on an object, in order to counteract that afflictive emotion. Such predominant afflictions are grouped in five classes—desire, hatred, obscuration, pride, and discursiveness. A person with predominant desire meditates on the object as ugly.

As an antidote to hatred, one meditatively cultivates love. As an antidote to obscuration, one meditates on dependent-arising. As an antidote to pride, one meditates on the divisions of the constituents. As an antidote to discursiveness, one meditates on the exhalation and inhalation of the breath. The Burmese tradition emphasizes concentration on the exhalation and inhalation of the breath.

Skillful objects of observation

There are five types of objects of observation for becoming skillful—the mental and physical aggregates, the constituents, the external and internal sense spheres, the twelve links of dependent-arising, and the appropriate and the inappropriate.

Objects of observation for purifying afflictive emotions

Objects—meditation on which serves to purify afflictive emotions—are of two types: meditation in which one views the present level as gross and a higher level as peaceful, and meditation on the four noble truths. Meditation on selflessness is included in the latter.

That is a brief, general explanation of objects of observation for cultivating calm abiding. Now, what specific object should we use? This is decided relative to your own disposition. As mentioned just above, those persons who are predominated by desire should meditate on ugliness, and those predominated by hatred should cultivate love. Those predominated by discursiveness would indeed do well to meditate on the exhalation and inhalation of the breath. Still, it is sometimes helpful not to have any such object but to concentrate on the mind itself, even though it is a little more difficult to achieve calm abiding observing the mind. Also, there is a danger of generating problems with the life-wind—anxiety, nervous breakdown. I have known some people who have worked at cultivating calm abiding within observing the mind, and in time they have become a little nervous.

Someone who has developed understanding of emptiness can take emptiness as the object and, within not analyzing, set the mind one-pointedly on it and achieve calm abiding. Also, according to the Mantra system, one meditates on one's own body as a divine body. Not involving Mantra, one can meditate on a Buddha body in front of oneself; similarly, a non-Buddhist could concentrate on Christ. Or, one could meditate on a drop of light, or a syllable—there are many such objects. This type of practice is prevalent throughout Buddhist and non-Buddhist systems.

When Buddhists, for instance, meditate on a Buddha's body, they imagine that the Buddha body is about four feet in front of them at the level of their eyebrows. Also, if possible, it is better to imagine the body as being very small; this makes it easier to gather the mind together on the object. In addition, it is helpful to meditate on the Buddha body as being heavy, as this assists in keeping the mind from becoming scattered. Also, it should be imagined as being very bright; this helps to keep laxity from occurring.

First of all, you should look at a properly crafted Buddha image, either a statue or a painting, in order to ascertain its features. To make a joke: If you use a poorly drawn figure with a twisted face, and so forth, then later when you become enlightened, you will become a Buddha with such a distorted figure!

You must stay with whatever you determine your object to be, not deviating from it. You cannot change the object day by day; the size, color, and shape must be fixed. Until you are qualified in meditation, you must use the same size and same shape of the object for the focus of your imagination.

While setting the mind on the object, what should you do? The meditative stabilization that you are trying to achieve has two attributes—stability and clarity. With regard to concentration, there is nothing fantastic about mere stability of mind—being able to stay on the object; what is very important is clarity, vividness of mind. Clarity here refers not just to the object but to the mind that is imagining the object; the mind itself must be very vivid. Not only that, but also there must be an *intensity* to the clarity—full alertness.

That which prevents stability is desirous excitement, which, for us, is the main form of scattering of the mind; such excitement is a scattering to an object of desire and thus is included within the category of desire. On the other hand, that which prevents the mind from becoming vividly clear is laxity. Therefore, initially, you need to stop the mind from being scattered and cause it to remain one-pointedly and vividly on the object.

If when placing your mind on the object, it becomes dull, clouded over, as if you were dozing in a chair, this is lethargy—a heaviness and cloudiness of mind. It is a cause of laxity, not laxity itself. In this case, the object is not clear. In another condition, however, the object is clear but the mind is not *very* clear, not *very* alert—the mind that is imagining the object is vivid, but it lacks intensity. If the factors of both mental clarity and intensity to that clarity are lacking, this is a case of the coarsest laxity. However, if mental clarity is present, but it lacks intensity, this is a middling form of laxity. The subtlest type of laxity occurs when the factor of mental clarity is intense but not fully so—there is a slight loss of intensity. It is considered to be one of the worst problems since it is very difficult to identify, as it is easily mistaken for a flawless state of meditative stabilization. You might wonder what fault there could be with coming under the influence of such subtle laxity since the object is clear, the mind is clear, and there is considerable intensity to this mental clarity. Even though if you remain in a state of subtle laxity for a long period of time, the mind becomes more and more collected and the breath in the nostrils even becomes more and more subtle, the problem is that your intelligence is becoming duller and duller—you are becoming stupid. Since this is the case, it is very important not to come under the influence of subtle laxity.

What techniques can be employed to prevent the onset of excitement and laxity? First, you have to hold to the object by way of mindfulness. Then, when you have developed strong mindfulness and its force has not deteriorated, this strong mindfulness will induce introspection; thus, one of the causes of introspection is powerful mindfulness. Introspection is a factor that inspects the mind to determine whether a fault is setting in or not. There are two types of introspection—a coarser form that is an inspection coming after excitement or laxity has set in and a more subtle form that operates before they set in. The uncommon cause of the development of strong introspection is to again and again perform this sort of inspection with a corner of the mind. The main force of the mind is set continuously on the object of imagination, but a corner of the mind inspects whether laxity or excitement are arising.

When the mind becomes very slack, desirous excitement will not be generated; to the extent that the mode of apprehension of the mind is lowered, to this extent the scattering of the mind will lessen, but there is danger of generating laxity. Similarly, if the mode of apprehension of the mind is too high, laxity will be removed, but there is a danger that desirous excitement will be generated. Thus, from your own experience, you have to arrive at a point where you recognize that when the mind becomes too heightened, there is a danger of generating excitement and, in reaction to this, you know to lower the mode of apprehension of the mind. Correspondingly, from your own experience, you need to learn to recognize the boundary of the mind's becoming too lowered such that there is a danger of generating laxity; you need to come to recognize immediately that the mode of apprehension of the mind must be heightened. These are the main activities.

Then, what are the techniques for heightening or lowering the mind? To heighten the mind, you think about something that enlivens it, but not an object that would generate desire. For instance, you could reflect on the value of developing the meditative stabilization of calm abiding or on the value of having attained a life as a human or on the value of having human intelligence. Through such reflection, your mind will gain courage, thereby causing its mode of apprehension to become heightened.

If, despite such a technique, laxity is not cleared away, it is better to end the session and go to a place that is bright or that is high with a vast view where you can see a great distance. Or, expose yourself to fresh air, or throw cold water on your face. Then, return to the session.

When the mind becomes too heightened and thus scattered, what will lower its mode of apprehension? As a technique to withdraw the mind inside, you should reflect on a topic that sobers the mind, such as the suffering of cyclic existence, or think, "In the past I have been ruined by distraction, and again now I will be ruined by distraction. If I do not take care now, it will not be good." This will lower the mode of apprehension of the mind.

Since this is the case, a person who is cultivating calm abiding needs to be in a state where such reflections will move the mind immediately. Therefore, prior to working at achieving calm abiding, it is necessary to have become convinced about many topics—such as those involved in the four establishments in mindfulness—through a considerable amount of analysis. In an actual session of cultivating calm abiding one is performing stabilizing meditation, not analytical meditation, but if one has engaged in considerable analysis of these topics previously, the force of the previous reflection remains with the mind and can be recalled. Thus, when you switch to such topics in order either to elevate or lower the mind, the mind will be immediately affected. In this way, if ascertainment has been generated previously, then reflecting on the value of meditative stabilization or the value of a human lifetime will immediately heighten the mind, and reflection on sobering topics such as the nature of the body or the ugliness of objects of desire will immediately lower its mode of apprehension. Also, sometimes when the mind is not clear, it can be refreshed by sending it out into space.

One has to recognize when laxity and excitement arise and needs to know the techniques for overcoming them. The appropriate antidote has to be implemented with respect to whatever is occurring—laxity or excitement. Still, when laxity and excitement do not arise, if you use too much introspection, there will be a danger of losing the object of observation; hence, at such a time, you need to employ techniques for just staying vividly and continuously on the object.

When meditating this way, you will pass through nine states of mind called "mental abidings."[5] At the first level, called "setting the mind,"[6] the mind is being set on the object of observation through the power of hearing about the value of meditative stabilization. Then, one comes to be able to set the mind more continuously on the object on which it is set; this is the second level, called "continuous setting."[7] Then, between the mind's being distracted and its being set on the object, distraction becomes less, and placement predominates; even though there are periods of slight distraction, immediately one is able to bring the mind back to the object. This is the third level, called "resetting."[8]

When initially placing the mind on an internal object of observation during the first level, meditators have the sense of having more conceptions than before, to the point of even being amazed at the amount of thought. In fact, we do not have more conceptions; we are just identifying how many conceptions we have. For instance, when doing Zazen, it seems that we have more saliva than usual and more itches. These are actually the same as usual, but usually we do not pay any attention to them. Then, during the second level, because you are able to set the mind on the object for a little while, even though conceptions are still generated, you have the sense that conceptuality rests a little now and then. With the third level, you have the sense that conceptuality has become tired; this means that conceptuality is no longer very active and is operating more slowly.

Then, from the fourth level, called "close setting,"[9] the object of observation is never lost; one is released from the danger of losing the object and remains on the object. However, from within being able to keep on the object of observation, subtle laxity and subtle excitement begin to occur. This state can be compared to a child in a classroom who, physically, is sitting on a chair but whose mind is thinking about something else. The main part of the mind is set on the object, but the mind is affected by subtle laxity and excitement. At this point, one has generated the power of mindfulness.

The next level is called "disciplining,"[10] at which point one has passed beyond the danger of gross laxity and excitement but the danger of subtle laxity is greater. It is necessary to generate the power of introspection. Then, at the time of the sixth level, called "pacifying,"[11] the danger of subtle excitement is greater due to the fact that on the previous level one exercised great caution with regard to laxity. Again, the antidote is the power of introspection, which, during the sixth level, develops to fullness such that it is well qualified.

The seventh is called "thorough pacifying";[12] at this time it is difficult for any sort of laxity or excitement to create problems. Still, strong exertion is needed. Even though neither laxity nor excitement can arise in any significant form, it is necessary deep down to have a tautness of mind that is concerned lest laxity or excitement occur. Then, with the eighth level, called "making one-pointed,"[13] at the beginning of the session one need only have the thought, "I must take care to keep laxity and excitement from arising," this being sufficient to prevent the occurrence of laxity and excitement.

The ninth level, called "setting in meditative equipoise,"[14] can be compared to the recitation of someone who is well trained in that particular recitation such that it comes spontaneously—it need only be begun, after which it goes by itself. For someone who is practicing Highest Yoga Tantra, it is possible at this point to practice the stage of completion. During the stage of generation, one achieves the factor of stability associated with these nine levels, but it is not necessary at this point to achieve a fully qualified calm abiding that is included within the preparations for the first concentration, if one is capable of the practices of the stage of completion.

I will not explain the six powers and the four mental engagements.[15] This afternoon we will discuss actual calm abiding.

8. ALTRUISM

Thursday Afternoon

QUESTION AND ANSWER PERIOD

QUESTION: You stated that in the Middle Way School all consciousnesses, except the wisdom consciousness directly realizing emptiness, are mistaken. Could you explain this?

ANSWER: The reason why all consciousnesses except those without dualistic appearance are necessarily mistaken is that forms and so forth appear to such consciousnesses to exist in their own right but are proved not to exist in their own right. To a wisdom consciousness directly realizing emptiness—this being a consciousness that has investigated whether an object exists in own right and has not found such an inherent nature—all that appears is a mere vacuity that is a negative, or absence, of the object of negation, inherent existence. Except for the aspect of a Buddha's wisdom that knows the many varieties of phenomena, any consciousness that perceives a conventional phenomenon necessarily is involved with the false appearance of the object as if it exists in its own right. Since the appearance factor of such a consciousness is involved with this mistake, the consciousness is said to be mistaken.

QUESTION: If we are to prove through reasoning the doctrines set forth in Buddhism, what reasoning is there to establish the stages of consciousness that one passes through in dying and rebirth?

ANSWER: These mainly are to be known through experiencing them. However, if one had to explain the levels of consciousness outside of the context of experience, there are many objects that are not very hidden phenomena *in general* but are very hidden, very obscure, *relative to a particular person.* For a person who has not experienced them, they are very hidden phenomena, and thus for that person, one would have to use the type of reasoning called "inference of belief" that involves investigation into scripture, as mentioned earlier. However, there are cases of people who remember their taking rebirth, as well as others who remember their death; for the latter, the levels of consciousness are not very hidden phenomena but are obvious.

QUESTION: You spoke the other day about *devaputra* demons who are always making obstacles for beings who want to overcome obscurations. For a practitioner of Great Vehicle Buddhism, what would you recommend to free oneself of these demons, if one knows that they are in fact inside oneself?

ANSWER: *Devaputra* demons are classified among the six categories of gods in the Desire Realm, specifically in the class called "Those Enjoying Control over Others' Emanations." We ourselves have formerly been born in that type of life within cyclic existence. All of us have acted as horrible demons, all of us! With regard to techniques that can be employed if one is being bothered by such a demon, in the Mantra system there are meditations of a wheel of protection, but the best of all techniques is to cultivate love. When Shākyamuni Buddha, from among the twelve great deeds of his lifetime, performed the deed of taming demons the night before his enlightenment, he did it by way of cultivating the meditative stabilization of love.

Sometimes, when one has a bad dream or nightmare and awakens, even if one repeats mantra or meditates on a wheel of protection, these will not help, but when one cultivates love, it cures the situation. This is the best technique.

QUESTION: How does one study Buddhism and maintain a daily practice, without becoming attached to it?

ANSWER: There are probably cases when even virtuous consciousnesses involve the assistance of the misconception of inherent existence. Therefore, it is said in some texts that the misconception of the transitory mental and physical aggregates as inherently existent I and mine can serve even as an aid in achieving Buddhahood—the reference being to initial practice. Therefore, when, for instance, you initially cultivate compassion, the conception of inherent existence is involved, but if you became concerned about this and decided, consequently, not to continue cultivating compassion, this would be a mistake, since, for the time being, there is no other choice. Thus, to overcome the conception of inherent existence and to overcome attachment, you cannot just withdraw your mind from objects; that will not overcome it. Rather, it is said that in order to reduce the force of the misconception of inherent existence, you have to ascertain the opposite of inherent existence, selflessness—mere withdrawal of the mind is not helpful. Hence, if you are becoming attached to your practice, you should work at overcoming this attachment through an additional practice. You should not stop practicing just because you notice the development of attachment to it.

However, when you have attachment to, for instance, material things, it is best to desist from that activity. It is taught that one should have few desires and have satisfaction—detachment—with respect to material things; it is not taught that one should be satisfied with practice of the path. The viewpoints are different; in the one case, the object with respect to which attachment is being generated is something to be discarded, whereas in the latter case it is something to be adopted. The distinction should be made from this perspective.

QUESTION: Does mindfulness of the body as having a nature of suffering prohibit regard for helpful maintenance of the body, and does it prohibit pleasure in its functioning at maximum potential?

ANSWER: When it is advised that one view the body as having a nature of suffering, it is not being suggested that one should neglect the body. As Āryadeva says in his *Four Hundred Stanzas on the Yogic Deeds of Bodhisattvas*:[1]

> Though the body is viewed as like an enemy,
> Nevertheless it should be protected.

In dependence upon this body, one can achieve great aims. As Shāntideva's *Engaging in the Bodhisattva Deeds* says:[2]

> Relying upon the boat of a human [body]
> Free yourself from the great river of suffering,

The body should be viewed as a favorable circumstance for bringing about others' welfare, due to which it has to be nourished and furthered within an attitude of non-attachment.

QUESTION: Why is it that non-virtuous emotions such as desire and hatred disappear when the wisdom of emptiness is realized, but virtuous emotions such as compassion do not?

ANSWER: This has to do with what I said earlier about whether the consciousness, the attitude, has a foundation of valid cognition or not. Even if at a time of feeling compassion, for instance, there can be a mixture with an afflictive emotion, the very basis of compassion is something that is founded in reason. When one gets angry, one has a reason such as, "This person has harmed me; so, I will get back at him/her in good style!" However, when you look into it in detail, the reasons are unfounded, and one is bringing trouble on oneself. In terms of a long-range perspective, it is better not to get angry.

In Mantra there is a practice of using anger in the path, but this does not refer to mere anger. The causal motivation is very strong compassion, although the motivation at the time of the action is anger. Enough on this for the time being.

ATTAINMENT OF CALM ABIDING

With regard to how long one should spend in a meditative session each day, it is said that at the beginning it is best for sessions to be short and frequent. When a beginner tries to meditate for a long period, a properly qualified meditation will not come, and, instead, one will become tired, with the resultant danger that the meditative stabilization will be faulty. Therefore, it is better to meditate for just ten or fifteen minutes, but to do this many times during the day.

The best time for meditation is the morning, but just like keeping a fire going so that it can be used at various times, you have to maintain the continuum of the meditation such that what is gained in earlier practice is not entirely lost by the time you begin the next session. A fully qualified person does not need much time to accomplish calm abiding; it can be done in a year or even several months. However, this is in terms of someone who has all of the concordant circumstances.

When one sustains meditative stabilization such as I was describing at the end of the last session, one is spontaneously set in the meditative stabilization of the ninth level, called "setting in meditative equipoise," free from the faults of laxity and excitement. Then, unfavorable states of mind and body—such that our minds and bodies usually are not serviceable in virtue—are removed gradually. At present, our minds are not usable in accordance with our wish, but through accustoming to the ninth level of meditative stabilization, this unserviceability diminishes in strength such that finally an antidote to it is generated, this being called "mental pliancy."

As a sign that mental pliancy is about to be generated, a tingly sensation is felt in the area of the brain. The feeling is not unpleasant; it is pleasant, and the reason why it is generated is that a special wind, an inner air, fills the body. The feeling is compared to that of a warm hand placed on top of the head after it has been shaved. This sign is said to occur just prior to the arising of mental pliancy, and, indeed, some people who have cultivated meditative stabilization have reported that it does.

In dependence upon the power of having generated this serviceability of mind, which is called "mental pliancy," a favorable wind, or energy, circulates in the body; it is a cause of generating physical pliancy. Through this wind's pervading all the parts of the body, the unserviceability of the body such that it cannot be directed to virtuous activities in accordance with one's wishes is removed, and physical pliancy is generated. The generation of physical pliancy, in turn, generates a bliss of physical pliancy, a sense of comfort throughout the body. Though it is indeed blissful, it has no connection with the bliss described in Mantra; it does not involve concentrated emphasis on important points in the body but is merely due to withdrawing the mind onto an object of observation—it is due to the power of just such meditative stabilization.

When the bliss of physical pliancy is generated, it makes the body blissful; this induces a bliss of mental pliancy, making the mind blissful. At first, this joyous mental bliss is a little too strong, but then gradually it becomes more steady, the element of excitement quieting down; at this point, one attains an unfluctuating pliancy. This is the point from which one has a fully qualified meditative stabilization of calm abiding.

When such mental meditative stabilization has been achieved, external good and bad objects, such as visible forms and so forth, that generate desire, hatred, and obscuration do not appear to be as solid as they usually do; through the force of having been familiarized with meditative stabilization, they appear to be less concrete. When, from the perspective of experiencing meditative stabilization, one views such objects, they seem to dissolve of their own accord, and the mind immediately withdraws inside. Consequently, at this time there is no danger at all from the usual scattering of the mind outside. Again, as external distractions lessen, one's mind remains experiencing its natural entity of mere luminosity and knowing; due to this, the internal generation of good and bad conceptions lessens. Even when conceptions are generated, they are like bubbles produced from water—they are not able to keep their own continuums going, they disappear immediately.

Another feature of calm abiding is that when one is in meditative equipoise, appearances of even one's own body and so forth do not occur. Also, one has the sense that the mind has become an immaculate vacuity such that it is indivisible from space.

CULTIVATION OF SPECIAL INSIGHT

What is the value of attaining of such calm abiding? Does it mark the attainment of any of the paths of the three vehicles—Hearer, Solitary Realizer, or Bodhisattva? As was mentioned earlier, the meditative stabilization of calm abiding is common to both Buddhists and non-Buddhists; hence, from the viewpoint of its own entity, it does not mark attainment of any of the paths. Nevertheless, even though it is not very elevated, the attainment of calm abiding has great purpose in that this level of concentration is very useful as a mental basis for higher realizations.

Then, in addition to attaining calm abiding, what paths should be cultivated? There are two modes of procedure of the path that can be accomplished in dependence upon a mind of calm abiding—mundane and supramundane.

Mundane Special Insight

The mundane type of special insight is common to both Buddhists and non-Buddhists. It involves meditative cultivation of a path that has the aspect of viewing the present level as gross and a higher level as more peaceful. To understand this, you need to know the presentation of the three realms and nine levels (see chart on page 146).

REALM	LEVEL
formless realm	peak of cyclic existence (ninth level) nothingness (eighth level) infinite consciousness (seventh level) infinite space (sixth level)
form realm	fourth concentration (fifth level) third concentration (fourth level) second concentration (third level) first concentration (second level)
desire realm	desire realm (first level)

Someone who wants to attain the first concentration—the second level—views his or her present level, the Desire Realm, as being gross and unpeaceful and considers the first concentration to be subtle and peaceful. An actual first concentration is attained by progressing through a series of seven "mental contemplations,"[3] the first of which—the "not-unable"[4]—is attained with the attainment of calm abiding. The feeling that accompanies this mental contemplation is neutral feeling. Then, to attain an actual first concentration, one must pass through the remaining six—the mental contemplation of individual knowledge of the character,[5] the mental contemplation arisen from belief,[6] the mental contemplation of thorough isolation,[7] the mental contemplation of withdrawal or joy,[8] the mental contemplation of analysis,[9] and the mental contemplation of final training.[10] Through these, the mental contemplation of the fruit of final training[11]—an actual first concentration—is attained.

Up to the level of attaining calm abiding, one meditates in the manner of stabilizing meditation, but with the mental contemplation of individual knowledge of the character, one begins analytical meditation, initiating the cultivation of special insight. In the mental contemplation of individual knowledge of the character, the individual characters being analyzed are the many qualities of the first concentration, which are viewed as being peaceful, and of the Desire Realm, which are viewed as being gross. Through analyzing these qualities over and over again, one gradually develops a power of mind such that one can overcome the manifest form of the coarser type of afflictive emotions with respect to the Desire Realm, these being divided into nine levels.[12] When one is able to suppress all nine levels of afflictive emotions with respect to the Desire Realm through the three mental contemplations of thorough isolation, withdrawal or joy, and final training, one attains an actual first concentration.

The same mode of procedure is used for attaining the second, third, and fourth concentrations, as well as the four formless absorptions of limitless space, limitless consciousness, nothingness, and the peak of cyclic existence. As was mentioned earlier, there is no definiteness with respect to cyclic existence; thus, from the Buddhist viewpoint, we are all persons who have experienced attainment of these minds. However, those states have deteriorated at present through the manifestation of a mind on the level of the Desire Realm.

SUPRAMUNDANE SPECIAL INSIGHT

In the supramundane path, one analyzes—with a mind of calm abiding—either the four noble truths in terms of what is to be adopted and what is to be discarded or, on a more subtle level, the emptiness of inherent existence in order to achieve supramundane special insight. Except for having switched the mode of thinking, practitioners meditatively cultivate special insight with the mind of calm abiding—that has already been attained—as their basis, and within this context they analyze the object, the four noble truths or emptiness, with individual investigation. Even though, in the process of achieving calm abiding, one has eliminated the laxity and excitement that would interfere with stabilizing meditation, here during the phase of using analytical meditation there is another level of laxity and excitement that interferes with the development of special insight. The laxity and excitement that occur when analyzing are not exactly like those that occurred earlier during cultivation of calm abiding, but it still is necessary again to pass through the four mental engagements.[13]

Gradually, the power of analysis itself is able to induce physical and mental pliancy similar to those explained earlier with respect to calm abiding, but to a greater degree. The generation of the bliss of physical and mental pliancy, induced through the power of analysis, marks the attainment of fully qualified special insight, and from this point on, one has a union of calm abiding and special insight. One now has powerful weapons for realizing the coarser and subtler levels of emptiness in order to overcome obstructions.

That concludes the explanation of the achievement of meditative stabilization within the topic of the four legs of manifestation.

Five faculties and five powers

The next group from within the thirty-seven harmonies with enlightenment are the five faculties—faith, effort, mindfulness, meditative stabilization, and wisdom. These are posited as the five faculties on the first two levels of the path of preparation, called "heat"[14] and "peak."[15] The same five, when they have increased in capacity such that they cannot be diminished by unfavorable circumstances—this being on the last two levels of the path of preparation, called "forbearance"[16] and "supreme mundane qualities"[17]—are posited as the five powers.

What are these five? In an interpretation common to the Hearer Vehicle and Great Vehicle, the first is *faith* with respect to what is to be adopted and what is to be discarded from among the four noble truths. *Effort* is enthusiasm for adopting and discarding what is appropriate among the four truths. *Mindfulness* is a non-forgetfulness with respect to such adopting and discarding. *Meditative stabilization* is one-pointedness of mind with respect to these, and *wisdom* is individual analysis of those.

In terms of the Great Vehicle as described in Maitreya's *Ornament for Clear Realization*,[18] the first is *faith* observing Buddha and so forth, but *faith* according to the uncommon interpretation of the Great Vehicle has unique qualities, in that refuge in Buddha and so forth is taken within the context of an intention involving all sentient beings; therefore, it is said that the objects of observation are omnipresent. Also, one is asserting Buddhahood to be one's own object of attainment. Also, what is to be realized is highest enlightenment. Through these qualities, the Great Vehicle form of refuge is said to outshine that of Hearers and so forth.

Then, *effort* is an enthusiasm for the practice of the six perfections—giving, ethics, patience, effort, concentration, and wisdom. *Mindfulness* is non-forgetfulness of the altruistic intention to become enlightened. *Meditative stabilization* is non-conceptual, and *wisdom* knows all phenomena as unapprehendable as truly established.

Similarly, when Bodhisattvas cultivate the four establishments in mindfulness, they cultivate them not just with respect to themselves but with respect to other sentient beings. In this way, except for differences in the scope of thought and slight differences in the procedure of the objects of observation, the thirty-seven harmonies with enlightenment are similarly practiced in all three vehicles— those of Hearers, Solitary Realizers, and Bodhisattvas.

Seven branches of enlightenment

The next set of practices are the seven branches of enlightenment, which occur during the path of seeing. I will not explain these in detail; in brief, they are mindfulness, differentiation of phenomena, effort, joy, suppleness, meditative stabilization, and equanimity.

Eightfold path

On the path of meditation, the eightfold path is attained. These are right view, right realization, right speech, right aims of actions, right livelihood, right effort, right mindfulness, and right meditative stabilization. I will not explain their entities.

Through practicing these thirty-seven harmonies with enlightenment, Hearers and Solitary Realizers can attain the state of a Foe Destroyer. Except for different interpretations of the meaning of emptiness in the schools of tenets, all agree in asserting the general mode of procedure of these thirty-seven.

SPECIAL FEATURES OF THE BODHISATTVA PATH

What is the Great Vehicle? What is the mode of procedure of the Bodhisattva path? We begin with the topic of the altruistic intention to achieve enlightenment in which one values others more than oneself. The Great Vehicle path requires the vast motivation of a Bodhisattva, who, not seeking just his or her welfare, takes on the burden of bringing about the welfare of *all* sentient beings. When persons generate this attitude, they enter within the Great Vehicle, and as long as it has not been generated, one cannot be counted among those of the Great Vehicle. This attitude really has great power; it, of course, is helpful for people practicing religion, but it also is helpful for those who are just concerned with the affairs of this lifetime. The root of happiness is altruism—the wish to be of service to others.

In terms of causal factors involved in generating this attitude, there are presentations of four causes, four conditions, and four powers, but I will not explain these here. Rather, let us talk about how to train in such an altruistic attitude. One mode of training was transmitted through Maitreya to Asaṅga—this being the seven cause and effect quintessential instructions; another was transmitted through Mañjushrī to Nāgārjuna and Shāntideva— the equalizing and switching of self and other.

What is the entity of a mind of the altruistic intention to become enlightened? As Maitreya's *Ornament for Clear Realization* says:[19]

> [Altruistic] mind generation is asserted to be a wish
> For complete perfect enlightenment for the sake of others.

It is an altruistically oriented mind wishing to become enlightened. It involves two aspirations; the main one is an aspiration to others' welfare, and the other, viewed as the means to bring this about, is an aspiration to one's own enlightenment.

In his *Clear Meaning Commentary*,[20] Haribhadra raises a hypothetical qualm about these two lines:[21]

> Two *aspirations*—for others' welfare and for one's own enlightenment—are involved, as is indicated by the word "wish" in the first line, and aspirations are mental factors. However, an [altruistic] *mind* generation must be a main mental consciousness. Therefore, it is unsuitable to characterize an [altruistic] *mind* generation with the term "aspiration."

In answer to this objection, he says that when altruistic *mind* generation is designated with the name "aspiration," this is a case of giving the name of the assisting mental factor that accompanies the main mental consciousness—the mental factor of aspiring to one's own highest enlightenment—to the mental consciousness itself. Also, in terms of the mental factor of aspiring to bring about others' welfare, which is a cause inducing an altruistic mind generation, the name of the cause is being given to the effect.

How many different types of the altruistic mind of enlightenment are there? From the viewpoint of entity, there are two—aspirational and practical minds of enlightenment. There are a few different interpretations of the difference between these by Indian and Tibetan scholars, but most say that as long as one has generated an altruistic intention to become enlightened but has not taken the Bodhisattva vows, the mind of enlightenment is aspirational. The reason is that during this period one mainly is just wishing, "If I could only attain the state of enlightenment!" Then, when this aspiration has been generated and one sees that attainment of the state of Buddhahood necessarily depends upon training in the Bodhisattva deeds, one endeavors to generate a strong wish to train in these deeds and learns about them. Thereupon, when the wish to train in the Bodhisattva deeds is generated in strong force, one makes a *decision* to train in them, taking the Bodhisattva vows. From that time on, the altruistic mind of enlightenment is not merely a salutary wish to attain Buddhahood but also involves a promise to train in the six perfections, which are the techniques for actually achieving Buddhahood. Thereupon, it is called a "practical mind of enlightenment," since it is a mind actually involved in the activities that are techniques or paths through which Buddhahood is attained.

The altruistic mind of enlightenment, in terms of its boundaries, is of four varieties:

1. Altruistic mind generation on the occasion of the two levels of practicing through belief, these being the paths of accumulation and preparation.
2. Altruistic mind generation of special pure thought on the seven impure grounds, these being the first seven Bodhisattva grounds.
3. Fruitional altruistic mind generation on the three pure grounds—the eighth, ninth, and tenth Bodhisattva grounds.
4. Unobstructed altruistic mind generation at Buddhahood.

As one progresses over the five paths—including the three levels of the path of accumulation, etc.—and the ten Bodhisattva grounds (the latter beginning with the path of seeing and stretching over the path of meditation), due to the fact that altruistic mind generation is accompanied by different assisting factors, there come to be twenty-two varieties of it. These do not need to be explained here.

How does a practitioner train in altruistic mind generation by way of the seven cause and effect quintessential instructions? The root of altruistic mind generation is compassion. In the process of generating strong compassion, as much as one has a sense of closeness, pleasantness, and dearness with regard to sentient beings who are troubled by suffering, to that degree one has compassion with respect to them. Since this is the case and since during this lifetime the most cherished, dear, and close person, in general, is one's mother, one should recognize all sentient beings as one's mother. However, it is said that this is only an illustration; you are to use whatever being is the dearest to your heart—whether this be your mother, your father, another family member, or a friend.

What are the seven cause and effect quintessential instructions? The seventh—altruistic mind generation—is the effect, whereas the first six—recognition of all sentient beings as mothers, reflecting on their kindness, developing an intention to repay their kindness, love, compassion, and the special altruistic attitude—are the causes. Also, if, prior to cultivating recognition of all sentient beings as mothers, you do not cultivate equanimity, your mind will be biased; therefore, equanimity is a preliminary step.

Earlier I explained about how cyclic existence knows no definiteness. I did not go into detail, but there are descriptions of eight types of suffering, six types of sufferings, and so forth. Among these is the indefiniteness of friends and enemies; it is completely obvious that such is the case in our own lifetime, is it not? Enemies, friends, and neutral persons are similar in that no one remains just an enemy, for instance, but sometimes becomes a friend, and so forth. Consequently, there is no way to decide unidirectionally that a certain person is just my enemy and hence should be discarded or that someone else is just my friend and hence should be cherished or that someone is just a neutral person and hence should be treated indifferently. Rather, all have equally acted as enemy, all have equally acted as friend, and all have equally remained as neutral persons. For example, if one person harmed you last year but helped you this year and another person helped you last year but harmed you this year, they would be equal, would they not? This is how you should think in meditation.

Also, in meditation, imagine that in front of you are three persons—an enemy whom you do not like, a friend whom you like, and a neutral person with respect to whom you are indifferent. At that time, in our minds we have (1) a sense of closeness for one of them, thinking, "This is my friend," (2) a sense of dislike even when imagining the enemy, and (3) a sense of ignoring the neutral person. Now, we have to think about the reasons why we generate these feelings—the reasons being that temporarily one of them helped us whereas the other temporarily harmed us, and the third did neither. However, when we think in terms of the long course of beginningless rebirth, none of us could decide that someone who has helped or harmed us in this life has been doing so for all lifetimes.

When you contemplate this way in meditation, eventually you arrive at a point where strong generation of desire or hatred appears to you to be just senseless. Gradually, such bias weakens, and you decide that one-sided classification of persons as friends and enemies has been a mistake.

At this point, you might begin to think that since everyone has equally helped and harmed you and thus bias is totally inappropriate, it might be better to stay in isolation without associating with anyone, but there would not be any comfort in that, would there? It is necessary to make connection with people, and if you are going to make a connection, it would be better to do it in a better way. In doing this, you should think that there is no way that you could forsake these beings, since there is not anyone who has not acted as the best of your friends—mother, father, and so forth.

At this point, the beginninglessness of rebirth is to be contemplated. Anyone who is born from a womb or born from an egg needs a mother, and since this is the case, by the reason of the fact that our births are innumerable, there must have been innumerable mothers.

If you have trouble coming to a conclusion on the positive side that everyone must have been your mother, then on the negative side see whether you can decide that any sentient being has not been your mother. No one could come to such a conclusion. Even if, when you think this way, you still cannot come to a decision and are doubtful, the safer position is better.

Then, you should think about how sentient beings, when they were your mother or best of friends, protected you with great kindness just as your mother has done in this lifetime. You need to reflect slowly and carefully about their kindness, not just superficially. You need to cause the form of this thought actually to be developed in your mind. I have given an illustration of how to extend these thoughts in meditation; thus, I will not go into detail for each step.

After reflecting on the kindness of sentient beings, the next step is to generate a sense of intending to repay that kindness. Then, when you have developed the thought, "I must repay their kindness," those persons whose kindness you want to repay appear to your mind in a very dear and close aspect; this is the fourth step— love, which is a sense of dearness and pleasantness with regard to every sentient being. Then, you are to think about how these persons are beset by suffering but want happiness. If earlier when studying the four noble truths you did not identify suffering well, there is no way for the fifth step of generating compassion to be anything but partial. For instance, it is because we have not identified the scope and extent of suffering well that we are in a state of bias, easily generating a certain degree of compassion for a person out on the street who is in an obviously destitute situation but not generating any compassion for another person in a very prosperous situation. This is a sign that we are attached to the marvels, the prosperity, of cyclic existence.

Indeed it is easier, when first generating compassion, to meditatively generate compassion while visualizing a sentient being who is in a very destitute situation, but, after that, it is necessary to reflect on persons who, although they presently are not undergoing suffering on an obvious level, are involved in actions that will bring about manifest suffering in the future or have accumulated such karmic predispositions in the past; though the effects are not currently being experienced, these prosperous persons have the causes. Therefore, initially, reflect on sentient beings who are undergoing the suffering of physical and mental pain, and cultivate compassion. Then, expand the meditation by reflecting on sentient beings who are undergoing the suffering of change. And then, reflect on how all sentient beings are under the sway of the pervasive suffering of being bound in a process of conditioning beyond their control.

Through this process, you will gradually develop a consciousness that, within taking cognizance of all sentient beings, has the subjective aspect of wishing that they be freed from suffering. This is called compassion. There are many different types of compassion—limitless compassion, great compassion, and mere compassion. Also, there is compassion that is mixed with desire; this is the kind that we usually have, for when some little thing goes wrong, we immediately get angry.

In terms of compassion being influenced by other understanding, there is compassion observing sentient beings who are understood merely to be in a situation of suffering, but there is a deeper level which observes sentient beings who are understood to be impermanent and to be without a coarse self of persons—a self-sufficient, substantially existent entity. Then, there is an even deeper level in which sentient beings are understood to be empty of inherent existence.

What is the distinctive feature of *great* compassion? It is compassion that has the capacity to induce the thought, "I myself will free all sentient beings from suffering!"—a great sense of will, not just a thought, "How nice it would be if all sentient beings could be free from suffering!" The powerful intention which it induces—the willingness to free all beings from suffering—is the special altruistic attitude, the sixth step.

When you generate this special altruistic attitude thinking that you yourself will bring about the welfare of all beings by freeing them from suffering and joining them with happiness, you then analyze whether or not in your present state you have the capacity to accomplish this. You see that at present you do not. Prior to this time, you have been working on developing an aspiration to bring about others' welfare; now, you turn to developing an aspiration to your own enlightenment. As mentioned earlier, *two* aspirations are required—for others' welfare and for your own enlightenment.

With respect to how to bring about such great beneficence for others, it is the general Buddhist procedure that one's own pleasure and pain are achieved by oneself and not from the outside and that, therefore, sentient beings themselves must understand and implement practices to bring about their own happiness. Thus, the most efficacious way to help others is through *teaching* what should be adopted in practice and what should be discarded from among current behavior. There is no way to do this unless you come to know all of the topics involved in what should be adopted in practice and what should be discarded—you must become omniscient. As mentioned earlier, there is no way to accomplish this except by removing the obstructions to omniscience, and one who has overcome, utterly and forever, the obstructions to omniscience is a Buddha.

This is the route through which you come to think that, in order to bring about the welfare of others in a full way, it is necessary to attain enlightenment. A Buddha is said to have two types of bodies, a Truth Body and Form Bodies. It is by way of the exalted activities of a Buddha's speech that others' welfare is accomplished, but such exalted activities of speech affect trainees only through the appearance of Form Bodies; this is the reason why Form Bodies are called "bodies for the sake of others." Furthermore, to attain such Form Bodies, it is necessary to be endowed with complete realization and complete abandonment in which all obstructions have been extinguished in the sphere of reality; such complete realization and abandonment comprise the Truth Body of a Buddha, which is therefore said to be the fulfillment of one's own welfare. In this way, there is a connection between the Form Body and the aspiration to bring about others' welfare and between the Truth Body of a Buddha and the aspiration to one's own enlightenment.

That completes discussion of the mode of training in the altruistic intention to become enlightened by way of the seven cause and effect quintessential instructions.

Equalizing and Switching Self with Others

The training of the mind by way of equalizing and switching self and other is set forth in great detail in Shāntideva's *Engaging in the Bodhisattva Deeds*. In this practice, one first establishes an equality between oneself and others by way of the fact that everyone equally wants happiness and does not want suffering. From among the ten chapters of Shāntideva's text, the topic of equalizing self and other is presented in the eighth; the basis that allows development of such an attitude is found in the sixth chapter on the cultivation of patience, in which the great importance and value of enemies is explained. Thus, the training needs to be done by way of combining these two chapters.

In the first chapter of the book, Shāntideva sets forth the benefits of an altruistic intention to become enlightened; one should reflect on these advantages over and over again. Then, it is necessary to accumulate the power of meritorious actions, and this mind of altruistic intention to become enlightened is assumed in a ceremony that involves a seven- or eight-branched service; therefore, the second chapter begins discussion of this multibranched service, taking the topic through the branch of disclosure of ill-deeds—this being the reason why the second chapter is called "Disclosure." In this chapter, Shāntideva explains in a very evocative way the topic of impermanence, that no matter how wonderful the present life comes to be, it is like having a dream about spending eight years in pleasure and then being awakened—there being nothing left from all of that enjoyment except objects of memory.

In the third chapter, Shāntideva explains the remaining from among the seven branches, whereupon he describes how generation of the mind of an altruistic intention to become enlightened is assumed in a ritual; this is the reason why it is entitled "Assuming the Mind of Enlightenment." Then, basically, he explains the six perfections—giving, ethics, patience, effort, concentration, and wisdom. The first, giving, is described in scattered places throughout the text; also, Shāntideva did not set forth a separate chapter on ethics, but he provided separate chapters—the fourth and the fifth—on conscientiousness and introspection, which are the means of purifying ethics. Patience is explained in the sixth chapter, and effort, in the seventh; his instructions on effort are particularly good in that he shows how to implement effort without falling to extremes.

In the eighth chapter, he sets forth mainly how to bring balance to the mind through the equalization and switching of self and other. In order to achieve such mental balance, it is necessary to withdraw the mind; thus, he speaks of the advantages of isolated places and the disadvantages of desires—it is in this context that he speaks to males about the faults of the female body. Then, in the ninth chapter he explains emptiness. There are many debates; the main of the non-Buddhist opponents at this point are the Sāṃkhyas, the Vedāntins, and the Mīmāṃsakas. Among the Buddhist schools, he refutes first the Sūtra School but then the Mind Only School at length. Then, when explaining the system of the Consequence School, he describes in a very full and marvelous way how objects do not exist ultimately but exist conventionally. Delineation of selflessness is done within the context of the four establishments in mindfulness, but in this case it is a reflection not on the nature of suffering, and so forth, of forms, feelings, mind, and phenomena but on their final nature, their emptiness. He also sets forth the way in which, upon actualizing Buddhahood, all activities are performed spontaneously without exertion.

The final, tenth chapter is on dedication. There is a story that when Shāntideva arrived at the point of the stanza in the ninth chapter, which says:[22]

> When functioning things and non-functioning things
> Do not abide in front of one's mind,

Then since no other aspect appears,
There is pacification in unapprehendability.

He rose up into the sky and traveled down to South India, after which he did not return to North India again. Thus, because his text was written down by his followers, there came to be two editions with different numbers of stanzas. There is also a story that some scholars went to South India to question Shāntideva about the text.

That is the basic structure of Shāntideva's *Engaging in the Bodhisattva Deeds*. We will pretend that it has been discussed in entirety; this is a real modern method, not taking much time! Tomorrow, I will talk briefly about how to train in equalizing and switching self and other.

9. Valuing Enemies

Friday Morning

Question and Answer Period

QUESTION: What is wrong with attachment? I feel that I would deny my humanity if I practiced non-attachment. What happens to my special love for my family?

ANSWER: A distinction must be made between afflictive desire and non-afflictive desire. Even with respect to the English term "attachment," when one thinks, "This is good; it is needed," the afflictive type of attachment is not necessarily involved; just a non-afflictive type of "attachment" might be present, but I am not sure about the import of the English term. In any case, when you have a mere recognition such as, "This is good; I want this. This is useful," such feelings are not afflictive.

Generally, there are three types of apprehension of objects—one is within the context of apprehending the object to exist inherently; another is within the context of apprehending the object not to exist inherently, and the third is without any qualification of either existing inherently or not existing inherently. We have the first and last types of apprehension—within qualifying objects to exist inherently or without any such qualification. Those who have realized the emptiness of inherent existence but have not yet completely overcome the conception of inherent existence have all three types.

Thus, in our continuums all awarenesses holding that an object is good, bad, and the like do not necessarily involve the conception of inherent existence. Although to all of our types of awarenesses objects necessarily *appear* to exist inherently, these consciousnesses do not necessarily *apprehend* those objects to exist inherently. Therefore, whether we use the terminology of desire, attachment, or others, there are cases of thinking, "This is good; it is needed," in which the ignorance conceiving of inherent existence is not involved. Such consciousnesses can even be conventional valid cognitions. For instance, when, viewing all sentient beings as close to us, we feel that all should have happiness, such a cognition is validly established. This sort of feeling or desire is unbiased in that it covers *all* sentient beings, whereas our present love which is limited to our own friends or our own family actually is, generally speaking, influenced by ignorant attachment. In fact, it is biased.

When we generate a reasoned form of love or "attachment," our humanness increases in strength. Thus, I doubt that if one becomes more detached, one would be denying one's humanity; instead of that, one would become more humane.

QUESTION: Buddhist teachers seem always to be able to laugh heartily. What within Buddhism opens the way for this warm humor?

ANSWER: Not all Buddhist teachers are known for laughing. The great Tibetan saint, Lang-ri-tangba,[1] was always crying; he was always thinking about the sufferings of sentient beings, and because he remained crying, he was called "Gloomy Face."

QUESTION: What is the reason for prostration and the vast number of repetitions of refuge and so forth?

ANSWER: Prostration is included among the seven-branched service, each of which serves as an antidote to factors in one's own mental continuum. *Prostration* serves to reduce pride, for the ground is low, and when you bow down, you are taking a low position. *Making offerings* counteracts miserliness. The *disclosure of* *ill deeds* is an antidote to the three poisons of desire, anger, and ignorance, these being what motivate ill deeds. *Admiring one's own and others' virtues* serves as an antidote to jealousy. *Requesting the turning of the wheel of doctrine* counteracts earlier actions of forsaking of the doctrine. *Supplicating the Buddhas not to disappear* counteracts ill deeds related with gurus. *Dedication of the merit of virtuous activities* is an antidote to wrong views; this is because one dedicates merit within the context of having realized that there are effects to one's actions.

QUESTION: How does the conception of a self of persons arise from a conception of a self of phenomena?

ANSWER: Nāgārjuna's *Precious Garland* says:[2]

> As long as one has conception of the aggregates [as
>   inherently existent],
> So long does one have conception of the I [as inherently
>   existent].

Since the mental and physical aggregates are the basis of designation of the person, the misconception of them as existing from their own side serves as a basis for considering the person designated in dependence upon them to exist from his/her own side.

Even the non-Consequentialist systems of tenets, despite asserting that phenomena are established from their own side, assert that the person is imputedly existent; however, they do not assert that whatever exists is necessarily imputedly existent, for they claim that some phenomena are substantially existent. They maintain that the basis of any imputed existent is necessarily substantially existent. Hence, they hold that the mental and physical aggregates are substantially existent. They say this because a person must be designated in dependence upon the mental and physical aggregates, there being no way an image of a person can appear to the mind without having first taken the aggregates to mind. This is the assertion of all schools except the Consequence School, which maintains that whatever exists is necessarily imputedly existent. Furthermore, what the lower systems mean by "imputedly existent" has a coarser import than the meaning of this term in the Consequence School.

According to the Consequence School, a person must be imputed, or designated, in dependence upon a basis of imputation, and, if one conceives the basis in dependence upon which a person is imputed—the mental and physical aggregates—to be inherently existent, one necessarily is drawn into considering the person that is imputed in dependence upon that basis of designation to be inherently existent. This is Nāgārjuna's meaning.

Still, a fine distinction needs to be made. In terms of the order of their production, first a conception of the mental and physical aggregates as inherently existent is produced, and, with this as a basis, a conception of the person as inherently existent is then produced. However, when emptiness is realized, one first realizes the emptiness of inherent existence of the person since it is easier to realize, and then later realizes the selflessness of phenomena. Now, a question needs to be asked. Does an awareness realizing the self-lessness of persons realize the selflessness of phenomena? If it does, it would follow that the awarenesses realizing selflessness would be single, but one consciousness cannot realize the two selflessnesses. Nevertheless, through realizing the emptiness of a single phenomenon, one can understand that all phenomena do not pass beyond this nature of an absence of inherent existence. Thus, it must be decided that a consciousness that specifically takes a person as the substratum and realizes its emptiness cannot itself realize the selflessness of the aggregates.

However, if a consciousness realizing the selflessness of persons does not realize the selflessness of the aggregates, then what is the meaning of Nāgārjuna's statement that if the selflessness of the aggregates is not realized, the misconception of a self of persons cannot be extinguished? In answer to this, it is said that an awareness realizing the absence of inherent existence of a person can, without depending on any other awareness, remove all superimpositions of the conception of inherent existence with respect to the mental and physical aggregates. In Indian texts, the most frequent illustrations of non-existents are the horns of a rabbit, a sky-flower, a child of a barren woman, and the hair of a turtle, and thus it is said that if you ascertain that a child of a barren woman does not exist, the very awareness realizing this—although it does not *conceive* that the eyes, ears, and so forth of the child of a barren woman do not exist—can, without depending on any other awareness, remove all false superimpositions that the eyes, ears, and so forth of the child of a barren woman exist.

Hence, Nāgārjuna's statement is taken as meaning that until one has discarded the tenet that superimposes inherent existence on the aggregates, it is impossible to generate an awareness that realizes the absence of inherent existence of the person designated in dependence upon the aggregates.

QUESTION: Is special insight necessarily an intellectual, logical analysis, or can it be achieved intuitively?

ANSWER: It is probably the case that one could not gain special insight without using any reasoning. As was mentioned the other day, when in the practice of Highest Yoga Mantra one arrives at a high level of realization, special insight is achieved just through stabilizing meditation, but, prior to that, one has performed a great deal of analytical reasoning. With this as a background, Highest Yoga Mantra has techniques whereby, even though at this point analysis is not actually done, one can develop all the potential that would be developed through further analysis.

QUESTION: What need is there for meditation if freedom from ignorance comes through logical analysis?

ANSWER: To remove ignorance, it is not sufficient just to understand that what is being misconceived by an ignorant consciousness actually does not exist. The mind has to be moved, has to undergo a deep transformation. The ignorance that misconceives things to be inherently existent is of two types, artificial and innate. The artificial form of ignorance is learned from mistaken systems of thought and is not inborn, whereas the innate form is inborn, not learned from the study of a system of thought. To overcome the innate type of ignorance, mere understanding is not sufficient; it is necessary to meditate repeatedly in order to become familiar with the profound meaning of the absence of inherent existence. Since this is the case, the meditative one-pointedness of a mind of calm abiding is needed.

QUESTION: If the Consequentialists assert that things are without inherent existence even conventionally, then in what way do things exist in the conventional mode? Are they merely misconceptions or phantoms of the mind? How are we to avoid the extreme of nihilism?

ANSWER: This will be explained this afternoon.

QUESTION: An engineer who is a Buddhist recently wrote a book in which he said that a robot or a computer might have a Buddha nature. Do you agree with this?

ANSWER: The Buddha nature is described solely in terms of living beings. If you could develop a computer that actually had a consciousness, it would be a different situation. However, if you thought of the Buddha nature as just an emptiness, then even a vase would have a Buddha nature.

QUESTION: Is it useful or possible for people of one tradition to follow a different tradition?

ANSWER: A distinction needs to be made between religion and culture. Religion is something that belongs to everybody; religion has no boundaries. The main question, the main factor, is what is suitable to your own mental disposition. Culture, on the other hand, is related with your own native environment, the heritage of earlier generations. For example, Buddhism is actually an Indian religion, and thus the cultural side was related with India, but when it went to other countries, it met the local culture and became, for instance, Tibetan Buddhism, Chinese Buddhism, Japanese Buddhism, and so forth. It is essentially the same Buddhism; yet, there have been happy marriages with local cultures, whereby it became specially suited for that country. In this way, a European Buddhism, an American Buddhism, and so forth will gradually develop. Similarly, Christianity, although belonging to the Middle East, was brought to Europe as well as to America, India, the Philippines, Japan, China, and even to Tibet, with the result that there are Christian communities throughout the world.

Training in Altruism

Yesterday, we discussed the altruistic intention to become enlightened, reaching the topic of the equalizing and switching of self and other. As Shāntideva says about equalizing self and other, everybody—oneself and all others—wants happiness and does not want suffering. For example, just as every part of our body is equally considered to be our body and to be equally protected from pain, so all sentient beings are equally to be protected from suffering.

From our own viewpoint, we can understand that the only reason why we must be separated from suffering is that we do not want suffering. There is no further reason; we have a wish that naturally comes from within—a wish to be free from suffering. All sentient beings have the same wish. Since this is the case, what is the difference between self and other? There is a great difference in number. No matter how important you are, you are just one simple person; for example, in my own case I am just a single Buddhist monk. But other people are infinite in number. Even without counting other planets, in this world alone others are limitless—several billion.

Now, if we consider which is more important, the benefit of the majority or the benefit of a minority of one, there is no argument, no question. The benefit of the majority is much more important than myself, a single person.

Like yourself, everyone else from their own side equally does not want suffering and equally wants happiness. For example, among ten ill people, each of them just wants happiness; from their side they are all ill, and they all want to be freed from their illness. Hence there is no possible reason for making a biased exception, treating a certain one better and neglecting the others. It is impossible to select one out for better treatment. Moreover, from your own viewpoint, all sentient beings, in terms of their connection with you over the course of lifetimes, have in the past helped you and in the future will help again. Thus, you also cannot find any reason from your own side to treat some better and others worse.

Also, from the viewpoint of the nature of yourself and others, both have a nature of suffering, a nature of impermanence, and so forth. Once all of us have a similar nature of deprivation, there is no sense in our being belligerent with each other; it is not worthwhile. Take, for example, a group of prisoners who are about to be executed. During their stay together in the prison, all of them will meet their end; thus, during their remaining few days there is no sense in quarreling with each other. Similarly, all of us are bound within the same nature of suffering and impermanence, conquered by ignorance; under such circumstances, it is clear that both self and other are in the same basic condition; thus, there is no reason to fight with each other. If oneself were completely pure and other beings were impure, then this might be a reason for looking down on others. But this is not the case! This is another reason to consider self and other to be equal.

We have the bias of considering some people to be enemies and others to be friends. If this really were true such that an enemy always remained an enemy and a friend always remained a friend, then there might be a reason to hate certain people and love others.

But, again, this is not the case. As was mentioned earlier, there is no certainty in relationships.

Also, if we hate other people, the result is not good either for others or for ourselves. Nothing helpful comes from it. Anger ultimately will not harm others; actually it hurts us. When you are very angry, even though you have good food, it is not tasty. You may even get irritated at food that otherwise would be tasty. Also, when you become angry, even the beautiful faces of your friends—your husband, wife, or children—give you irritation, not because they are bad but because something is wrong with your own attitude. This is very clear. Using common sense, consider what the usefulness of anger and hatred is.

If we think along these lines, there is absolutely no reason to be angry. When an unfortunate event happens, we can face and handle a problem or tragedy more effectively without anger. The usefulness of anger is practically zero. As I mentioned earlier, it is possible within a compassionate causal motivation for an action to be done with an immediate motivation of hatred; however, that is a different situation. The type of upset that comes within affection and the type of upset that comes within hatred are different. With a causal motivation of deep love and compassion, it is possible—in order to bring about a certain action—for the immediate motivation at the time of the action itself to involve anger; however, the action basically comes out of concern for the particular person. In order to stop the person from a stupid deed, sometimes a harsh word is needed, in the course of which anger may be needed, but this anger is not the basic, causal motivation. On the other hand, strong actions that come solely out of hatred are of no use at all.

We are always talking about how human beings are superior to animals since animals cannot think as humans can; our human brain, therefore, is an endowment. Animals also can practice anger and attachment very well, but only human beings can judge and reason; this is a real human quality. Also, humans can develop infinite love, whereas animals such as dogs or cats can have only a limited form of affection and love for their offspring and so forth. Also, their affection is present for a certain period of time, but when a puppy, for instance, becomes grown up, the sense of affection disappears. Human beings, on the other hand, can think much more deeply and much more in the distance. When you become angry, however, all of these fine potentialities are lost. Thus, anger is the real destroyer of our good human qualities; an enemy with a weapon cannot destroy these qualities, but anger can. Anger is our real enemy.

Again, if we consider the other side—love, compassion, and concern for other people—these are *real* sources of happiness. With love and compassion, even if you are living in a very uncomfortable place, the external circumstances will not disturb you. With hatred, however, even if you have the best of facilities, you will not be happy. Thus, since we all want happiness, if we really do want it, we must follow a right method to achieve it. This type of thought is not particular to Buddhist or religious thinking but is common sense.

With a selfish attitude, oneself is important, and others are not so important. According to Shāntideva's advice, a technique to help in turning this attitude around is to imagine—in front of yourself as an unbiased observer—your own selfish self on one side and a limited number of other beings on the other side—ten, fifty, or a hundred. On one side is your proud, selfish self, and on the other side are a group of poor, needy people. You are, in effect, in the middle—as an unbiased, third person. Now, judge. Is this one, single, selfish person more important? Or is the group of people more important? Think. Will you join this side or that side? Naturally, if you are a real *human* being, your heart will go with the group because the number is greater and they are more needy. The other one is just a single person, proud and stupid. Your feeling naturally goes with the group. By thinking, thinking, thinking in this way, selfishness gradually decreases, and respect for others grows. This is the way to practice.

I usually advise that even if you want to be selfish, then be wisely selfish, not narrowly selfish! Wise people think of others, serve others sincerely as much as they can—not in order to cheat them, but sincerely. Regard yourself as a secondary factor. The ultimate result will be that you will get the maximum benefit. Clear? This is how to be wisely selfish!

Through fighting, killing, stealing, or harsh words—forgetting other people's welfare, always thinking of yourself, "I, I, I,"—the result will be your own loss; you will become a loser. Others may speak nice words in front of you, but behind your back they will not speak so nicely. This itself shows that you are losing. Therefore, the practice of altruism is not religious but the authentic way of human life, the real human quality. Being a believer or a non-believer, a Buddhist or non-Buddhist, is secondary, not important. The important thing is that, as human beings, we live purposeful, meaningful lives. Eating just makes excrement; that is not the purpose of our life! The purpose of life is the development of a good, warm heart, whereby we become good human beings. With this quality, you will lead your whole life meaningfully, purposefully; you will be the friend of everyone, the helper of everyone.

Through such thought, we can get a real sense of being brothers and sisters. Full of hatred, "brothers" and "sisters" are just words, nothing, but with an altruistic motivation, our big human community will become one harmonious, friendly, just, and honest family. This is our aim. Whether we achieve it in this life or not is a different matter; in any case, the attempt is worthwhile. This is my belief; I usually call such an attitude a universal religion. Not necessarily this or that religion, it is universal. Do you agree that these things are important? Complicated theories are not necessary; think with common sense. By thinking properly, we can convince ourselves that the practice of altruism, of love and compassion, is worthwhile, necessary, and most important.

Taking and Giving

When a Buddhist practitioner who has thought in this way sees sentient beings troubled by suffering, he or she wonders what can be done to help these beings. All of these sufferings are due to their own karma, and thus one is limited in how much one can help them directly. However, one can voluntarily and enthusiastically, from the depths of the heart, make the wish and imagine with great will, "May their suffering as well as its causes ripen within me." This is called the practice of taking others' suffering within emphasizing compassion.

Correspondingly, from the depths of one's heart one can wish and imagine that whatever few virtues one has accumulated, which will produce pleasurable effects, be given to other sentient beings, without the slightest regret. This is called the practice of giving away one's own happiness within emphasizing love. Although such mental imagining does not actually bring about these results, it helps with regard to increasing determination and willpower.

A person who has become accustomed to this practice can, at the time of an illness or unfortunate happening, implement it, thereby both keeping one's suffering from getting worse and developing courage. In my limited experience, these practices are really sources of courage, sources of inner strength. I think that this may have some connection with the question earlier today about why Buddhist teachers can be jovial. If you worry, it does not help, does it?

As far as my own motivation is concerned, I am sincere; I will do whatever I can. Whether something is achieved or not is a different matter; thus, I have no regret. It is better to be focused on larger issues than smaller ones; a lifetime even of a hundred years is very small, not important. Now I am forty-six; if I remain another forty or even fifty years, that time will not be very important compared to the infinite future. Also, compared to the problems of limitless sentient beings, my own are nothing. If you look at problems, suffering, very closely, they become very big, complicated, and unbearable. But when you look from a distance, they become smaller, not worth too much worry. When you concentrate on the bigger issues, the small ones come and go, come and go—that is their nature; they do not cause much concern.

Patience

As I mentioned yesterday, one of the most important practices is that of tolerance, patience. Tolerance can be learned only from an enemy; it cannot be learned from your guru. At these lectures, for instance, you cannot learn tolerance, except perhaps when you are bored! However, when you meet your enemy who is really going to hurt you, then, at that moment you can learn tolerance. Shāntideva makes a beautiful argument; he says that one's enemy is actually a good spiritual guide because in dependence upon an enemy one can cultivate patience, and in dependence upon patience one accumulates great power of merit. Therefore, it is as if an enemy were purposefully getting angry in order to help you accumulate merit.

However, Shāntideva posits someone who objects—this person being a manifestation of one's own inner afflictive emotions. The objector says, "That is not so. The enemy does not have an attitude of helping me; thus, there is no reason for me to be nice to him/her." Shāntideva answers, "It is not necessary for something to have an intention to help in order for it to help; for instance, we have faith in and very much want true cessations of sufferings and the true paths that bring these about, but they do not have any intention to help. Nevertheless, because they help, we respect them."

Then, the manifestation of one's own afflictive emotions, seeming to accept this, makes a further objection, "But an enemy has an intention to harm, whereas true cessations and true paths, even if they do not have an intention to help, also do not have an intention to harm. Therefore, I cannot respect an enemy." Shāntideva answers, "Because they have an intention to harm, they are called harmers, enemies. If they did not have an intention to harm, they would not even be called by that name. If they were like doctors, you would not get upset and thus would not have a chance to practice patience. Thus, since enemies are necessary for the practice of patience, an enemy is needed, and for someone to be an enemy, that person needs an intention to harm. Consequently, it is unsuitable to respond angrily; rather, an enemy should be respected."

Also, when someone strikes us, we immediately get angry at that person, but Shāntideva reasons differently: "If you consider what is actually harming you by creating suffering, then it is not the person but the weapon, be this a stick, the person's arm, or whatever. Still, even if you consider what indirectly brings about harm, the main source is not the person, it is the afflictive emotions in that person's mental continuum. Therefore, if you are going to get angry, either you should get angry at the weapon or at the motivation, the person's anger, not the person him/herself." This is very true. The actual pain is created by the weapon, but we foolishly do not get angry at the weapon, though indeed we sometimes do this as when bumping into an object! In the past when I was occupied with fixing up cars, I had a friend who, while working under a car, hit his head on the chassis; he yelled, "Yah! Yah!" He got so angry he hit the car twice with his head!

Besides such exceptions, generally we do not get upset at the weapon; we particularly choose the person. However, without anger, the person will not hit you; thus, it is because of the anger that he/she took the action. Therefore, if we think properly about the real source, the troublemaker is anger. We should get upset, not at the person, but at the afflictive emotion in the person.

Also, about angry persons, Shāntideva gives advice to consider whether anger is the nature of the person or is something adventitious—peripheral to the person's nature. If it is the nature of the person, then just as we do not get angry at fire even if it burns our hand because it is the very nature of fire to burn, so we should not get angry at the person. Again, if it is adventitious or peripheral, then just as when a cloud covers the sun, we do not get angry at the sun but see that the problem is with the cloud, so one should not get angry at the person but get upset with the person's afflictive emotion.

Also, one can think that one's own body has a nature of suffering and that the weapon has a nature of suffering, and thus when these two come together, pain is produced. Hence, half the fault is one's own. Then, just as one gets angry at the other person, so one should get angry at oneself.

Thus, as you can see, many worthwhile and meaningful ideas can be gained from reading Shāntideva's work—very useful for self-discipline and self-awareness. I practice according to Shāntideva's book; it is very, very helpful.

Through such reflections, one can develop a very strong sense of altruism. It is not absolutely necessary that you recognize other sentient beings as mothers. In contemplations such as those just discussed, the main reason for altruism is just that others want happiness; since this is sufficient, there is no fault even if you do not put emphasis on recognizing other beings as mothers. For, even in recognizing other beings as mothers, they come to be valued because they are *your own* mothers, and this involves considering yourself to be important. However, when the cherishing of others is achieved with the sole reason being that others want happiness and do not want suffering, there is no connection with considering yourself to be important. In particular, when you are able to generate a strong sense of respect for an enemy, all the rest of the people are easy since it is hardest to engender a sense of cherishing enemies.

That completes our discussion of cultivating altruism by way of the equalizing and switching self and other.

BODHISATTVA DEEDS

Then, when one has trained in such an altruistic intention to become enlightened to the point where a moderate degree of experience has been developed, one makes a promise never to forsake it. Through making such a promise, the aspirational intention to become enlightened becomes more steady.

Having done this, one trains in causes to keep this aspiration from deteriorating in this and future lifetimes, after which one trains in the wish to engage in the Bodhisattva deeds, the six perfections—giving, ethics, patience, effort, concentration,

and wisdom. There are many explanations about the six perfections in terms of their entities, precise enumeration, precise
order, coarse and subtle forms, etc., but I will not go into these
here. All of the practices of Bodhisattvas are contained in the
six perfections, which, in turn, are contained in the three types
of ethics—restraining ill deeds, the composite of virtuous practices, and bringing about others' welfare. The root of the ethics of
Bodhisattvas is the restraining of self-centeredness. Thus, it is said
that the root of all of Buddha's teaching is compassion, for in the
vehicles of Hearers and Solitary Realizers it is within the context
of compassion that they restrain from harming others, and Bodhisattvas not only refrain from harming others but also seek to help
others. In this way, the whole of Buddhism can be included in two
sentences: "If you can, help others. If you cannot, at least do not
harm them." The essence of the Buddhist vehicles is contained, in
an abbreviated way, in this advice.

WISDOM IN THE MIND ONLY SCHOOL

There is not much time left; so, I will not discuss the perfections
of giving, ethics, patience, effort, and concentration separately but
will speak briefly about wisdom, the topic of the view. There are
basically three types of wisdom—(1) wisdom realizing conventionalities, specifically the five sciences of medicine, art, logic, lin-
guistics, and the inner sciences; (2) wisdom realizing the mode of
subsistence of phenomena; and (3) wisdom realizing how to bring
about the welfare of sentient beings. Here, I will speak about the
second, the wisdom realizing the ultimate, even though, to some
extent, we have already discussed it.

From among the four Buddhist schools of tenets, the principal ones are the Mind Only School and the Middle Way School
because they assert both a selflessness of persons and a selflessness of phenomena. The Mind Only School, also called the Yogic
Practice School,[3] asserts the last of the three wheels of doctrine to
be definitive. In the *Sūtra Unravelling the Thought,* itself a sūtra

of the third wheel, it is said that the first two wheels of doctrine require interpretation. Specifically, it is said that if one asserted the literal rendering of the middle wheel of doctrine in which it is said, "All phenomena are without entityness; all phenomena are unproduced, unceasing, quiescent from the start, and naturally thoroughly passed beyond sorrow," one would fall to an extreme of nihilism. Since this is the case, the intended meaning of the middle wheel sūtras needs to be understood in dependence upon the third wheel.

Then, what, according to the Mind Only School, is the meaning of the teaching in the middle wheel that all phenomena are without entityness? In the Questions of Paramārthasamudgata Chapter of the *Sūtra Unravelling the Thought*, it is said that the teaching in the middle wheel that all phenomena are without entityness was given in consideration of three types of lack of entityness. Three different types of non-entityness are posited individually with respect to three classes of phenomena called the three natures—imputational, other-powered, and thoroughly established natures. Imputational natures are without entityness in the sense that they are not established by way of their own character; this is because imputational natures are only imputed by conceptuality and are not established by way of their own character. Still, the meaning of being only imputed by conceptuality as it is explained in the Mind Only School differs greatly from how it is explained in the Consequence School. The Proponents of Mind Only view imputational natures as not existing by way of their own character, but according to the Consequentialists' own description of the meaning of something's existing by way of its own character, the Proponents of Mind Only still have in their mental continuums such a conception even with respect to imputational natures.

Other-powered natures, that is to say, compounded phenomena, are without the entityness of self-production. This is because they are produced through the force of other causes and conditions and are not produced under their own power.

Thoroughly established natures, which are the emptinesses of all phenomena that are the final objects of observation of paths of purification, are ultimate non-entitynesses. This is because they are the ultimate and are the lack of entityness of the object of negation in the view of selflessness. In this way, thoroughly established natures are the final natures of phenomena, and thus other-powered natures are the bases of those emptinesses. A thoroughly established nature is an other-powered nature's emptiness of the imputational nature, the latter being the object of negation.

Since it is said that other-powered natures are empty of the imputational nature, what is the imputational nature? This is a very deep topic that requires a great deal of explanation, but, in brief, the imputational nature of a form, for instance, is a form's being established by way of its own character as the referent of a conceptual consciousness.[4] Such a nature does not at all exist; a form is empty of existing this way.

That phenomena are established by way of their own character as the referents of a conceptual consciousness is refuted by the reasoning set forth in Asaṅga's *Compendium of the Great Vehicle*:[5]

1. Because an awareness [of the name of an object] does not exist prior to [learning its] name,
2. Because many [names are used for one object], and
3. Because [a name is] not restricted [to one object].

> There are the contradictions that [if a bulbous splayed based thing able to hold fluid, for instance, were established through the force of its own mode of subsistence as the basis of the verbal convention "pot," (1) that which is designated "pot," for instance, would exist in] the essence of that [bulbous thing; (2) one object which has many names would have to be] many entities; and (3) the essences [of many objects, such as persons, which have the same name] would be mixed. Therefore, it is proven [that objects are not established by way of their own character as the referents of a conceptual consciousness].

If a form, for instance, were established by way of its own character as the referent of a conceptual consciousness or of a name, then prior to learning its name, an awareness thinking "This is a form" would have to be generated just by looking at it. However, this is not the case; prior to learning a name, we do not know the names of objects. Also, when one object has many names, it absurdly would have to be many objects, and when many objects have one name, they would absurdly have to be one object. Through such proofs, it can be ascertained that forms and so forth do not exist by way of their own character as the referents of a conceptual consciousness.

To our awarenesses—take, for instance, an eye consciousness apprehending blue—not only does it seem as if the patch of blue is established by way of its own character as the referent of a conceptual consciousness but also the patch of blue appears to be another factuality, external to the eye consciousness, that casts its image to the consciousness. However, the Mind Only School explains that, due to the activation of predispositions that have been accumulated since beginningless time in the mind-basis-of-all, the patch of blue, for instance, *appears* to be an external object but in fact is not. When, through reasoning, one sees that all phenomena, although appearing to be separate entities from the consciousnesses apprehending them, are the same entities as those consciousnesses and are not different entities, one realizes emptiness. The Mind Only School presents such a view of non-duality, which in this context means the emptiness of apprehending subject and apprehended object as different entities or the emptiness of objects beings established by way of their own character as the referents of a conceptual consciousness.

When one realizes that objects do not exist as entities external to the consciousness apprehending them, they cease to serve as such solid bases of desire, hatred, and so forth. In this way, the view of the Mind Only School is helpful, and indeed many scholars in India achieved high realizations in dependence upon it. Also, many yogis and great adepts of the Mantra Vehicle initially made use of this system. Thus, nowadays also it could be that this view would be appropriate for certain persons. Hence, even though from the viewpoint of the Consequence School, the view of the Mind Only School is susceptible to refutation, if it is suitable for one's mind, it is suitable to practice it.

We will continue this afternoon.

10. Wisdom

Friday Afternoon

Question and Answer Period

QUESTION: To accomplish the completion of the path requires a full commitment of study, instruction, and meditation so that one might offer the highest gift to people, the teachings. Working to provide shelter, food, and protection for those in need also can demand one's full commitment. Therefore, how can one balance these two requirements so that one can swiftly attain the capability of offering the teachings while not neglecting the immediate material needs of sentient beings?

ANSWER: One has to do as much of both of these as one can. This is my own position, for I myself try to do certain practices but at the same time carry out work that essentially benefits others. For people whose circumstances are similar to mine, the most important aspect is to cultivate a good motivation and to carry out your daily program within it. Early in the morning as well as late in the night, you should spend at least half an hour in practice—meditation, recitation, daily yoga, or the like. Then, while working during the day, you should remember the motivation.

Each morning before working, you should establish a determination to carry out today's work in accordance with the teaching and for the maximum usefulness to other beings. In the evening, before going to bed, check what you have done during the day, whether or not you actually acted in accordance with that initial determination. If indeed your activities remained within the scope of that motivation, you will become further encouraged, "Now, I have done well; I fulfilled my wish. At least one day has not been wasted." If something went wrong, then use self-criticism, "Oh, this is very bad; despite my knowledge and ability, due to carelessness or laziness, I did not fulfill my intention." Criticize and scold yourself this way, and form an intention to change the situation in the future. That is how to perform daily practice.

QUESTION: Does emptiness also mean fullness?

ANSWER: It seems so. Usually, I explain that emptiness is like a zero. A zero itself is nothing, but without a zero you cannot count anything; therefore, a zero is something, yet zero.

QUESTION: How can one reconcile the practice of viewing others' faults as being mere projections of one's own faulty mind with the need to compassionately help others clear away the faults they have?

ANSWER: With regard to this, it is necessary to understand that even though in both the Autonomy and the Consequence Schools—the two divisions of the Middle Way School—all phenomena are only imputed by conceptuality, everything that conceptuality posits to exist does not necessarily exist. If one held that things are whatever conceptuality makes them to be, this would be an extreme of nihilism. For example, even if a conceptual consciousness considers yellow to be white or white to be yellow, this does not make it so. Therefore, although there are no phenomena not imputed by conceptuality, whatever conceptuality posits as existing does not necessarily exist. More will be said about this later.

QUESTION: Since all beings are developing at different levels at all times, when a practitioner of the Great Vehicle vows not to enter into nirvana until all beings are liberated, how is it possible to fulfill this vow?

ANSWER: Three modes of generating an altruistic intention to become enlightened are described—like a king, like a boatman, and like a shepherd. In the first, that like a king, one first seeks to attain a high state after which help can be given to others. In the second, like a boatman, one seeks to cross the river of suffering together with others. In the third, like a shepherd, one seeks to relieve the flock of suffering beings from pain first, oneself following afterward. These are indications of the style of the altruistic motivation for becoming enlightened; in actual fact, there is no way that a Bodhisattva either would want to or could delay achieving full enlightenment. As much as the motivation to help others increases, so much closer does one approach Buddhahood.

QUESTION: When using a deity as the object of concentration, is it best to focus on the visualization or on the mantra or on both?

ANSWER: If the visualization is very steady, there is no way that visualization and recitation of mantra could be done together. During such steady visualization, recitation of mantra cannot be performed. In the ritual texts for these meditations, it is said that first one should meditate, and then if, after meditating, one becomes tired, one should recite mantra for the sake of resting. Most people, however, do not visualize the deity and, instead, make recitation of mantra the main activity; in that case, when they tire, they do not have any way of resting except to leave the session!

QUESTION: Is there any way that Buddhists and Communists can work together? Or are their philosophies completely opposed? Do they share any common goals?

ANSWER: This is a serious matter. For quite some time I have thought about this. I believe that, despite the differences, there is common ground between Marxism and Buddhism in general and Great Vehicle Buddhism in particular, and, in any case, it is far better to find common ground on which dialogue can be conducted.

The reason is that more than a quarter of humankind lives in an area stretching from the Buriat Republic in Siberia in the USSR to the border of Thailand; in these places the people are Buddhist deep down in their being, while, at the same time, the countries are governed by Communist states. The past few decades of history show that neither Buddhism nor Communism can dominate the other completely. Also, if they remain in hostile opposition to each other, this will bring more suspicion and more suffering, a complete loss of mental peace. Therefore, if a workable common ground can be found for dialogue, this may bring more openness and less rigidity to Marxism. I believe that original Marxism was more pure but that it gradually became involved with nationalism and global power politics. Similarly, the Buddhist side must be more realistic by being more open and flexible. I think that if both sides do this, the two can work together.

QUESTION: Yesterday, you stated that suicide was equal to killing a deity. Does this apply to the Buddhist monks that burned themselves in protest against the Vietnam war?

ANSWER: My reference was to those with Mantra vows who are engaged in the practice of meditating on themselves as deities. In general, however, it is difficult to make judgments about individual situations. If, in the Vietnamese example, the motivation were anger, it would be a mistaken deed, but if the motivation was strong altruism to be of service to the Buddhist teaching and to the Vietnamese people, the situation would be different.

On this final day, I would like to express my appreciation for your many questions that have indicated strong interest. There has not been sufficient time to answer all of them, but some of them probably were addressed in the course of the lectures.

WISDOM IN THE MIDDLE WAY SCHOOL

The Middle Way School takes the middle wheel of doctrine to be its root teachings. When this School says that all phenomena are not truly established, the Proponents of Truly Existent Things view this as an extreme of nihilism. Nāgārjuna, in the twenty-fourth chapter of his *Treatise on the Middle*, states the position of such an objector:[1]

> If all these are empty,
> There would be no arising and no disintegration;
> It would follow that for you [Proponents of the Middle Way School]
> The four noble truths would not exist.

The objector's position is:

> If, as you say, all phenomena are empty of true existence, then the four noble truths would be impossible. When the four truths are impossible, the Three Jewels—Buddha, doctrine, and spiritual community—are impossible. In that case, training in the path, entering the path, attaining the fruits of the path and so forth would be impossible. Not only that, if all phenomena were empty of inherent existence, no presentations of any of the phenomena of the world could be posited. If phenomena do not have inherent existence, their very entities would be non-existent. Without any entity, no phenomenon could be posited as existing.

What is Nāgārjuna's answer?[2]

> If all this is not empty,
> There would be no arising and no disintegration;

It would follow that for you [Proponents of Inherent
Existence]
The four noble truths would not exist.

Nāgārjuna answers that in a system in which things are *not* empty
of inherent existence, everything would be impossible. Then, he
says that the objector has not understood well the meaning of the
emptiness of inherent existence. What does a system that asserts
an emptiness of inherent existence mean by this? Emptiness has
the meaning of dependent-arising. To prove that things are empty
of inherent existence, Nāgārjuna uses the reason that they are
dependent-arisings. He does not use as a reason that things are
utterly devoid of the capacity to perform functions. Far from that,
dependent-arising is asserted, and it is used as the reason proving
that things are empty of inherent existence.

Because the other systems do not assert an emptiness of inherent
existence, they assert that phenomena inherently exist, in which
case objects must be established under their own power, and hence
it is contradictory for them to depend upon conditions. Consequently, dependent-arising becomes impossible in their systems.
Once dependent-arising is not feasible, all the presentations of
cyclic existence and nirvana, good and bad, are impossible. However, all of us assert the dependent-arising of the cause and effect of
favorable and unfavorable phenomena; there is no way that this can
be denied. Since this is the case, the absence of inherent existence
also definitely should be asserted.

What is the middle? It is the center free from the two extremes
of permanence and nihilism. Texts that delineate the meaning of
the middle just as it is are called texts of the middle way, and an
awareness that realizes this is called a view of the middle way. The
Middle Way School has two internal subdivisions—an Autonomy
School and a Consequence School. It seems that the names of these
two subschools were designated by Tibetan scholars; however, the
reasons for designating groups of scholars with these names are
clear in Indian texts. Nāgārjuna's student Buddhapālita wrote a

commentary on Nāgārjuna's *Treatise on the Middle,* in which he used many consequences in explaining the refutation of production from self and production from other. The master Bhāvaviveka criticized Buddhapālita's commentary, saying that it was not sufficient just to state consequences, that it was also necessary to state autonomous reasons. The basis of Bhāvaviveka's system is that phenomena are empty of true establishment, but, in addition to this, he asserts that, conventionally, phenomena are established by way of their own character. This is how he came to be called an Autonomist, and how Buddhapālita came to be called a Consequentialist.

Later, there came to be a system of asserting the view of the Middle Way School in which the Middle Way assertion that all phenomena do not truly exist is accepted and in which the Mind Only reasoning refuting external objects is accepted. The person who explicated this view in a clear way was the master Shāntarakṣhita. Thus, there came to be two subdivisions within the Autonomy School—a Sūtra Autonomy Middle Way School[3] and a Yogic Autonomy Middle Way School.[4]

Chandrakīrti composed a commentary on Nāgārjuna's *Treatise on the Middle* in which he indicated that Buddhapālita's system was correct; he responded to the criticisms that Bhāvaviveka had made of certain points in Buddhapālita's system. He showed that it was not suitable for Proponents of the Middle Way School to assert autonomous syllogisms in which the three aspects of a reason are established under their own power. Indeed, there are many debates between Chandrakīrti and Buddhapālita, the principal of which is over whether there are commonly appearing subjects—Bhāvaviveka holding that there are and Chandrakīrti holding that there are not. The root of all of these controversies is that Chandrakīrti does not assert that conventionally objects are established by way of their own character, whereas Bhāvaviveka does. The non-Consequentialist schools maintain that the valid cognitions that establish the three modes of a reason are necessarily non-deceptive in terms of the appearance of objects as being established by way of their own character, but the Consequentialists maintain that it is not possible for these valid cognitions to be non-deceptive—they are necessarily mistaken in this respect. Since this is the case, there is no way that the mode of establishment by valid cognition can be asserted similarly in the systems of the parties of a debate when the participants are a Consequentialist and a non-Consequentialist.

For this reason, when Consequentialists debate with Proponents of Inherent Existence in an attempt to prove that a phenomenon such as a sprout is without inherent existence, it would not be sufficient if the reason did not fulfill the three modes, and thus indeed the reasons that they state are endowed with these three modes. However, in terms of how a reason is certified by valid cognition, in the Consequence School this valid cognition is nevertheless a mistaken consciousness with respect to the appearance of the object's being established by way of its own character, but such a valid cognition is not accepted by the opponent. Similarly, the opponent asserts that the reason and so forth are certified by valid cognitions that are not mistaken with respect to the appearance of the object's being established by way of its own character, and thus such valid cognitions are, for Consequentialists, non-existent.

Since this is the case, it is said that, for the time being, the Consequentialist makes use of the mode of establishment by valid cognition that is renowned to the opponent—a Proponent of Inherent Existence—to establish the three modes of the reason, for the sake of proving that a phenomenon does not inherently exist. This is why the reasons that Consequentialists use are called "other-renowned reasons." Nevertheless, in actual fact the valid cognitions that establish the three modes of a logical reason and that exist in the continuum of a Proponent of Inherent Existence are mistaken consciousnesses with respect to the appearance of the object's being established by way of its own character, but for their own minds they think that the three modes of the reason are established by consciousnesses that are *not* mistaken with respect to the appearance of the object's being established by way of its own character. They cannot distinguish between the existence of an object and its existence by way of its own character, and thus until they can refute the establishment of objects by way of their own character, they cannot understand that their valid cognitions actually are mistaken with respect to the appearance of the object's being established by way of its own character. Thus, Consequentialists are willing to accept that there are valid cognitions in the *continuums* of Proponents of Inherent Existence, but these valid cognitions do not exist in the manner in which they are described in the *systems* of the Proponents of Inherent Existence. The Consequentialists, therefore, are *not* saying that there are no valid cognitions in the *continuums* of Proponents of Inherent Existence that can certify the existence of the three modes of a reason, the subject, and so forth.

In this way, there came to be a division within the Middle Way School into Autonomy and Consequence Schools. However, in the texts of both of these subschools the same vocabulary of an "absence of inherent existence" and an "absence of existence by way of the object's own character" is used, as is the phrase "when analyzed, phenomena are not found." Still, despite the usage of the same terminology, the thought behind their usage differs. For example, when the master Bhāvaviveka refutes the assertion by the Mind Only School that the imputational nature is established by way of its own character, it is clear that he thinks that all phenomena are conventionally established by way of their own character. He says (in paraphrase), "When you say that imputational natures are not established by way of their own character, does 'imputational natures' refer to the conceptual consciousnesses that are the imputers or does it refer to the factors that are imputed? If it refers to the conceptual consciousnesses that are the imputers, then conceptual consciousnesses would not be established by way of their own character, in which case they would be utterly non-existent." Thus, it is clear that, in his own system, Bhāvaviveka asserts that conceptual consciousnesses are established by way of their own character conventionally.

Similarly, Bhāvaviveka posits the mental consciousness as an illustration of the self; that he does this suggests that, for him, when the self is sought among the mental and physical aggregates, the mental consciousness is found to be the self. From the perspective of the Consequence School, Bhāvaviveka—because of this assertion that the mental consciousness is an illustration of the self, or person—is hard pressed to respond to the proofs that the Mind Only School sets forth to establish the existence of a mind-basis-of-all in each being's continuum. In any case, according to the Consequence School, just the mere I is posited as an illustration of a person, that is to say, something that is a person; they maintain that there is nothing—from among the mental and physical aggregates that are the bases of designation of a person—that can be found to be the person. Once the mere I is posited as the person, the Mind Only School's proofs of a mind-basis-of-all cannot challenge this position. These topics are very deep and a little complicated, but we will not pursue them further here.

When the Consequentialists delineate selflessness, they make a division into a selflessness of persons and a selflessness of other phenomena. In terms of the order of realization, one ascertains first the selflessness of persons and then the selflessness of other phenomena, for it is said that it is easier to realize the selflessness of persons first because of certain features of the substratum, the person.

Then, in "selflessness" what is the self that does not exist? If you do not understand this, then as Shāntideva's *Engaging in the Bodhisattva Deeds* says:[5]

> Without contacting the imagined existent
> Its non-existence is not apprehended.

Without knowing what "self" is, one cannot know selflessness.

In general, phenomena are of two types, positive and negative. Negative phenomena are such that without taking an object of negation to mind, the absence that is the emptiness of that object of negation cannot appear to the mind. Negative phenomena, again, are of two types—those that suggest a positive phenomenon in place of the object of negation and those that do not. Those that suggest a positive phenomenon in place of the object of negation are called affirming negatives,[6] whereas those that do not are called non-affirming negatives.[7] Also, affirming negatives can indicate positive phenomena in place of their object of negation either explicitly, implicitly, both explicitly and implicitly, and contextually. Selflessness, however, is a non-affirming negative. It is a mere elimination of self.

What is the "self" that does not exist? As Chandrakīrti says in his *Commentary on (Āryadeva's) "Four Hundred Stanzas on the Yogic Deeds of Bodhisattvas"*:[8]

> Here "self" is an inherent existence[9] of phenomena, that is, non-dependence on another. The non-existence of this is selflessness.

Therefore, the object of negation, called "self," is an existence of things under their own power without depending on others. Tibetan lamas have been very skillful in drawing out the meaning of these topics. The Seventh Dalai Lama says:[10]

> For a consciousness made crazy by sleep, there are dream objects.
> For those affected by magic, there are horses, elephants and so forth.
> Aside from mere appearances, there are no factually established phenomena there—
> They are only imputed by consciousness.

The various objects that appear in dreams as well as those that appear in magic shows are just appearances to the mind; except for that, such actual objects do not exist in those places; these are only imputed by consciousness. The reference here is to ordinary dreams, not special dream bodies and so forth.

Similarly, self and other, cyclic existence and nirvana,
All phenomena are only imputed by consciousnesses
    and terms.
Aside from that, none of them in the least exist by
    themselves
Right with their own bases of designation.
Nonetheless, that for the six consciousnesses of common
    beings
Overwhelmed by the thick sleep of ignorance,
Whatever appears seems to be established in its own right
Can be determined by watching our own bad minds.

This mode of subsistence in which the I and so forth appear
To a mistaken consciousness to be established from their
    own side
Is the subtle object of negation. Therefore, value greatly
The refutation of it, without any remainder, for your mind.

Whatever we perceive seems to exist from its own side. For example, when I look at all of you in the audience, each of you seem to exist from your own side; it does not at all appear as if these appearances are imputed by my consciousness.

If things did exist from the side of the object, then when they are sought analytically, they should become more and more evident. For example, when seeking analytically for my self, the only place where such could sensibly be sought is here in this area where this body is. It can be decided that the place of the existence of my self must be with this self's mental and physical aggregates and not anywhere else. Then, when this self is sought from the top of my head to the soles of my feet, it is not at all found.

In the same way, without analysis and investigation, we have a common impression of "my mind" and "my body," and indeed the mind and the body belong to the I; however, aside from mind and body, there is no I. Similarly, no matter what phenomenon is sought analytically, it cannot be found among its bases of designation. Take, for instance, a physical phenomenon; it necessarily has directional parts. When the parts and the whole appear to a conceptual consciousness, they appear separately as the thing that possesses the parts and the parts that are possessed. If whole and parts truly existed in the manner in which they appear to such a consciousness, then whole and parts would have to be different entities. If their mode of appearance and their mode of existence were concordant, they would have to be separate; however, when the whole is analyzed, once the parts are removed, a phenomenon that is the whole is not to be found.

Moreover, analyzing the parts of a part, one eventually reaches the level of subtle particles. The lower schools of tenets assert that gross objects are composed of an aggregation of indivisibly small particles; however, if there were directionally partless particles, then no matter how many of these aggregated—a hundred, thousand, million, or billion—they would not amount to anything more than one particle. For, when two directionally partless particles come together, since they do not have sides—and they cannot have sides if they are directionally partless—there could not be the distinction of their touching each other in one part and not in another. Thus, they have to be together in all respects and hence could be no bigger than one particle. If, however, they have directional sides, then they have parts, and the assertion they are partless must be abandoned. This is why the Consequence School holds that even the smallest particles have directional parts; even if parts cannot be physically split off, mentally any particle can be divided into directional parts. Even though when a physical object is divided into its parts, it eventually is reduced to something non-physical, whatever is physical—even the smallest particle—necessarily has directional parts.

A consciousness similarly has temporal parts. The lower systems assert smallest moments of consciousness that are partless, but let us consider two such partless moments of consciousness—the former being the direct cause of the second moment of consciousness, which is its direct effect. If another moment of consciousness intervened between these two, they could not be said to be direct cause and direct effect. However, if another moment of consciousness does not intervene between these two, since the two are partless, they would have to be together in all respects, in which case they could not form a continuum. Thus, partless moments of consciousness that form a continuum are not tenable.

If, on the other hand, one can distinguish between parts of the two moments that "touch" and parts that do not, then no matter how subtle these are conceived to be, each of the moments comes to have temporal parts, that is to say, former and later parts, and thus is not partless. This is why the Consequence School holds that even the smallest units of time have temporal parts just as material particles have directional parts.

In the Consequence School, all phenomena are asserted necessarily to have parts. Any phenomenon exists in dependence upon its parts—is designated in dependence upon its parts. Once this is the case, everything is dependently designated and hence has to be devoid of being established under its own power, independently.

In a similar fashion, effects are produced from causes—a sprout is produced from a seed—but that an effect is produced from a cause is posited within the framework of non-analysis and non-investigation, because, except for such, when the mode of production is analyzed to find the object designated in the expression, "A sprout is produced from a seed," one finds that a sprout is not produced from causes that are the same entity as itself, nor from causes that are inherently established as different entities from itself, nor from something that is both, nor causelessly. However, if production did exist inherently, it should become clearer when sought analytically among its possibilities, but when the object designated is sought, it is not found among the possibilities for inherently existent production.

Again, production must be of an existent; a non-existent, such as the horns of a rabbit, cannot be produced. However, if the existent exists under its own power, it does not need to depend upon causes. Thus, a non-existent cannot be produced, and something that exists under its own power does not need to be produced.

Since this is the case, when production and so forth are analyzed in this manner, they cannot be posited.

For example, when the activity of going is analyzed as Nāgārjuna does in the first stanza of the second chapter of his *Treatise on the Middle*, it cannot be found:

> Respectively, the gone-over is not being gone over,
> The not-yet-gone-over is also not being gone over,
> A being-gone-over separate from the gone-over
> And the not-yet-gone-over is not known.

Similarly, time exists, but the past and the future have to be posited in dependence upon the present, and thus when the present moment is sought analytically, it is half past and half future. Except for the past and the future, there is no present.

This is how things are when they are analyzed in this way; they cannot be found. In term of higher objects, a Buddha cannot be found; emptiness cannot be found; there is not anything that can be found.

Then, is everything non-existent? If things did not exist, they could not affect us, some helping and others harming. Help and harm do exist. Though they cannot be found under analysis, there are signs of their existence. When, with respect to any phenomenon, the object designated is sought, it is not found in the place where it was thought to exist; however, that it is non-existent is contradicted by experience. Therefore, since it is the case that the phenomenon being sought certainly exists but is not found under analysis, it can be concluded that it is not established under its own power but exists through the force of other conditions. What are those conditions? Conceptual consciousnesses that designate phenomena. Thus, it is inevitably established that phenomena exist through the force of, or in dependence upon, imputation by conceptuality.

Then, what is the meaning of something's existing? It cannot be an existence that is findable upon such analysis. Rather, there are three criteria for existence:

1. The object is renowned among conventions.
2. There is no contradiction from a conventional valid cognition.
3. There is no contradiction from a valid cognition analyzing the ultimate.

An object that fulfills these three criteria is posited as existing conventionally. Therefore, the existence of an object is dependent upon other factors and is not something constituted within itself.

While it is the mode of being or mode of subsistence of phenomena that they cannot be found under analysis, phenomena appear in a contrary way as if they exist objectively in their own right. Objects appear in a manner that is discordant with their own mode of being, seeming to exist in their own right whereas they do not, and we adhere to them as existing in accordance with how they appear. We have a type of consciousness that remains believing in what is actually an appearance at variance with the nature of phenomena—ourselves and other phenomena—a sense of independent existence, of not depending on other conditions. This nondependence on other conditions is called "self";[11] it is the self, the status of things, that does not exist. A consciousness that adheres to such a mode of existence of things is called a misconception of self; such a consciousness which misapprehends things as existing inherently is the chief erroneous consciousness.

Among the reasonings proving that things do not inherently exist, the foremost is dependent-arising. As was explained earlier, dependent and independent are mutually exclusive and contradictory—a dichotomy. If two items are a dichotomy, when it is eliminated that something is one of them, it is established that it is the other. Similarly, when it is established that something is one of them, it is eliminated that it is the other. Thus, since dependent and independent are a dichotomy, when one perceives damage to the position of things' being independent or under their own power, there is no other option except that things are dependent.

Once things exist in a dependent manner, they are devoid of having the independence of being under their own power. Once they are devoid of having the independence of being under their own power, they have a nature of being empty of such independence, which is called "self." This emptiness of "self" is the mode of subsistence of phenomena.

When one is not satisfied with the mere appearance of phenomena—oneself, others, and so forth—but analyzes to determine their mode of establishment, one cannot find anything. What does that consciousness—which has become an awareness analyzing the ultimate—find? It finds the final reality of these phenomena—oneself, others, and so forth—their emptiness of inherent existence. Since it is the object found by a reasoning consciousness analyzing the final mode of being, the emptiness of inherent existence is called the "highest-object-truth," the ultimate truth.[12] The objects that are the substrata of the ultimate truth which is the final nature are called "conventional truths";[13] these are objects found by valid awarenesses that do not enter into such investigation and analysis. These two—the final nature of the object and the substratum of that final nature—are posited within one basis.

The final nature of a sprout is an object found by a consciousness analyzing the mode of subsistence of the sprout, and, relative to the sprout, this emptiness of inherent existence is its ultimate nature, but when the final nature of the sprout is taken as the substratum and its mode of establishment is analyzed, it also is not found. The final nature of the sprout has become the substratum, and the final nature of the final nature of the sprout is found. It is in this sense that the emptiness of emptiness is set forth.

As reasonings specifically directed at the Autonomists, the Consequentialists state the following:

1. If objects are asserted to be established by way of their own character conventionally, then it would absurdly follow that things are destroyed by a Superior's meditative equipoise realizing emptiness.

2. Also, it would absurdly follow that conventionally things could withstand analysis and that production would not be refuted ultimately.

3. Similarly, that all phenomena are self-empty in the sense of being empty of their own inherent existence would absurdly be incorrect.

Due to the fact that the view is explained this way as being an emptiness of inherent existence, the Consequence School comes to have many unique tenets, but I will not go into them here. What I have described over the past few days have been just the outlines of topics. Those of you who are interested should look into these matters over a long period of time. I too am a student of these subjects; so, all of us should keep up our studies.

MANTRA

The view of emptiness and the attitude of an altruistic intention to become enlightened are the foundation of Mantra also, for through development of the awareness realizing emptiness, one achieves the Truth Body of a Buddha, and through development of the altruistic intention to become enlightened, one achieves the Form Bodies of a Buddha. This is how highest enlightenment is achieved. The profound, distinctive feature of Mantra is to be found in the quick and powerful achievement of a meditative stabilization that is a union of calm abiding and special insight, and the main technique in dependence upon which such meditative stabilization is attained is to meditate, not on an external object of observation, but on an internal one—one's own body as a divine body. Moreover, one's own body, visualized as the body of a deity, is taken as the substratum, and its final nature—its emptiness of inherent existence—is ascertained. This combination of realization of emptiness and an altruistically appearing body is called the non-dual yoga of the profound and the manifest—the profound being emptiness and the manifest being altruistic appearance in divine form. This yoga is the main practice in tantra, its general mode of procedure.

In the three lower tantra sets—Action, Performance, and Yoga Tantras—this yoga forms the basis of the practice but with slight variations in the particular rites of deity yoga that each tantra set and even individual tantras have. For all of the Mantra paths, it is necessary first to receive initiation, which ripens, or matures, one's continuum through a threefold process that involves special articles (such as vajra, bell, a vase, and water), mantras, and meditative stabilization; through this combination, the mental continuum becomes transformed into a higher state, making it serviceable. To receive initiation, a qualified lama is needed, and thus the lama comes to be very important; however, it is equally important for the lama to have the necessary qualifications. If the "lama" is not qualified, it is not good; there is danger, and, therefore, Buddha put great emphasis on the qualifications of a guru. In particular, in tantra it is said that before considering someone to be your lama, it is necessary to investigate even for a period of twelve years whether the person has the qualifications of a lama. This indicates how important proper analysis is; the import is that one should not rush into these matters.

There are many types and levels of initiation, but they need not be explained here. Having attained initiation, one must keep the pledges and vows.

In Highest Yoga Mantra, factors that we already have in our continuums in the common state are used as the means for achieving Buddhahood through engaging in special techniques. As explained earlier, the foundations of tantric practice are an altruistic intention to become enlightened and an understanding of emptiness as described either in the Mind Only School or the Middle Way School. With these as a basis, the experiences of birth, death, and intermediate state are transformed through techniques of Highest Yoga Mantra into factors of enlightenment. The roots of this process are the very subtle wind and mind mentioned earlier—death, intermediate state, and rebirth being manifestations of them. Because the three states of death, intermediate state, and rebirth in the ordinary state have a correspondence with the Truth Body, Complete Enjoyment Body, and Emanation Body of the enlightened state, through techniques of the path, the three ordinary states can be utilized to provide an opportunity for transformation into the Three Bodies of Buddhahood. With this purpose in mind, death is called the Truth Body of the ordinary state; the intermediate state is called the Complete Enjoyment Body of the ordinary state; and rebirth is called the Emanation Body of the ordinary state.

Also, during practice of the path, there are corresponding states called the Truth Body, Complete Enjoyment Body, and Emanation Body of the time of the path. These paths, in turn, are divided into two levels—a stage of generation and a stage of completion. The first is achieved mainly through imagination; in the second, the stage of completion, actual changes are brought about in the physical structure of channels, winds, and drops of essential fluid, the process utilizing the very subtle fundamental mind as a path-consciousness. To accomplish this, it is necessary first to untie knots in the structure of channels, the essential aim being to stop the grosser levels of wind and consciousness. When these path-techniques bring about a cessation of all coarser levels of wind and consciousness, the clear light becomes manifest, and it is transformed into a path-consciousness realizing emptiness. When one is able to utilize the clear light as an exalted wisdom consciousness directly realizing the emptiness of inherent existence, one can extinguish both the artificial and the innate forms of the afflictive obstructions simultaneously, whereby the ignorance conceiving inherent existence is completely destroyed. Also, when the clear light has been manifested, one has easy access to the substantial cause of a Buddha's Form Body.

That concludes a brief outline of Mantra.

THE TIBETAN ORDERS

In Tibet, the main religious orders are Ñying-ma, Śa-ḡya, Ḡagyu, and Ge-luk. From the standpoint of the view of emptiness, all are of the Consequence School. All have paths that are a union of sūtra and tantra, all of them having the essentials of Highest Yoga Mantra. How do they differ? They differ in their time of formation as well as in their vocabulary and topics emphasized. In these ways, their respective traditions have come to vary a little, but, from the viewpoint of a person who knows these systems well, they basically are getting at the same thing.[14] There is no time to go into detail. If you look into the matter over the years, you will understand.

CONCLUSION

In conclusion, I am very, very glad to have had the opportunity to explain a little about the Buddhism which we Tibetans practice and which we have preserved for many centuries. As you have heard in these lectures, in reality Tibetan Buddhism is a full and complete form of Buddhism. We practice teachings of the Hearer Vehicle as well as of the Great Vehicle in both its Sūtra and Mantra forms—all of the Tantra Vehicle including Highest Yoga Tantra. In reality, Tibetan Buddhism is not some sort of semi-Buddhism but is, in fact, a complete form of Buddhism.

My final word is that Buddhist practitioners must practice sincerely, as much as we can. If we cannot, it is a different matter, but within our own reach it is necessary and useful to implement the teachings. If the teachings remain in books, they have no value, but when they are absorbed and practiced, you can actually feel what emptiness, for instance, means. In my own experience, when I started studying about emptiness, though I repeated the word a thousand times, it was just a word. But when you practice, thinking and thinking and thinking, the word becomes weightier; it also influences your entire outlook toward problems, toward both happiness and suffering.

For Christians and followers of other religions, it is the same; you must practice your own teaching. At the same time, certain points—such as meditation—from among those that I have explained over the last few days, can be adopted as techniques for enhancing your own practice. Also, basic altruism—love and compassion—are completely the same; all teachings carry the same basic message. Altruism is essential also for nonbelievers; it is suitable for everybody. So, please implement these teachings.

In simple words, we all are human beings, and we should be good, not bad, human beings. If we become bad human beings, we ourselves will lose peace completely, as will others around us due to our own fault, our own mischief. Such a situation would be very unfortunate; so, we must try to become good human beings, good members of the human family.

NOTES

1. The Buddhist Analytical Attitude

1. *dbu ma pa, mādhyamika.*
2. *sems tsam pa, cittamātra.*
3. *dkon mchog gsum, triratna.*
4. See, for instance, the *Udānavarga,* XII.8 and XXIII.10ff. For a translation, see Gareth Sparham, *The Tibetan Dhammapada: Sayings of the Buddha* (London: Wisdom, 1986).
5. *ye shes chos sku, jñānadharmakāya.*
6. *ngo bo nyid sku, svabhāvikakāya.*
7. *chos sku, dharmakāya.*
8. *chos kyi dbyings, dharmadhātu.*
9. *chos mngon pa, abhidharma.*
10. *mdo sde, sūtrānta.*
11. *'dul ba, vinaya.*
12. *theg pa chen po'i mdo sde rgyan, mahāyānasūtrālaṃkāra;* XI.1. The Sanskrit is: piṭakatrayaṃ dvayaṃ vā samāgrahataḥ kāraṇairnavabhiraṣṭam. See S. Bagchi, ed., *Mahāyāna-Sūtrālaṃkāra of Asaṅga,* Buddhist Sanskrit Texts, No.13, (Darbhanga: Mithila Institute, 1970): 55.
13. *'phags pa, ārya.*
14. *sa, bhūmi.* These stages are called "grounds" because they serve as bases for the generation of other qualities much as the ground, or earth, serves as the basis of all that grows, and so forth.
15. *mos spyod kyi sa, adhimukticaryābhūmi.*
16. *phyag rgya chen po, mahāmudrā.*
17. The eight grounds of Hearers are the ground of lineage, the ground of the eighth, the ground of seeing, the ground of diminishment, the ground of freedom from desire, the ground of realizing completion, the ground of Hearers, and the ground of Solitary Realizers.
18. *rgyun zhugs, srotāpanna.*

19. *lan gcig phyir 'ong, sakṛdāgāmin.*

20. *phyir mi 'ong, anāgāmin.*

21. *dgra bcom pa, arhan.* With respect to the translation of *arhant (dgra bcom pa)* as "Foe Destroyer," I do this to accord with the usual Tibetan translation of the term and to assist in capturing the flavor of oral and written traditions that frequently refer to this etymology. Arhats have overcome the foe which is the afflictive emotions *(nyon mongs, kleśa)*, the chief of which is ignorance, the conception (according to the Consequence School) that persons and phenomena are established by way of their own character.

The Indian and Tibetan translators were also aware of the etymology of *arhant* as "worthy one," as they translated the name of the "founder" of the Jaina system, Arhat, as *mchod 'od*, "Worthy of Worship" (see Jam-yang-shay-ba's *Great Exposition of Tenets*, ka 62a.3). Also, they were aware of Chandrakīrti's gloss of the term as "Worthy One" in his *Clear Words: sadevamānuṣāsurāl lokāt pūnārhatvād arhannityuchyate* (Poussin, 486.5), *lha dang mi dang lha ma yin du bcas pa'i 'jig rten gyis mchod par 'os pas dgra bcom pa zhes brjod la* (409.20, Tibetan Cultural Printing Press edition; also, P5260, Vol. 98 75.2.2), "Because of being worthy of worship by the world of gods, humans, and demi-gods, they are called Arhats." Also, they were aware of Haribhadra's twofold etymology in his *Illumination of the Eight Thousand Stanza Perfection of Wisdom Sūtra.* In the context of the list of epithets qualifying the retinue of Buddha at the beginning of the sūtra (see Unrai Wogihara, ed., *Abhisamayālaṃkārālokā Prajñā-pāramitāvyākhyā, The Work of Haribhadra* [Tokyo: The Toyo Bunko, 1932–5; reprint ed., Tokyo: Sankibo Buddhist Book Store, 1973], 8.18), Haribhadra says:

> They are called *arhant* [= Worthy One, from root *arh* "to be worthy"] since they are worthy of worship, religious donations, and being assembled together in a group, etc. (W9. 8–9: *sarva evātra pūjā-dakṣiṇā-gaṇa-parikarṣādy-ārhatayārhantaḥ*; P5189, 67.5.7: *'dir thams cad kyang mchod pa dang // yon dang tshogs su 'dub la sogs par 'os pas na dgra bcom pa'o*).

Also:

> They are called *arhant* [= Foe Destroyer *arihan*] because they have destroyed *(hata)* the foe *(an)*. (W10.18: *hatāritvād arhantaḥ*; P5189, 69.3.6. *dgra rnams bcom pas na dgra bcom pa'o*).

(My thanks to Gareth Sparham for the references to Haribhadra.) Thus, we are not dealing with an ignorant misconception of a term, but a considered preference in the face of alternative etymologies—"Foe Destroyer" requiring a not unusual *i* infix to make *arihan, ari* meaning enemy and *han* meaning to kill, and thus "Foe Destroyer." Unfortunately, one word in English cannot convey both this meaning and "Worthy of Worship"; thus, I have gone with what clearly has become the predominant meaning in Tibet. (For an excellent discussion of the two etymologies of Arhat in Buddhism and Jainism, see L.M. Joshi's "Facets of Jaina Religiousness in Comparative Light," L.D. Series 85, [Ahmedabad: L.D. Institute of Indology, May 1981]: 53–58.)

22. *gnas ma'i bu pa.*
23. *dgongs pa nges par 'grel pa'i mdo, saṃdhinirmocanasūtra;* P774, Vol. 29; Toh 106, Dharma Vol.18. The Tibetan text has been edited and translated into French by Étienne Lamotte in *Saṃdhinirmocanasūtra: l'explication des mystères,* (Louvain: Université de Louvain, 1935).
24. *kun btags pa'i rang bzhin, parikalpitasvabhāva.*
25. *rang gi mtshan nyid kyis grub pa, svalakṣaṇasiddha.*
26. *yongs grub kyi rang bzhin, pariniṣpannasvabhāva.*
27. *gzhan dbang gi rang bzhin, paratantrasvabhāva.*
28. For more on this topic, see the last part of chapter nine.
29. *rgyal po la gtam bya ba rin po che'i phreng ba, rājaparikathāratnāvalī.* For an English translation, see Nāgārjuna and the Seventh Dalai Lama, *The Precious Garland and the Song of the Four Mindfulnesses* (New York: Harper and Row, 1975). This point is made in stanza 392, p. 76.
30. Chapter one.
31. Stanzas 367–398.
32. *rtog ge 'bar ba, tarkajvālā.* This is Bhāvaviveka's commentary on his *Heart of the Middle (dbu ma snying po, madhya-makahṛdaya).* For a partial English translation of the latter (chap. III. 1–136), see Shotaro Iida, *Reason and Emptiness* (Tokyo: Hokuseido, 1980).
33. *byang chub sems dpa'i spyod pa la 'jug pa, bodhicāryāvatāra.* For translations into English see Stephen Batchelor, *A Guide to the Bodhisattva's Way of Life* (Dharamsala: Library of Tibetan Works and Archives, 1979), and Marion Matics. *Entering the Path of Enlightenment* (New York: Macmillan, 1970). For a contemporary commentary see Geshe Kelsang Gyatso, *Meaningful to Behold* (London: Wisdom Publications, 1980).
34. *nges don, nītārtha.*

35. *drang don, neyārtha.*
36. *bye brag smra ba, vaibhāṣika.*
37. *mdo sde pa, sautrāntika.*
38. *sems tsam pa, cittamātra.*
39. *dbu ma pa, mādhyamika.*
40. For a slightly different Sanskrit version of this, see Robert A. F. Thurman, *Tsong Khapa's Speech of Gold in the Essence of True Eloquence* (Princeton: Princeton University Press, 1984), n. 12, p.190.
41. Dzong-ka-ba *(tsong kha pa,* 1357–1419) makes this statement in the introductory part of his *The Essence of the Good Explanations*:

> Therefore, in the end, the differentiation [between the interpretable and the definitive] must be made just by stainless reasoning, because if a speaker asserts a tenet contradicting reason, [that person] is not suitable to be a valid being [with respect to that topic] and because the suchness of things also has reasoned proofs which are establishments by way of [logical] correctness.

42. *mngon rtogs rgyan, abhisamayālaṃkāra;* IV.3ab. The Sanskrit is:

> hetau mārge ca duḥkhe ca nirodhe ca yathākramam

See Th. Stcherbatsky and E. Obermiller, ed., *Abhisamayālankāra-Prajñāpāramitā-Upadeśa-śāstra,* Bibliotheca Buddhica XXIII (Osnabrück: Biblio Verlag, 1970), p. 18. For a translation into English of the text, see Edward Conze, *Abhisamayālankāra,* Serie Orientale Roma (Rome: Is. M.E.O., 1954).

43. *theg pa chen po rgyud bla ma'i bstan bcos, mahāyānottaratantraśāstra;* IV.55 (as per Obermiller). The title could also be rendered as *Great Vehicle Treatise on the Later Scriptures.* For English translations, see E. Obermiller, "Sublime Science of the Great Vehicle to Salvation," *Acta Orientalia,* 9 (1931), pp. 81–306; and J. Takasaki, *A Study on the Ratnagotravibhāga* (Rome: Is. M.E.O., 1966). In the Sanskrit edition by E. H. Johnston and T. Chowdhury, *The Ratnagatravibhāga Mahāyānottaratantraśāstra* (Patna: Bihar Research Society, 1950), this is IV.52 (p. 106):

> vyādhijñeyo vyādhihetuḥ praheyaḥ
> svāsthyaṃ prāpyaṃ bheṣajaṃ sevyamevam
> duḥkhaṃ hetustannirodho 'tha mārgo
> jñeyaṃ heyaḥ sparśitavyo niṣevyaḥ

44. For instance, in the syllogistic statement, "The subject, a person, is empty of inherent existence because of being a dependent-arising," that the sign is established as being a property of the subject means that a person is a dependent-arising; that the forward pervasion is established means, roughly speaking, that whatever is a dependent-arising is necessarily empty of inherent existence; and that the counterpervasion is established means, roughly speaking, that whatever is not empty of inherent existence is not a dependent-arising.

2. THE SITUATION OF CYCLIC EXISTENCE

1. *thal 'gyur pa, prāsaṅgika.*
2. *'phags pa, āryan.* This term refers to someone who has reached the path of seeing, at which time emptiness is directly realized for the first time.
3. *rigs, gotra.*
4. *zag bcas kyi las, sāsravakarma.*
5. *nyon mongs, kleśa.*
6. IX.41ab.
7. *mngon pa kun btus, abhidharmasamuccaya.* This point is made at the beginning of the section entitled "Compendium of Ascertainments." For a translation into French, see *La compendium de la super-doctrine (philosophie) (Abhidharmasamuccaya) d'Asaṅga,* translated by Walpola Rahula (Paris: École Française d'Extrême-Orient, 1971; rpt. 1980), p. 59. For the Sanskrit, see P. Pradhan, ed., *Abhidharma Samuccaya* (Santiniketan: Visva-Bharati, 1950) and N. Tatia, ed., *Abhidharmasamuccayabhāsyam,* Tibetan-Sanskrit Works Series, No.17 (Patna: K.B. Jayaswal Research Institute, 1976).
8. *nam mkha' mtka' yas, ākāśānantya.*
9. *rnam shes mtha' yas, vijñānānantya.*
10. *ci yang med, ākiṃcaya.*
11. *srid rtse, bhavāgra.*
12. *rgyal chen rigs bzhi, cāturmahārājakāyika.*
13. *sum cu rtsa gsum, trayastriṃśa.*
14. *'thab bral, yāma.*
15. *dga' ldan, tuṣita.*
16. *'phrul dga', nirmāṇarati.*
17. *gzhan 'phrul dbang byed, paranirmitavaśavartin.*
18. For more detailed presentations of the levels of cyclic existence, see Herbert V. Guenther, *The Jewel Ornament of Liberation by sGam-po-pa*

(London: Rider, 1963; rpt. Berkeley: Shambala, 1971): 55–73, and Lati Rinbochay's explanation in Lati Rinbochay, Denma Lochö Rinbochay, Leah Zahler, Jeffrey Hopkins, *Meditative States in Tibetan Buddhism* (London: Wisdom Publications, 1983): 23–47.

19. *chos mngom pa'i mdzod, abhidharmakośa*; chapter three. For a translation into French, see Louis de La Vallée Poussin, *L'Abhidharmakośa de Vasubandhu* (Paris: Geuthner, 1923–31). For a Sanskrit edition, see *Abhidharmakośa & Bhāsya of Ācārya Vasubandhu with Sphuṭārtha Commentary of Ācārya Yaśomitra*, Swami Dwarikadas Shastri, ed., Bauddha Bharati Series no.5 (Banaras: Bauddha Bharati, 1970).

20. *lag na rdo rje dbang bskur ba'i rgyud chen mo, vajrapāṇyabhiṣekamahātantra.*

21. *dmigs rkyen, ālambanapratyāya.*

22. *nyer len gyi rgyu, upādānahetu.*

23. *bdag rkyen, adhipatipratyāya.*

24. *de ma dag rkyen, anantaryapratyāya.*

25. That is to say, when he died.

26. For a brief explanation of these, see John Avedon, *Interview with the Dalai Lama* (New York: Littlebird Publications, 1980), p. 23.

27. *'das log.*

28. *The Tibetan Book of the Dead*, compiled and edited by W.Y. Evans-Wentz (London: Oxford University Press, 1960). See also, *The Tibetan Book of the Dead: The Great Liberation through Hearing in the Bardo*, translated with commentary by Francesca Fremantle and Chögyam Trungpa (Boulder: Shambhala, 1975).

3. The Psychology of Cyclic Existence

1. *rdzogs chen.*

2. For discussion of this process, see chapter four.

3. *lhag med myang das, nirupadhiśeṣanirvāṇa.*

4. *dga' ldan, tuṣita.*

5. *[mchog gi] sprul sku, nirmāṇakāya.*

6. *longs spyod rdzogs pa'i sku, saṃbhogakāya.*

7. *chos sku, dharmakāya.*

8. *rang bzhin, prakṛti.*

9. *spyi'i gtso bo, sāmānyapradhāna.*

10. *skyes bu, puruṣa.*

11. *bsam pa'i las.*

12. *sems pa'i las.*

13. *sems byung sems pa.*
14. These are called "non-fluctuating" because, unlike fluctuating actions which in general impel rebirth in a certain type of transmigration but can bear their results in another type of transmigration as a form of pleasure or pain, these impel rebirth in the Form or Formless Realms and must bear their results in those transmigrations.
15. *sgra spyi, śabdasāmānya.*
16. *don spyi, arthasāmānya.*
17. *tshad ma, pramāṇa.*
18. The prefix *pra* in *pramāṇa.*
19. *rang mtshan, svalakṣaṇa.*
20. *spyi mtshan, sāmānyalakṣaṇa.*
21. *snang yul, *pratibhāsaviṣaya.*
22. *'jug yul, *pravṛttiviṣaya.* In the case of an eye consciousness apprehending blue, roughly speaking, the blue is its appearing object as well as its object of operation. A conceptual consciousness apprehending blue also has blue itself as its object of operation; its appearing object, however, is a generic image of blue.
23. I.e., the fact that the form *appears* to exist inherently.

4. More about Consciousness and Karma

1. By the Ga-dam-ba Ge-shay Lang-ri-tang-ba *(bka' gdams pa dge bshes blang ri thang pa),* 1054–1123. For a translation of this text as well as a commentary by the Dalai Lama, see The Fourteenth Dalai Lama, His Holiness Tenzin Gyatso, *Kindness, Clarity, and Insight* (Ithaca: Snow Lion, 1984), pp. 100–115.
2. *gzhal bya'i gnas gsum.*
3. *mngon gyur, abhimukhī.*
4. *cung zad lkog gyur, *kiṃcidparokṣa.*
5. *shin tu lkog gyur, *atyarthaparokṣa.*
6. *tshad ma rnam 'grel gyi tshig le'ur byas pa, pramāṇavartikakārikā.* For a Sanskrit edition, see *Pramāṇavarttika of Āchārya Dharmakīrtti,* Swami Dwarikadas Shastri, ed. (Varanasi: Bauddha Bharati, 1968).
7. *mngon mtho, abhyudaya.* The term refers to the status of humans, demigods, and gods which is elevated *(abhi + ud)* relative to animals, hungry ghosts, and hell-beings within the six types of lives in cyclic existence.
8. *nges legs, niḥśreya.*
9. Chapter one. The bracketed additions are from Kay-drup's commentary,

Extensive Explanation on the Great Treatise (Dharmakīrti's) "Commentary on (Dignāga's) 'Compendium on Valid Cognition'" (rgyas pa'i bstan bcos tshad rna rnam 'grel gyi rgya cher bshad pa rigs pa'i rgya mtsho) [n.d., blockprint in library of HH the Dalai Lama], 135b.6.

10. *bstan bcos bzhi brgya pa zhes bya ba'i tshig le'ur byas pa, catuḥśatakaśāstrakārikā;* XII.5. The bracketed additions are from Gyel-tsap's commentary, *Explanation of (Āryadeva's) "Four Hundred": Essence of Good Explanation (bzhi brgya pa'i rnam bshad legs bshad snying po)* [n.d., blockprint in library of H.H. the Dalai Lama], 90b.3–91a.3. For an edited Tibetan text and Sanskrit fragments along with English translation, see Karen Lang, *Āryadeva's Catuḥśataka: On the Bodhisattva's Cultivation of Merit and Knowledge,* Indiske Studier VII (Copenhagen: Akademisk Forlag, 1986).

11. The more common traditional name for "tantra" is "mantra."

12. For more on this topic, see Tenzin Gyatso and Jeffrey Hopkins, *The Kālachakra Tantra: Rite of Initiation for the Stage of Generation* (London: Wisdom Publications, 1985), pp. 120–122.

13. *kun gzhi rnam par shes pa, ālayavijñāna.*

14. *nyon mongs can gyi yid, kliṣṭamanas.*

15. *kun 'gro, sarvatraga.*

16. *yul nges, viniyata.*

17. *dge ba, kuśula.*

18. *rtsa nyon, mūlakleśa.*

19. *nye nyon, upakleśa.*

20. *gzhan 'gyur, aniyata.*

21. *tshor ba, vedanā.*

22. *'du shes, saṃjñā.*

23. *sems pa, cetanā.*

24. *yid la byed pa, manaskāra.*

25. *reg pa, sparśa.*

26. I.21.

27. I.7–22.

28. *'dun pa, chanda.*

29. *mos pa, adhimokṣa.*

30. *dran pa, smṛti.*

31. *ting nge 'dzin, samādhi.*

32. *shes rab, prajñā.*

33. *dad pa, śraddhā.*

34. *ngo tsha shes pa, hrī.*

35. *khrel yod pa, apatrāpya.*
36. *ma chags pa, alobha.*
37. *zhe sdang med pa, adveṣa.*
38. *gti mug med pa, amoha.*
39. *brtson 'grus, vīrya.*
40. *shin tu sbyangs pa, prasrabdhi.*
41. *bag yod pa, apramāda.*
42. *btang snyoms, upekṣā.*
43. *rnam par mi 'tshe ba, avihiṃsā.*
44. *'dod chags, rāga.*
45. *khong khro, pratigha.*
46. *nga rgyal, māna.*
47. *ma rig pa, avidyā.*
48. *the tshom, vicikitsā.*
49. *lta ba [nyon mongs can], dṛṣṭi.*
50. *'jig tshogs la lta ba, satkāyadṛṣṭi.*
51. *mthar 'dzin pa'i lta ba, antagrāhadṛṣṭi.*
52. *lta ba mchog 'dzin, dṛṣṭparāmarśa.*
53. *tshul khrims dang brtul zhugs mchog 'dzin, śilavrataparāmarśa.*
54. *log lta, mithyādṛṣṭi.*
55. *phra rgyas, anuśaya.*
56. *kho ba, krodha.*
57. *'khom 'dzin, upanāha.*
58. *'chab pa, mrakṣa.*
59. *'tshig pa, pradāśa.*
60. *phrag dog, irsyā.*
61. *ser sna, mātsarya.*
62. *sgyu, māyā.*
63. *g.yo, śāṭhya.*
64. *rgyags pa, mada.*
65. *rnam par 'tshe ba, vihiṃsā.*
66. *ngo tsha med pa, āhrīkya.*
67. *khrel med pa, anapatrāpya.*
68. *rmugs pa, styāna.*
69. *rgod pa, auddhatya.*
70. *ma dad pa, āśraddhya.*
71. *le lo, kausīdya.*
72. *bag med pa, pramāda.*
73. *brjed nges pa, muṣitasmṛtitā.*

74. *shes bzhin ma yin pa, saṃprajanya.*
75. *rnam par g.yen ba, vikṣepa.*
76. *gnyid, middha.*
77. *'gyod pa, kaukṛtya.*
78. *rtog pa, vitarka.*
79. *dpyod pa, vicāra.*
80. For a listing of these, see Lati Rinbochay and Jeffrey Hopkins, *Death, Intermediate State, and Rebirth in Tibetan Buddhism* (London: Rider, 1979; rpt. Ithaca: Snow Lion, 1980): 38–41.
81. II.219cd.
82. *dbu ma la 'jug pa, madhyamakāvatāra,* I.3. For an edited Tibetan text, see *Madhyamakāvatāra par Candrakīrti,* publiée par Louis de la Vallée Poussin, Bibliotheca Buddhica IX (Osnabrück: Biblio Verlag, 1970). For a French translation of Chandrakīrti's own commentary (up to VI.165), see Louis de la Vallée Poussin, *Muséon* 8 (1907): 249–317; *Muséon* 11 (1910), pp. 271–358; and *Muséon* 12 (1911): 235–328. For a German translation of the remainder of the sixth chapter (VI.166–226), see Helmut Tauscher, *Candrakīrti-Madhyamakāvatāraḥ und Madhyamakāvatārabhāṣyam* (Wien: Wiener Studien zur Tibetologie und Buddhismuskunde), 1981.
83. "Supreme mundane qualities" (*chos mchog/ 'jig rten pa'i chos mchog, laukikāgradharma*) indicates that this level is the supreme of levels while one is still an ordinary being, for the next level is the path of seeing at which point one becomes a Superior (*'phags pa, āryan*).
84. *sā lu'i ljang pa'i mdo, śālistambasūtra;* P876, vol. 34.
85. *Fundamental Treatise on the Middle, Called "Wisdom"* (*dbu ma'i bstan bcos/ dbu ma rtsa ba'i tshig le'ur byas pa shes rab ces bya ba, madhyamakaśāstra/prajñānāmamūlamadhyamakakārikā*), P5224, vol. 95. For edited Sanskrit texts, see *Nāgārjuna, Mūlamadhyamakakārikāḥ,* J.W. de Jong, ed. (Adyar: Adyar Library and Research Centre, 1977); and Chr. Lindtner in *Nāgārjuna's Filosofiske Vaerker,* Indiske Studier 2, pp. 177–215 (Copenhagen: Akademisk Forlag, 1982). For English translations, see Frederick Streng, *Emptiness: A Study in Religious Meaning* (Nashville, New York: Abingdon Press, 1967); also Kenneth Inada, *Nāgārjuna: A Translation of his Mūlamadhyamakakārikā* (Tokyo: The Hokuseido Press, 1970); and David J. Kalupahana, *Nāgārjuna: The Philosophy of the Middle Way* (Albany: State University Press of New York, 1986). For an Italian translation, see R. Gnoli, *Nāgārjuna: Madhyamaka Kārikā, Le stanze del cammino di mezzo,* Enciclopedia di autori classici 61 (Turin:

P. Boringhieri, 1961). For a Danish translation, see Chr. Lindtner in *Nāgārjuna's Filosofiske Vaerker,* Indiske Studier 2, pp. 67–135 (Copenhagen: Akademisk Forlag, 1982).

86. XVI.9cd.

87. XVI.12.

5. CESSATION AND BUDDHA NATURE

1. *Engaging in the Bodhisattva Deeds,* III.21.

2. *dbu ma'i snying po'i tshig le'ur byas pa, madhyamakahṛdayakārikā;* P5255, vol. 96. For a partial English translation (chap. III. 1–136), see Shotaro Iida, *Reason and Emptiness* (Tokyo: Hokuseido, 1980).

3. *byang chub sems pa'i sa, bodhisattvabhūmi;* P5538, vol. 110. For a Sanskrit edition, see *Bodhisattvabhumi (being the XVth Section of Asangapada's Yogacarabhumi),* edited by Nalinaksha Dutt, Tibetan Sanskrit Works Series, vol. 7 (Patna: K.P. Jayaswal Research Institute, 1966). For a translation of the Chapter on Suchness, the fourth chapter of Part I which is the fifteenth volume of the *Grounds of Yogic Practice,* see Janice D. Willis, *On Knowing Reality* (Delhi: Motilal, 1979).

4. *de bzhin gshegs pa thams cad kyi sku gsung thugs kyi gsang chen gsang ba 'dus pa zhes bya ba brtag pa'i rgyal po chen po, sarvatathāgatakāyavākcittarahasyaguhyasamājanāmamahākalparāja;* P81, vol. 3.

5. Also known as the *Chakrasaṃvara Tantra (dpal 'khor lo sdom pa'i rgyud kyi rgyal po dur khrod kyi rgyan rmad du 'byung ba, śrī cakrasaṃbaratantrarājādbutaśmaśanālaṃkāranāma);* P57, vol. 3. For an English translation, see *Shrīchakrasambhāra Tantra, a Buddhist Tantra,* Tantrik Texts, under the general editorship of Arthur Avalon, vol. vii. Ed. by Kazi Dawa-Samdup (London: Luzac; Calcutta: Thacker, Sprink, 1919).

6. *kye'i rdo rye zhes bya ba rgyud kyi rgyal po, hevajratantrarāja;* P10, vol. 1. For a translation into English, see D.L. Snellgrove, ed. and tr., *Hevajra Tantra,* Parts I and II (London: Oxford University Press, 1959).

7. *'dod pa.*

8. *'dod chags.*

9. Dzok-chen (*rdzogs chen*).

10. Stanzas 148–170.

11. In chapter eight.

12. VI.34.

13. *Commentary on (Dignāga's) "Compendium on Valid Cognition,"* II.120.

14. *rang bzhin gnas rigs, prakṛtisthagotra.*

15. *'phags pa'i rigs, āryagotra.*
16. *rgyas gyur kyi rigs, paripuṣṭhagotra.*
17. *rang bzhin myang 'das.*
18. *gung thang dkon mchog bstan pa'i sgron me,* 1762–1823.
19. *rang rkya thub pa'i rdzas yod du 'dzin pa.*

6. PATHS AND THE UTILIZATION OF BLISS

1. *zhi gnas, śamatha.*
2. XVIII.2.
3. XVIII.4.
4. *mngon rtogs, abhisamaya.*
5. *byang phyogs, bodhipakṣa.*
6. Stanzas 148–170.
7. Chapter eight.
8. *zag cas kyi chos, sāsravadharma.*
9. VIII.12: *gang la 'di skyo yod min pa// de la zhi gus ga la yod//,* (Varanasi: Pleasure of Elegant Sayings, 1974), Vol. 18, 122.2. Sanskrit: *udvego yasya nāstīha bhaktis tasya kutaḥ shive,* Lang, p.609.
10. *zhi gnas, śamatha.*
11. The discussion is found in chapter eight of the sūtra.
12. VIII.4.

7. TECHNIQUES FOR MEDITATION

1. VI.28.
2. *gti mug, moha.*
3. *Engaging in the Bodhisattva Deeds,* VII.17–19.
4. *dbus dang mtha' rnam par 'byed pa, madhyāntavibhaṅga;* IV.3b. The Sanskrit is:

   pañcadoṣaprahāṇā 'ṣṭasaṃskārā 'sevanā 'nvayā

   See Ramchandra Pandeya, ed., *Madhyānta-Vibhāga-Śāstra* (Delhi: Motilal Banarsidass, 1971): 129. For a partial English translation of the text, see T. Stcherbatsky, *Madhyānta-Vibhaṅga* (Calcutta: Indian Studies Past and Present, 1971).
5. *sems gnas dgu, navākārā cittasthiti.*
6. *sems 'jog pa, cittasthāpana.*
7. *rgyun du 'jog pa, saṃsthāpana.*

8. *slan te 'jog pa, avasthāpana.*
9. *nye bar 'jog pa, upasthāpana.*
10. *dul bar byed pa, damana.*
11. *zhi bar byed pa, śamana.*
12. *nye bar zhi bar byed pa, vyapaśamana.*
13. *rtse gcig tu byed pa, ekotīkaraṇa.*
14. *mnyam par 'jog pa, samādhāna.*
15. For brief descriptions of these by the Dalai Lama, see his *The Buddhism of Tibet and The Key to the Middle Way* (London: George Allen and Unwin, 1975), pp. 39–40, and *Opening the Eye of New Awareness*, translated by Donald Lopez, (London: Wisdom Publications, 1985), pp. 66–69.

8. ALTRUISM

1. II.1ab.
2. VII.14.
3. *yid byed, manaskāra.*
4. *mi lcog med, anāgamya.* This is also called the "mental contemplation of a mere beginner" (*las dang po pa tsam kyi yid byed*).
5. *mtshan nyid so sor rig pa'i yid byed, lakṣaṇapratisaṃvedīmanaskāra.*
6. *mos pa las byung ba'i yid byed, adhimokṣikamanaskāra.*
7. *rab tu dben pa'i yid byed, prāvivekyamanaskāra.*
8. *dga' ba sdud pa'i yid byed, ratisaṃgrāhakamanaskāra.*
9. *dpyod pa yid byed, mīmāṃsāmanaskāra.*
10. *sbyor mtha'i yid byed, prayoganiṣṭhamanaskāra.*
11. *sbyor mtha'i 'bras bu'i yid byed, prayoganiṣṭhahalamanaskāra.*
12. Big, middling, and small are each divided into big, middling, and small.
13. See chapter 7, note 15.
14. "Heat" (*drod, ūṣmagata*) indicates that the fire of the non-conceptual wisdom of the path of seeing will soon be generated.
15. "Peak" (*rtse mo, mūrdhagata*) indicates that one has reached the peak, or end, of the instability (susceptibility to destruction) of roots of virtue.
16. "Forbearance" (*bzod pa, kṣānti*) indicates a meditative serviceability with emptiness, lack of fear of emptiness, etc.
17. "Supreme mundane qualities" (*chos mchog/ 'jig rten pa'i chos mchog, laukikāgradharma*) indicates that this level is the supreme of levels while one is still an ordinary being, for the next level is the path of seeing at which point one becomes a Superior (*'phags pa, ārya*).
18. *mngon rtogs rgyan, abhisamayālaṃkāra*, IV.33–34ab.

19. I.18ab. The Sanskrit is: *cittotpādaḥ parārthāya samyaksaṃbodhikāmatā.* See Th. Stcherbatsky and E. Obermiller, ed., *Abhisamayālaṃkāra-Prajñāpāramitā-Upadeśa-Śāstra,* Bibliotheca Buddhica XXIII, (Osnabrück: Biblio Verlag, 1970), p.4.

20. *Clear Meaning Commentary/Commentary on (Maitreya's) "Ornament for Clear Realization, Treatise of Quintessential Instructions on the Perfection of Wisdom"* ('*grel pa don gsal/shes rab kyi pha rol tu phyin pa'i man ngag gi bstan bcos mngon par rtogs pa'i rgyan ces bya ba'i 'grel pa, sputhārtha/abhisamayālaṃkāranāmaprajñāpāramitopadeśaśāstravṛtti*), P5191, Vol.90.

21. Paraphrasing Haribhadra who is commenting on the stanza cited just above.

22. IX.35 (34 in Batchelor).

9. VALUING ENEMIES

1. *glang ri thang pa,* 1054–1123.

2. Stanza 35.

3. *rnal 'byor spyod pa pa, yogācāra.*

4. *rang 'dzin rtogs pa'i zhen gzhir rang gi mtshan nyid kyis grub pa.*

5. P5549, vol.112, 224.4.1. Lamotte's edition, vol. 1, p. 36 (24); his translation into French, vol. 2, pp. 118–119. The bracketed additions are drawn from Jam-ȳang-shay-b̄a Ngak-wāng-dzön-drü (*'jam dbyangs bzhad pa ngag dbang brtson grus,* 1648–1721), *Great Exposition of Tenets/ Explanation of "Tenets," Sun of the Land of Samantabhadra Brilliantly Illuminating All of Our Own and Others' Tenets and the Meaning of the Profound [Emptiness], Ocean of Scripture and Reasoning Fulfilling All Hopes of All Beings* (*grub mtha' chen mo/ grub mtha'i rnam bshad rang gzhan grub mtha' kun dang zab don mchog tu gsal ba kun bzang zhing gi nyi ma lung rigs rgya mtsho skye dgu'i re ba kun skong*), (Musoorie: Dalama, 1962), nga 44b.6–45a.3; and Ngak-wāng-b̄el-den (*ngag dbang dpal ldan,* born 1797), *Annotations for (Jam-ȳang-shay-b̄a's) "Great Exposition of Tenets," Freeing the Knots of the Difficult Points, Precious Jewel of Clear Thought* (*grub mtha' chen mo'i mchan 'grel dka' gnad mdud grol blo gsal gces nor*), (Sarnath: Pleasure of Elegant Sayings Press, 1964), *dngos* 186.6–187.4.

10. WISDOM

1. XXIV.1.
2. XXIV.20.
3. *mdo sde spyod pa dbu ma rang rgyud pa,*
   *sautrāntikasvātantrikamādhyamika.
4. *rnal 'byor spyod pa dbu ma rang rgyud pa,*
   *yogācārasvātantrikamādhyamika.
5. IX.140. The Sanskrit is:

   kalpitaṃ bhāvam aspṛṣṭvā tadabhāvo na gṛhyate

   See Vidhushekara Bhattacharya, ed., *Bodhicaryāvatāra*, Bibliotheca
   Indica Vol. 280 (Calcutta: The Asiatic Society, 1960): 221.
6. *ma yin dgag, paryudāsapratiṣedha.*
7. *med dgag, prasajyapratiṣedha.*
8. *byang chub sems dpa'i rnal 'byor spyod pa gzhi brgya pa'i rgya cher 'grel pa,*
   bodhisattvayogacaryācatuḥśatakaṭīkā. P5266, vol. 98, 103.4.4, chapter 12.
9. *rang bzhin, svabhāva.*
10. Gel-sang-gya-tso (*bskal bzang rgya mtsho,* 1708–57). The citation is from
    an untitled song found in *blo sbyong dang 'brel ba'i gdams pa dang snyan*
    mgur gyi rim pa phyogs gcig tu bkod pa don ldan tshangs pa'i sgra dbyangs,
    which comprises part 17 in volume ca of the 1945 'bras-spungs redaction
    of the Collected Works (gsuṅ 'bum) of the Seventh Dalai Lama Blo-
    bzaṅ-bskal-bzaṅ-rgya-mtsho, vol. 1. (Gangtok: Dodrup Sangye, 1975),
    397–502; this citation is 418.1–418.4. The work has been translated by
    Glenn H. Mullin as *Songs of Spiritual Change* (Ithaca: Snow Lion, 1982);
    this particular song is found on pp. 53–55. Many thanks to Tsepak Rig-
    zin of the Library of Tibetan Works and Archives for the citation.
11. *bdag, ātman.*
12. *don dam bden pa, paramārthasatya.*
13. *kun rdzob bden pa, saṃvṛtisatya.*
14. For discussion of this topic, see the final chapter of the Dalai Lama's
    Kindness, Clarity, and Insight.

BIBLIOGRAPHY

Sūtras and tantras are listed alphabetically by English title in the first section. Indian and Tibetan treatises are listed alphabetically by author in the second section; other works are listed alphabetically by author in the third section.

"P," standing for "Peking edition," refers to the *Tibetan Tripiṭaka* (Tokyo-Kyoto: Tibetan Tripiṭaka Research Foundation, 1956).

SŪTRAS AND TANTRAS

Chakrasaṃvara Tantra
dpal 'khor lo sdom pa'i rgyud kyi rgyal po dur khrod kyi rgyan rmad du 'byung ba
śrīcakrasaṃbaratantrarājādbutaśmaśanālaṃkāranāma
P57, vol. 3
Translation: *Shrīchakrasambhāra Tantra, a Buddhist Tantra*. Tantrik Texts, under the general editorship of Arthur Avalon, vol. vii. Ed. by Kazi Dawa-Samdup. London: Luzac; Calcutta: Thacker, Sprink, 1919.

Perfection of Wisdom Sūtras
prajñāramitāsūtra
shes rab kyi pha rol tu phyin pa'i mdo
P vols. 12–21
See: E. Conze. *The Large Sūtra on Perfect Wisdom*. Berkeley: U. Cal., 1975.

Sūtra Unravelling the Thought
saṃhinirmocanasūtra
dgongs pa nges par 'grel pa'i mdo
P774, vol. 29; Toh 106; Dharma vol. 18
Edited Tibetan text and French translation: Étienne Lamotte, *Saṃdinirmocanasūtra: l'explication des mystères*. Louvain: Université de Louvain, 1935.

SANSKRIT AND TIBETAN WORKS

Āryadeva ('*phags pa lha,* second to third century, C.E.)
  Four Hundred/Treatise of Four Hundred Stanzas
  catuḥśatakaśāśtrakārikā
  bstan bcos bzhi brgya pa zhes bya ba'i tshig le'ur byas pa
  P5246, vol. 95
  Edited Tibetan and Sanskrit fragments along with English trans-
  lation: Karen Lang. *Āryadeva's Catuḥśataka: On the Bodhisat-
  tva's Cultivation of Merit and Knowledge.* Indiske Studier VII.
  Copenhagen: Akademisk Forlag, 1986.
  Italian translation of the last half from the Chinese: Giuseppe
  Tucci, "La versione cinese del Catuḥśataka di Āryadeva, con-
  fronta col testa sanscrito et la traduzione tibetana." *Rivista degli
  Studi Orientalia* 10 (1925), pp. 521–567.

Asaṅga (*thogs med,* fourth century)
  Compendium of Manifest Knowledge
  abhidharmasamuccaya
  chos mngon pa kun btus
  P5550, vol. 112
  French translation: Walpola Rahula. *La compendium de la
  super-doctrine (philosophie) (Abhidharmasamuccaya) d'Asaṅga.*
  Paris: École Française d'Extrême-Orient, 1971.

  Compendium of the Great Vehicle
  mahāyānasaṃgraha
  theg pa chen po bsdus pa
  P5549, vol. 112
  French translation and edited Chinese and Tibetan texts: Étienne
  Lamotte, *La somme du grand véhicule d'Asaṅga,* rpt. 2 vol. Pub-
  lications de l'Institute Orientaliste de Louvain, vol.8. Louvain:
  Université de Louvain, 1973.

Five Treatises on the Grounds
  Grounds of Yogic Practice
  yogācārabhūmi
  rnal 'byor spyod pa'i sa
  P5536–5538, vol. 109–10
  Translation of the Chapter on Suchness, the fourth chapter of
  Part I of the *Grounds of Bodhisattvas (byang chub sems dpa'i sa,*

bodhisattvabhūmi), which is the fifteenth volume of the *Grounds of Yogic Practice:* Janice D. Willis. *On Knowing Reality.* Delhi: Motilal, 1979.

Compendium of Ascertainments
nirṇayasaṃgraha/viniścayasaṃgrahaṇī
rnam par gtan la dbab pa bsdu ba
P5539, vol. 110–11

Compendium of Bases
vastusaṃgraha
gzhi bsdu ba
P5540, vol. 111

Compendium of Enumerations
paryāyasaṃgraha
rnam grang bsdu ba
P5543, vol. 111

Compendium of Explanations
vivaraṇasaṃgraha
rnam par bshad pa bsdu ba
P5543, vol. 111

Bhāvaviveka *(legs ldan 'byed,* c.500–570?)
Blaze of Reasoning, a Commentary on the "Heart of the Middle Way"
madhyamakahṛdayavṛttitarkajvālā
dbu ma'i snying po'i 'grel pa rtog ge 'bar ba
P5256, vol. 96
Partial English translation (chap. III. 1–136): S. Iida. *Reason and Emptiness.* Tokyo: Hokuseido, 1980.

Heart of the Middle Way
madhyamakahṛdayakārikā
dbu ma'i snying po'i tshig le'ur byas pa
P5255, vol. 96
Partial English translation (chap. III. 1–136): S. Iida. *Reason and Emptiness.* Tokyo: Hokuseido, 1980.

Chandrakīrti *(zla ba grags pa,* seventh century)
[Auto]commentary on the "Supplement to (Nāgārjuna's) 'Treatise on the Middle'"

madhyamakāvatārabhāṣya
dbu ma la 'jug pa'i bshad pa/dbu ma la 'jug pa'i rang 'grel
Ps263, vol. 98
Also: Dharamsala: Council of Religious and Cultural Affairs, 1968
Edited Tibetan: Louis de la Vallée Poussin. *Madhyamakāvatāra par Candrakīrti.* Bibliotheca Buddhica IX. Osnabrück: Biblio Verlag, 1970.
French translation (up to VI. 165): Louis de la Vallée Poussin. *Muséon* 8 (1907), pp. 249–317; *Muséon* 11 (1910), pp. 271–358; and *Muséon* 12 (1911), pp. 235–328.
German translation (VI.166–226): Helmut Tauscher. *Candrakīrti-Madhyamakāvatāraḥ und Madhyamakāvatārabhāsyam.* Wien: Wiener Studien zur Tibetologie und Buddhisrmuskunde, 1981.

Clear Words, Commentary on (Nāgārjuna's) "Treatise on the Middle"
mūlamadhyamakavṛttiprasannapadī
dbu rna rtsa ba'i 'grel pa tshig gsal ba
Ps260, vol. 98
Also: Dharamsala: Tibetan Publishing House, 1968.
Sanskrit: *Mūlamadhyamakakārikās de Nāgārjuna avec la Prasannapadā Commentaire de Candrakīrti.* Louis de la Vallée Poussin, ed. Bibliotheca Buddhica IV. Osnabrück: Biblio Verlag, 1970.
English translation (Ch.I, XXV): T. Stcherbatsky. *Conception of Buddhist Nirvāṇa.* Leningrad: Office of the Academy of Sciences of the USSR, 1927; revised rpt. Delhi: Motilal Banarsidass, 1978, pp. 77–222.
English translation (Ch.II): Jeffrey Hopkins. "Analysis of Coming and Going." Dharamsala: Library of Tibetan Works and Archives, 1974.
Partial English translation: Mervyn Sprung. *Lucid Exposition of the Middle Way, the Essential Chapters from the Prasannapadā of Candrakīrti translated from the Sanskrit.* London: Routledge, 1979, and Boulder: Prajñā Press, 1979.
French translation (Ch.II–IV, VI–IX, XI, XXIII, XXIV, XXVI, XXVII): Jacques May. *Prasannapadā Madhyamaka-vṛtti, douze chapitres traduits du sanscrit et du tibétain.* Paris: Adrien-Maisonneuve, 1959.
French translation (Ch.XVIII–XXII): J.W. de Jong. *Cinq chapitres de la Prasannapadā.* Paris: Genthner, 1949.

French translation (Ch.XVII): É. Lamotte. "Le Traité de l'acte de Vasubandhu, Karmasiddhiprakarana," *MCB 4* (1936), 265–288. German translation (Ch.V and XII–XVI): St. Schayer. *Ausgewhälte Kapitel aus der Prasannapadā.* Krakow: Naktadem Polskiej Akademji Umiejetnosci, 1931. German translation (Ch.X): St. Schayer. "Feuer und Brennstoff." *Rocznik Orientalistyczny* 7 (1931), pp. 26–52.

Commentary on (Āryadeva's) "Four Hundred Stanzas on the Yogic Deeds of Bodhisattvas"
bodhisattvayogacaryācatuḥśatakaṭīkā
byang chub sems dpa'i rnal 'byor spyod pa gzhi brgya pa'i rgya cher 'grel pa
P5266, vol. 98; Toh 3865, Tokyo sde dge vol. 8
Edited Sanskrit fragments: Haraprasād Shāstri, ed. "Catuḥśatika of Ārya Deva," Memoirs of the Asiatic Society of Bengal, III no. 8 (1914), pp. 449–514.
Also (Ch. 8–16): Vidhusekhara Bhattacarya, ed. *The Catuḥśataka of Āryadeva: Sanskrit and Tibetan Texts with Copious Extracts from the Commentary of Candrakīrti,* Part II. Calcutta: Visva-Bharati Bookshop, 1931.

Supplement to (Nāgārjuna's) "Treatise on the Middle"
madhyamakāvatāra
dbu rna la 'jug pa
P5261, P5262, vol. 98
Edited Tibetan: Louis de la Vallée Poussin. *Madhyamakāvatāra par Candrakīrti.* Bibliotheca Buddhica IX. Osnabrück: Biblio Verlag, 1970.
English translation (Ch. I–V): Jeffrey Hopkins in *Compassion in Tibetan Buddhism.* Ithaca, NY: Gabriel Snow Lion, 1980.
English translation (Ch. VI): Stephen Batchelor, trans., in Geshé Rabten's *Echoes of Voidness.* London: Wisdom, 1983, pp. 47–92.
See also references under Chandrakīrti's *[Auto] commentary on the "Supplement."*

Dharmakīrti *(chos kyi grags pa,* seventh century)
Seven Treatises on Valid Cognition
Analysis of Relations
sambandhaparīkṣā

'brel pa brtag pa
P5713, vol. 130

Ascertainment of Valid Cognition
pramāṇaviniścaya
tshad ma rnam par nges pa
P5710, vol. 130

Commentary on (Dignāga's) "Compendium on Valid Cognition"
pramāṇavartikakārikā
tshad ma rnam 'grel gyi tshig le'ur byas pa
P5709, vol. 130
Also: Sarnath, India: Pleasure of Elegant Sayings Press, 1974.
Sanskrit: Swami Dwarikadas Shastri, ed. *Pramāṇavarttika of Āchārya Dharmakīrti.* Varanasi: Bauddha Bharati, 1968.

Drop of Reasoning
nyāyabinduprakaraṇa
rigs pa'i thigs pa zhes bya ba'i rab tu byed pa
P5711, vol.130
English translation: Th. Stcherbatsky. *Buddhist Logic.* New York: Dover Publications, 1962.

Drop of Reasons
hetubindunāmaprakaraṇa
gtan tshigs kyi thigs pa zhes bya ba rab tu byed pa
P5712, vol. 130

Principles of Debate
vādanyāya
rtsod pa'i rigs pa
P5715, vol. 130

Proof of Other Continuums
saṃtānāntarasiddhināmaprakaraṇa
rgyud gzhan grub pa zhes bya ba'i rab tu byed pa
P5716, vol. 130

Dzong-ka-ba Lo-sang-drak-ba (*tsong kha pa blo bzang grags pa*, 1357–1419)
Treatise Differentiating the Interpretable and the Definitive, The Essence of the Good Explanations

drang ba dang nges pa'i don rnam par phye ba'i bstan bcos legs
bshad snying po
P6142, vol. 153
Sarnath: Pleasure of Elegant Sayings Press, 1973 [on the cover in
roman letters is *Dan-ne-leg-shed nying-po*]
English translation: Robert Thurman. *Tsong Khapa's Speech of Gold
in the Essence of True Eloquence.* Princeton: Princeton University Press, 1984.

Gyel-tsap-dar-ma-rin-chen (*rgyal tshab dar ma rin chen*, 1364–1432)
    *Commentary on (Maitreya's) "Great Vehicle Treatise on the Sublime
    Continuum"/ Commentary on (Maitreya's) "Treatise on the Later
    Scriptures of the Great Vehicle"*
    theg pa chen po rgyud bla ma'i ṭīkka
    [n.d., blockprint in library of H.H. the Dalai Lama]

    *Explanation of (Āryadeva's) "Four Hundred": Essence of Good
    Explanation*
    bzhi brgya pa'i rnam bshad legs bshad snying po
    blockprint in the library of H.H. the Dalai Lama, no other data

    *Explanation of (Shāntideva's) "Engaging in the Bodhisattva Deeds":
    Entrance of Conqueror Children*
    byang chub sems dpa'i spyod pa la 'jug pa'i rnam bshad rgyal sras
    'jug ngogs
    Varanasi: 1973

Haribhadra (*seng ge bzang po*, late eighth century)
    *Clear Meaning Commentary/Commentary on (Maitreya's) "Orna-
    ment for Clear Realization, Treatise of Quintessential Instructions
    on the Perfection of Wisdom"*
    spuṭhārthābhisamayālaṃkāranāmaprajñāpāramitopadeśaśāstravṛtti
    'grel pa don gsal/shes rab kyi pha rol tu phyin pa'i man ngag gi bstan
    bcos mngon par rtogs pa'i rgyan ces bya ba'i 'grel pa
    P5191, vol. 90

Jam-yang-shay-ba Ngak-wang-dzön-drü ('*jam dbyangs bzhad pa ngag
dbang brtson grus*, 1648-1721)
    *Great Exposition of Tenets/ Explanation of "Tenets," Sun of the Land
    of Samantabhadra Brilliantly Illuminating All of Our Own and*

Others' Tenets and the Meaning of the Profound [Emptiness], Ocean of Scripture and Reasoning Fulfilling All Hopes of All Beings
grub mtha' chen mo/ grub mtha'i rnam bshad rang gzhan grub mtha' kun dang zab don mchog tu gsal ba kun bzang zhing gi nyi ma lung rigs rgya mtsho skye dgu'i re ba kun skong
Musoorie: Dalama, 1962.
English translation (beginning of the chapter on the Consequence School): Jeffrey Hopkins in *Meditation on Emptiness*. London: Wisdom Publications, 1983.

Kay-drup-ge-lek-bel-sang *(mkhas grub dge legs dpal bzang, 1385–1438)*
Extensive Explanation of the Great Treatise (Dharmakīrti's) "Commentary on (Dignāga's) 'Compendium of Teachings on Valid Cognition'"
rgyas pa'i bstan bcos tshad ma rnam 'grel gyi rgya cher bshad pa rigs pa'i rgya mtsho
[n.d., blockprint in library of H.H. the Dalai Lama]

Maitreya *(byams pa)*
Five Doctrines of Maitreya
Great Vehicle Treatise on the Sublime Continuum/Treatise on the Later Scriptures of the Great Vehicle
mahāyānottaratantraśāstra
theg pa chen po rgyud bla ma'i bstan bcos
P5525, vol. 108
Sanskrit: E. H. Johnston (and T. Chowdhury), ed. *The Ratnagotravibhāga Mahāyānottaratantraśāstra*. Patna: Bihar Research Society, 1950.
English translation: E. Obermiller. "Sublime Science of the Great Vehicle to Salvation." *Acta Orientalia*, 9 (1931), pp. 81–306. Also: J. Takasaki. *A Study on the Ratnagotravibhāga*. Rome: IS. M.E.O., 1966.

Differentiation of Phenomena and the Final Nature of Phenomena
dharmadharmatāvibhaṅga
chos dang chos nyid rnam par 'byed pa
P5523, vol. 108

Differentiation of the Middle and the Extremes
madhyāntavibhaṅga
dbus dang mtha' rnam par 'byed pa

P5522, vol. 108
Sanskrit: *Madhyānta-vibhāga-śāstra.* Ramchandra Pandeya, ed.
Delhi: Motilal Banarsidass, 1971.
Partial English translation: Th. Stcherbatsky. *Madhyānta-Vibhaṅga*
Calcutta: Indian Studies Past and Present, 1971.

Ornament for Clear Realization
abhisamayālaṃkāra
mngon par rtogs pa'i rgyan
P5184, vol. 88
Sanskrit text: Th. Stcherbatsky and E. Obermiller, ed. *Abhisamayālaṃkāra-Prajñāpāramitā-Upadeśa-Śāstra.* Bibliotheca Buddhica XXIII. Osnabrück: Biblio Verlag, 1970.
English translation: Edward Conze. *Abhisamayālaṃkāra.* Serie
Orientale Roma. Rome: Is. M.E.O., 1954.

Ornament for the Great Vehicle Sūtras
mahāyānasūtrālaṃkāra
theg pa chen po'i mdo sde rgyan gyi tshig le'ur byas pa
P5521, vol. 108
Sanskrit text: S. Bagchi, ed. *Mahāyāna-Sūtrālaṃkāra of Asaṅga.*
Buddhist Sanskrit Texts, No. 13. Darbhanga: Mithila Institute,
1970.
Sanskrit text and translation into French: Sylvain Levi.
*Mahāyānasūtrālaṃkāra, exposé de la doctrine du grand véhicule
selon le système Yogācāra.* 2 vol. Paris: 1907, 1911.

Nāgārjuna (*klu sgrub,* first to second century, C.E.)
Six Collections of Reasoning
Precious Garland of Advice for the King
rājaparikathāratnāvalī
rgyal po la gtam bya ba rin po che'i phreng ba
P5658, vol. 129
Sanskrit, Tibetan, and Chinese in: Michael Hahn, *Nāgārjuna's
Ratnāvalī, vol. 1, The Basic Texts (Sanskrit, Tibetan, and Chi-
nese).* Bonn: Indica et Tibetica Verlag, 1982.
English translation: Jeffrey Hopkins in Nāgārjuna and the Sev-
enth Dalai Lama, *The Precious Garland and the Song of the
Four Mindfulnesses.* New York: Harper and Row, 1975.

Refutation of Objections
vigrahavyāvartanīkārikā
rtsod pa bzlog pa'i tshig le'ur byas pa
P5228, vol. 95; Toh 3828, Tokyo sde dge vol. 1
Edited Sanskrit text: E. H. Johnston, *The Ratnagotravibhāga Mahāyānottaratantraśāstra*. Patna: Bihar Research Society, 1950.
English translation: K. Bhattacharya in *The Dialectical Method of Nāgārjuna*. New Delhi: Motilal Banarsidass, 1978.
Edited Tibetan and Sanskrit: in Chr. Lindtner, *Nagarjuniana*. Indiske Studier 4, pp. 70–86. Copenhagen: Akademisk Foriag, 1982.
Translation from the Chinese version of the text: G. Tucci in *Pre-Diṅnāga Buddhist Texts on Logic from Chinese Sources*. Gaekwad's Oriental Series, 49. Baroda: Oriental Institute, 1929.
French translation: S. Yamaguchi, "Traité de Nāgārjuna pour écarter les vaines discussion (Vigrahavyāvartanī) traduit et annoté," *Journal Asiatique* 215 (1929), pp. 1–86.

Seventy Stanzas on Emptiness
śūnyatāsaptatikārikā
stong pa nyid bdun cu pa'i tshig le'ur byas pa
P5227, vol. 95; Toh 3827, Tokyo sde dge vol. 1
Edited Tibetan and English translation: Chr. Lindtner in *Nagarjuniana*. Indiske Studier 4, pp. 34–69. Copenhagen: Akademisk Foriag, 1982.

Sixty Stanzas of Reasoning
yuktiṣaṣṭikākārikā
rigs pa drug cu pa'i tshig le'ur byas pa
P5225, vol. 95; Toh 3825, Tokyo sde dge vol. 1
Edited Tibetan with Sanskrit fragments and English translation: Chr. Lindtner in *Nagarjuniana*. Indiske Studier 4, pp. 100–119. Copenhagen: Akademisk Foriag, 1982.

Treatise Called the Finely Woven
vaidalyasūtranāma
zhib rno rnam par 'thag pa zhes bya ba'i mdo
P5226, vol. 95

Treatise on the Middle/ Fundamental Treatise on the Middle, Called "Wisdom"
madhyamakaśāstra/prajñānāmamūlamadhyamakakārikā
dbu rna'i bstan bcos/ dbu rna rtsa ba'i tshig le'ur byas pa shes rab ces bya ba
P5224, vol. 95
Edited Sanskrit: *Nāgārjuna, Mūlamadhyamakakārikāḥ.* J.W. de Jong, ed. Adyar: Adyar Library and Research Centre, 1977. Also: Chr. Lindtner in *Nāgārjuna's Filosofiske Vaerker.* Indiske Studier 2, pp. 177–215. Copenhagen: Akademisk Forlag, 1982. English translation: Frederick Streng. *Emptiness: A Study in Religious Meaning.* Nashville, New York: Abingdon Press, 1967. Also: Kenneth Inada. *Nāgārjuna: A Translation of his Mūlamadhyamakakārikā.* Tokyo, The Hokuseido Press, 1970. Also: David J. Kalupahana. *Nāgārjuna: The Philosophy of the Middle Way.* Albany: State University Press of New York, 1986. Italian translation: R. Gnoli. *Nāgārjuna: Madhyamaka Kārikā, Le stanze del cammino di mezzo.* Enciclopedia di autori classici 61. Turin: P. Boringhieri, 1961. Danish translation: Chr. Lindtner in *Nāgārjuna's Filosofiske Vaerker.* Indiske Studier 2, pp. 67–135. Copenhagen: Akademisk Forlag, 1982.

Ngak-ŵang-ḃel-den (*ngag dbang dpal ldan,* b. 1797), also known as Ḃelden-chö-jay (*dpal ldan chos rje*)
Annotations for (Jam-ŷang-shay-ba's) "Great Exposition of Tenets," Freeing the Knots of the Difficult Points, Precious Jewel of Clear Thought
grub mtha' chen mo'i mchan 'grel dka' gnad mdud grol blo gsal gees nor
Sarnath: Pleasure of Elegant Sayings Press, 1964.

Shāntideva (*zhi ba lha,* eighth century)
Compendium of Instructions
śikṣāsamuccayakārikā
bslab pa kun las btus pa'i tshig le'ur byas pa
P5272, vol. 102

English Translation: C. Bendall and W.H.D. Rouse. *Śikṣā Samuccaya*. Delhi: Motilal, 1971.

Engaging in the Bodhisattva Deeds
bodhi[sattva]caryāvatāra
byang chub sems dpa'i spyod pa la 'jug pa
P5272, vol. 99
Sanskrit and Tibetan texts: Vidhushekara Bhattacharya, ed. *Bodhicaryāvatāra.* Bibliotheca Indica, vol. 280. Calcutta: The Asiatic Society, 1960.
English translation: Stephen Batchelor. *A Guide to the Bodhisattva's Way of Life.* Dharamsala: Library of Tibetan Works and Archives, 1979. Also: Marion Matics. *Entering the Path of Enlightenment.* New York: Macmillan, 1970.
Contemporary commentary by Geshe Kelsang Gyatso. *Meaningful to Behold.* London: Wisdom Publications, 1980.

Vasubandhu (*dbyig gnyen*)
Treasury of Manifest Knowledge
abhidharmakośakārikā
chos mngon pa'i mdzod kyi tshig le'ur byas pa
P5590, vol. 115
Sanskrit text: P. Pradhan, ed. *Abhidharmakośabhāsyam of Vasubandhu.* Patna: Jayaswal Research Institute, 1975.
French translation: Louis de la Vallée Poussin. *L'Abhidharmakośa de Vasubandhu.* 6 vols. Bruxelles: Institut Belge des Hautes Études Chinoises, 1971.

OTHER WORKS

Bagchi, S., ed. *Mahāyāna-Sūtrālanmkāra of Asaṅga.* Buddhist Sanskrit Texts, No.13. Darbhanga: Mithila Institute, 1970.
Bendall, C., and Rouse, W.H.D. *Śikṣā Samuccaya.* Delhi: Motilal, 1971.
Chandra, Lokesh, ed. *Materials for a History of Tibetan Literature.* Śatapiṭaka series, vol. 28–30. New Delhi: International Academy of Indian Culture, 1963.
Conze, E. *The Large Sūtra on Perfect Wisdom.* Berkeley: U. Cal., 1975.
Das, Sarat Chandra. *A Tibetan-English Dictionary.* Calcutta, 1902.

Dutt, Nalinaksha, ed. *Bodhisattvabhumi (being the XVth Section of Asangapada's Yogacarabhumi).* Tibetan Sanskrit Works Series, vol. 7. Patna: K.P. Jayaswal Research Institute, 1966.

Evans-Wentz, W.Y., compiled and edited. *The Tibetan Book of the Dead.* London: Oxford University Press, 1960.

Fremantle, Francesca, and Trungpa, Chögyam. *The Tibetan Book of the Dead: The Great Liberation through Hearing in the Bardo.* Boulder: Shambhala, 1975.

Guenther, Herbert V. *The Jewel Ornament of Liberation by sGampo-pa.* London: Rider, 1963; rpt. Berkeley: Shambala, 1971.

Gyatso, Tenzin, Dalai Lama XIV and Hopkins, Jeffrey. *The Kālachakra Tantra: Rite of Initiation.* Translated and introduced by Jeffrey Hopkins. London: Wisdom Publications, 1985.

Gyatso, Tenzin, Dalai Lama XIV. *Kindness, Clarity, and Insight.* Jeffrey Hopkins, trans. and ed.; Elizabeth Napper, co-editor. Ithaca, N.Y.: Snow Lion Publications, 1984.

Gyatso, Tenzin, Dalai Lama XIV. *My Land and My People.* New York: McGraw-Hill, 1962; rpt. New York: Potala Corporation, 1977.

Gyatso, Tenzin, Dalai Lama XIV. *Opening the Eye of New Awareness.* Translated by Donald Lopez. London: Wisdom Publications, 1985.

Hopkins, Jeffrey. *Meditation on Emptiness.* London: Wisdom, 1983.

Iida, Shotaro. *Reason and Emptiness.* Tokyo: Hokuseido, 1980.

Johnston, E. H. (and T. Chowdhury), ed. *The Ratnagotravibhāga Mahāyānottaratantraśāstra.* Patna: Bihar Research Society, 1950.

Joshi, L.M. "Facets of Jaina Religiousness in Comparative Light," L.D. Series 85, [Ahmedabad: L.D. Institute of Indology, May 1981], pp. 53–8.

Lamotte, Étienne. *Saṃdhinirmocanasūtra: l'explication des mystères.* Louvain: Université de Louvain, 1935.

Lang, Karen. *Āryadeva's Catuḥśataka: On the Bodhisattva's Cultivation of Merit and Knowledge.* Indiske Studier VII. Copenhagen: Akademisk Forlag, 1986.

Lati Rinbochay, Denma Lochö Rinbochay, Leah Zahler, Jeffrey Hopkins. *Meditative States in Tibetan Buddhism.* London: Wisdom Publications, 1983.

Lati Rinbochay and Jeffrey Hopkins. *Death, Intermediate State and Rebirth in Tibetan Buddhism.* London: Rider and Co., 1979.

Mullin, Glenn H. *Songs of Spiritual Change.* Ithaca: Snow Lion, 1982.

Obermiller, E. "Sublime Science of the Great Vehicle to Salvation." *Acta Orientalia,* 9 (1931), pp. 81–306.

Poussin, Louis de la Vallée. *L'Abhidharmakośa de Vasubandhu.* 6 vols. Bruxelles: Institut Belge des Hautes Études Chinoises, 1971.

Poussin, Louis de La Vallée, trans. *Madhyamakāvatāra.* *Muséon* 8 (1907), pp. 249–317; 11 (1910), pp. 271–358; and 12 (1911), pp. 235–328.

Poussin, Louis de La Vallée, ed. *Mūlamadhyamakakārikās de Nāgārjuna avec la Prasannapadā Commentaire de Candrakīrti.* Bibliotheca Buddhica IV. Osnabrück: Biblio Verlag, 1970.

Pradhan, P., ed. *Abhidharmakośabhāsyam of Vasubandhu.* Patna: Jayaswal Research Institute, 1975.

Rahula, Walpola. *La compendium de la super-doctrine (philosophie) (Abhidharmasamuccaya) d'Asaṅga.* Paris: École Française d'Extrême-Orient, 1971.

Shastri, Swami Dwarikadas, ed. *Pramāṇavarttika of Āchārya Dharmakīrti.* Varanasi: Bauddha Bharati, 1968.

Snellgrove, David L., trans. *Hevajra Tantra, A Critical Study,* Parts I and II. London: Oxford University Press, 1959.

Snellgrove, D.L., and Richardson, Hugh. *Cultural History of Tibet.* New York: Praeger, 1968.

Sparham, Gareth. *The Tibetan Dhammapada: Sayings of the Buddha.* London: Wisdom, 1986.

Stcherbatsky, Th., and Obermiller, E., ed. *Abhisamayālaṃkāra-Prajñāpāramitā-Upadeśa-Śastra.* Bibliotheca Buddhica XXIII. Osnabrück: Biblio Verlag, 1970.

Takasaki, J. *A Study on the Ratnagotravibhāga.* Rome: IS. M.E.O., 1966.

Thurman, Robert A. F. *Tsōng Khapa's Speech of Gold in the Essence of True Eloquence.* Princeton: Princeton University Press, 1984.

Willis, Janice D. *On Knowing Reality.* Delhi: Motilal, 1979.

Wogihara, Unrai, ed. *Abhisamayālaṃkārālokā Prajñā-pāramitāvyākhyā. The Work of Haribhadra.* Tokyo: The Toyo Bunko, 1932–5; reprint ed., Tokyo: Sankibo Buddhist Book Store, 1973.

BOOKS BY THE DALAI LAMA

CORE TEACHINGS OF THE DALAI LAMA SERIES

The Complete Foundation: The Systematic Approach to Training
the Mind

An Introduction to Buddhism

Our Human Potential: The Unassailable Path of Love, Compassion,
and Meditation

Perfecting Patience: Buddhist Techniques to Overcome Anger

Perfecting Wisdom: How Things Appear and How They Truly Are

Refining Gold: Stages in Buddhist Contemplative Practice

Stages of Meditation: The Buddhist Classic on Training the Mind

Where Buddhism Meets Neuroscience: Conversations with the Dalai
Lama on the Spiritual and Scientific Views of Our Minds

(*more forthcoming*)

ALSO AVAILABLE FROM SHAMBHALA PUBLICATIONS

Answers: Discussions with Western Buddhists

The Bodhisattva Guide: A Commentary on *The Way of the Bodhisattva*

The Buddhism of Tibet

Dzogchen: Heart Essence of the Great Perfection

From Here to Enlightenment: An Introduction to Tsong-kha-pa's Classic Text *The Great Treatise on the Stages of the Path to Enlightenment*

The Gelug/Kagyu Tradition of Mahamudra

The Great Exposition of Secret Mantra, Volume 1: Tantra in Tibet

The Great Exposition of Secret Mantra, Volume 2: Deity Yoga

The Great Exposition of Secret Mantra, Volume 3: Yoga Tantra

The Heart of Meditation: Discovering Innermost Awareness

Kindness, Clarity, and Insight

The Pocket Dalai Lama

The Union of Bliss and Emptiness: Teachings on the Practice of
Guru Yoga

INDEX